The Strange Bestiary

CREDITS

Writers/Designers Bruce R. Cordell, Monte Cook, and Robert J. Schwalb
Creative Director Shanna Germain
Editor and Proofreader Ray Vallese
Lead Artist Matt Stawicki
Graphic Designer Bear Weiter

Artists Brenoch Adams, Milivoj Céran, Nicholas Cloister, Dreamstime.com, Jason Engle, Cory Trego-Erdner, Erebus, David Hueso, Guido Kuip, Brandon Leach, Eric Lofgren, Patrick McEvoy, Brynn Metheney, Grzegorz Pedrycz, Mike Perry, John Petersen, Michael Phillippi, Roberto Pitturru, Scott Purdy, Nick Russell, Joe Slucher, Lee Smith, Michael Startzman, Matt Stawicki, Cyril Terpent, Tiffany Turrill, Chris Waller, Cathy Wilkins, Ben Wootten

Monte Cook Games Editorial Team Scott C. Bourgeois, David Wilson Brown, Eric Coates, Gareth Hodges, Ryan Klemm, Jeremy Land, Laura Wilkinson, George Ziets

Printed in Canada

Table of Contents

INTRODUCTION: STRANGE BEINGS

In the beginning was a singularity. Not a stable one, because it exploded, creating our universe. Some time after that, but billions of years before now, aliens known as the Precursors arose. They modified—or perhaps created—exotic space-time to create a network that scientists on Earth today call dark energy. This newly fashioned dark energy network was used by the Precursors to travel between planets, solar systems, and even galaxies of the universe. Then something went about as wrong as things can go. The transport system malfunctioned. The Precursors and their civilization were destroyed. The dark energy network raced out of control, accelerating the expansion of the entire universe.

Fast-forward to now. The few people on Earth aware of the true nature of the dark energy network call it the Strange, the Chaosphere, or "the thing that'll finally kill us all." That's because creatures live in the network, many of them terrifyingly powerful, though even the least are scary as hell. Most other alien civilizations that discovered the Strange were subsequently destroyed by the creatures living within it.

Speaking of Hell, one of the qualities of the Strange is its ability to host limited worlds called recursions that have alternate laws of physics. Earth is filthy with recursions seeded from human imagination, which means more than a few recursions are crawling with demons. Wizards and dragons live in other recursions. Some limited worlds feature plasma swords and intelligent robots. Several recursions host terrors spawned by horror flicks and novels, described in campfire stories and tall tales, and written about on clay tablets. Vampires, kaiju, ghosts, killer robots, things that hide in mirrors, ogres, psychic parasites, cyborg warriors, demigods, posthumans, and many, many more monstrosities live in the recursions "beneath" Earth. Even stranger things abide in the dark energy network beyond, things born in the mind of no human being.

This bestiary describes them for you. Enjoy.

DESIGNING CREATURES FOR THE STRANGE

Designing creatures for The Strange is intentionally very easy. At its most basic, a creature—like any NPC—is just a level. That tells you all you need, and then you just layer in the description. You can describe a terrible slavering beast with three clawed limbs, a mouth like a sphincter, and some kind of blue jelly covering its flesh, but "behind the screen" (so to speak) all you have is "level 5."

The Strange corebook gives a brief discussion on designing new creatures in chapter 19 (page 352). Basically, all the GM really needs to know is that creatures can work however he wants them to. But for those who would like more details, suggestions, guidelines, and food for thought, this chapter is for you.

Creatures don't follow the same rules that player characters do. They don't have stat Pools, don't use Effort, and aren't as limited in what they can do in an action because their form, size, and nature can vary so wildly.

LEVEL

A creature's level is a measure of its power, defense, intelligence, speed, and ability to interact with the world around it. Generally, it's an indicator of toughness in combat, although it's certainly possible to have a lower-level creature be a tougher opponent than a slightly higher one, particularly in certain circumstances. Level isn't an abstract tool to match NPCs to PCs for "appropriate" encounters. Instead, it's an overall rating of a creature to show how it fits into the context of the world. There is no rule that says a certain ability should be given only to a creature of a certain level, and there is no rule dictating how many abilities a creature of a given level should have. But keep the spirit of the system in mind: lower-level creatures are less dangerous.

Obviously, a creature's level is its most important feature. For some creatures, it is the only feature. If you know the level, you have everything you need. Level determines how hard it is to hit, how hard it is to dodge or resist, how much damage it does, and how much health it has (typically, three times its level). It tells you how hard the creature is to interact with, fool, or intimidate, and how well it can run, climb, and so on. Level even tells you how fast it acts in terms of initiative.

Of course, you're free to modify any of this as fits the creature, either for what you want it to do in an encounter or—even better—to try to ensure that it makes sense in the story and the world. A really big creature should have more health but be easier to hit in combat, for example.

In general, level is the default stat for a creature, with pretty much everything else being an exception (that is, you can derive what you need from the level, but exceptions are what make creatures unique and interesting). To determine a level, figure out an appropriate rating (on a scale of 1 to 10) for the creature for most things. Don't base its level on the one thing it does best because you can portray that as a modification. Level is the baseline.

HEALTH

Since creatures don't have stat Pools, you have to determine how much damage they can take, and that's health. Health should make sense. Really big creatures should have lots of health, and tiny ones should have very little. You can also "cheat" a bit and give a creature that's really good in combat more health than its physicality might suggest to represent the fact that it's no pushover and not easily defeated.

Although there are many, many variables, it's safe to think—as a baseline—that a group of four low-tier PCs is likely to dish out about 10 points of damage in a round. This figure assumes that the group includes a paradox with Exception, a vector and a spinner with medium weapons, and a vector with a heavy weapon. The paradox deals 4 points of damage, the first vector 5 points (medium weapon and the Pierce move), the spinner 4 points (medium weapon), and the second vector 7 points (heavy weapon and Pierce). That's a total of 20 points, and we can assume that they hit their target with a bit better than 50 percent accuracy if they are fighting a level 3 or 4 foe and using Effort. This very rough estimate tells you that a creature with a health of 11 or less will be wiped out in a single round (Armor figures hugely into this, however, so see below). A creature with a health of 12 to 22 will last for two rounds. A creature with a health of 23 to 33 will last three. And so on.

Throughout this book, you'll see page references to various items accompanied by this symbol. These are page references to The Strange *corebook, where you can find additional details about that item, place, rule, NPC, or creature. Usually, it isn't necessary to look up the referenced items in the corebook; it's an optional way to learn more about the situation. The exception is if a cypher or creature stat is referenced, in which case you'll want the corebook nearby.*

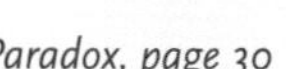

Paradox, page 30

Exception, page 32

Vector, page 25

Spinner, page 38

For PCs who are third or fourth tier, you can add about 6 points to the average damage figure, based on using Effort to increase damage. At fifth and sixth tiers, you can figure that the PCs will deal about 20 to 25 points of damage each round.

Again, these are rough estimates based on averages. They don't figure in high dice rolls, using lots of Effort, cyphers, artifacts, or GM intrusions. They're useful as a rule of thumb to determine how hard or easy you want the fight to be. A single-round fight is kind of a pushover. A fight that lasts two to four rounds is interesting. Going five or six rounds is a tough fight. Combat encounters that go on longer than that can start to drag unless the creature is really interesting or the encounter offers something unique (for example, it occurs on a precipice over a river of toxic sludge, or the PCs have to protect a sickly NPC while dealing with their foes).

In other words, creature health is the knob to adjust when determining how long you want a combat encounter to last.

DAMAGE

It's important to remember that damage is based on the creature's level, not other factors. So a level 6 creature that fires a medium handgun inflicts 6 points of damage, not 4 points. You can adjust the damage to fit the creature's attack, but the level should always be the baseline. A massive, strong creature will deal more damage than its level might suggest, and a creature with especially large claws or a powerful bite might do so as well. A particularly skillful combatant will deal more damage, too. Only very rarely should a creature deal less damage than its level.

Remember that more PCs have Armor than don't, so it's difficult (but not impossible) for creatures that deal only 1 or 2 points of damage to challenge the characters.

You can compare the determinations you made about the creature's health to figure out how much damage it will deal to the PCs in an encounter. Again, if you figure 50 percent accuracy, the creature will deal its damage every other round. So if a creature has enough health to last three rounds, on average, it will deal its damage twice.

Creatures that make more than one attack on their turn potentially deal their damage with each attack, which can greatly affect damage output.

ARMOR

Armor doesn't depend on level. The default is no Armor.

Armor represents a suit of physical armor, thick skin, metal plating, scales, a carapace, mental wards, or any other type of similar protection. Armor does not represent other things that might make a creature hard to damage, such as intangibility (that's represented in other ways).

Armor greatly influences how long a creature can last in a combat encounter. The Armor rating reduces the damage the creature suffers each round. So take our four characters mentioned above, who inflict 4, 5, 4, and 7 points of damage, respectively. Give their foe 3 points of Armor, and now they inflict 1, 2, 1, and 4 points of damage. On an average round, they'll inflict a total of 4 points of damage, and a creature with 11 health will last for three rounds, not one. (Of course, against such a foe, smart PCs will use Effort to increase their damage.)

Don't give every creature Armor, though. If everything has 2 points of Armor, then all attacks just deal 2 fewer points of damage, and that's not terribly interesting. Sometimes a creature with lots of health and no Armor can be an interesting encounter, too.

MOVEMENT

Other than Armor, the only thing that level doesn't tell you is how fast a creature moves. However, unless there's a really good reason to do otherwise, just assume that it can move a short distance as an action. Typically, flying creatures can move a long distance in the air and a short distance (or less) on the ground.

Creatures that can move a long distance as an action are usually large beings with a big stride. Small creatures can be very quick, but that doesn't always mean they move a long distance in a single round.

MODIFICATIONS

Health, damage, and almost everything else in the creature's entry can include exceptions to the default assumptions based on the creature's level. Modifications are a catch-all of these exceptions. Basically, they are tasks that the creature performs at something other than its normal level.

A level 2 tree-dwelling beast might be level 4 when it comes to climbing. A level 3 creature with a heightened sense of smell and good hearing is probably level 4 or 5 when it comes to perception. Tiny, quiet creatures are usually a level or two higher at stealth.

Not all modifications are positive. If you make a huge creature that is little more than a beast, you might want to lower its level for things like resisting trickery. A big, lumbering brute would likely be worse at stealth than its level would suggest. A stupid creature might be terrible at

STATTING ANIMALS

Normal animals, whether on Earth or in a recursion, are typically fairly simple in terms of stats. Most are just a level, or a level with a single modification. Although there are exceptions, anything smaller than a dog is likely level 1. The Strange is not a game where a rat is meant to be a meaningful foe—although a swarm of rats might be a little scary. A few examples follow:

Rat: level 1

Hawk: level 2; flies a long distance each round

Dog: level 2, level 3 for perception

Dog, Guard: level 3, level 4 for attacks and perception

Rattlesnake: level 2; bite inflicts 3 points of Speed damage that ignores Armor

Horse: level 3; moves a long distance each round

Bear, Black: level 3, level 4 for attacks

Bear, Grizzly: level 5; health 20; Armor 1

perception. Modifications that modify creatures down are just as interesting as those that modify them up.

Don't bother considering modifications in too much detail. Only think about things that will come up at the table. Figuring out how good a creature is at basket weaving or how much it knows about tidal pools probably isn't worth the effort unless those elements play directly into your encounter.

COMBAT

Combat is simply where we note what the creature does in a fight, how it reacts to combat, and—most important—any special combat-related abilities it might have. There are no hard-and-fast rules here. In fact, it's very much the opposite. This is the place where you note how the creature makes its own rules. Multiple attacks in a single action? Fine. Poison? Good. Mental powers? Interesting. If you're designing a creature for your own use, just make simple notes for how you want a combat encounter to play out so it fits the role you want it to have in the grand scheme. Use (or create) the mechanics to replicate what you want the creature to do, not the other way around.

MOTIVE, ENVIRONMENT, INTERACTION, USE, LOOT

The bestiary provides these entries for creatures, but for a GM's home-brewed creature, they probably aren't necessary. After all, you made the creature, so you know how to use it and where it's found, and you probably have a good idea of how the PCs can interact with it.

MAKING CREATURES REALLY DANGEROUS

Although a high-level creature is already pretty dangerous, there are a few things you can do to turn any creature into a threat to the PCs (if that's something you want to do—not every encounter should carry a risk of instant death for everyone in the group).

The Damage Track: First and foremost, moving PCs down the damage track rather than (or in addition to) dealing damage is a sure way to put fear into the heart of a player. It doesn't matter how many points you have in your Pools or what abilities you have—it's still just three steps to death on the damage track.

Attacks That Do More Than Damage: Attacks that do more than just deal damage make it

OTHER CONSIDERATIONS

Those are all the main sections in a creature's stat entry, but there are other things to think about.

Creature Size: Consider creature size very carefully. For those that are quick and hard to hit, increase the difficulty to attack them by one step. Large, slow creatures should be easier to hit, so decrease the difficulty to attack them by one step.

Multiple Attacks: No matter how big and tough it is, a single creature will have a hard time holding its own against a group of foes like the PCs. Giving a creature multiple attacks as a single action—so that it can attack some or all of the characters at once—goes a long way toward making it a suitable foe for a group of opponents.

However, creatures with multiple attacks that appear in groups can simply be annoying, as the combat encounter will take quite a while to resolve (and require lots of defense rolls). Instead, if a creature needs to take on a group of opponents, give it an option for doing so. Maybe it attacks with a bite normally, but it can emit a mental blast in a radius to affect more than one target.

Ignoring Armor: Attacks that ignore Armor are interesting because they really scare players. Such attacks might be from intense heat, out-of-phase tentacles, or something so sharp that it cuts right through whatever the PC is wearing.

Use your discretion, however. For example, if Armor comes from a force field, a fiery blast seems less likely to ignore it. And use this kind of thing sparingly because if everything ignores Armor, Armor loses its meaning.

Poison and Disease: A level 1 creature could be poisonous, but its venom should inflict a few points of damage at most. The venom of a level 6 creature, on the other hand, might knock a PC down a step on the damage track or put him into a coma if he fails a Might defense roll.

Other Special Abilities: In The Strange, a creature can have almost any kind of power or ability you want to dream up. Basically, it comes down to what kind of roll the player makes—an Intellect defense roll to ward off a weird mind attack, a Speed defense roll to dodge a barrage of spikes, a Might defense roll to resist a cellular disintegration, or perhaps something else. The difficulty of the roll and the damage dealt by the attack is based primarily on the level of the creature, although this can be modified if it seems appropriate.

Maybe there's no roll involved. The creature just walks through the wall, teleports, or melts the metal object it holds in its clutches. Although some of these abilities can give a creature a tactical advantage in a combat encounter, they're just as often there to make it more interesting.

This means that a creature's level is probably more important than any particular ability when it comes to determining its "toughness." And it also means that you don't have to save the cool abilities just for high-level creatures.

clear that a player should spend points from his Pool to avoid them. If an attack deals 3 points of damage, does it make sense to spend 3 points to use a level of Effort to avoid it? Maybe—in some situations, losing points from your Speed Pool might be better than losing them from your Might Pool. But spending points to avoid moving a step down the damage track? That makes more sense. Spending Intellect points to avoid being mind-controlled? Again, very fitting.

Ignoring Armor: Bypassing the PCs' primary defense mechanism is scary.

Multiple Attacks: Creatures that can attack all the PCs at once, whether with multiple arms or a radius or aura effect, can be very challenging. Sometimes a group's tactics rely on one or two characters going toe to toe with the enemy while the others hang back. Those PCs in the back might not be prepared for an attack that affects them as well.

Longer Than Long-Range Attacks: Most PCs have limited options at long range, but what if the creature can attack them from a quarter mile away with mental blasts or homing missiles? Now they have an entirely different kind of encounter to deal with.

Ardeyn, page 160

Ruk, page 190

All Song, page 192

Cataclyst, page 238

FITTING THE CREATURES INTO THE SETTING

The ideas behind a creature are just as important as its combat stats—or perhaps more important. How does it fit into the world? What role will it play in your story? What's right and what's wrong for The Strange?

The important thing to keep in mind is to maintain the flavor of the recursion where the creature lives. Ardeyn creatures are magic, but not quite standard fantasy. Ruk creatures are biotech horrors and beings associated with the All Song. Cataclyst creatures are likely radioactive mutants. And so on. Creatures from the Strange itself should always be the most bizarre and alien creatures in the setting—things humans can barely comprehend, let alone understand.

These flavor choices should be overt and obvious, not a hidden facet of the creature's backstory that the players won't ever discover. Remember that if it's not out there in the open, the PCs likely won't ever learn about it. Thus, less is more when it comes to creatures. Don't worry about where it came from—worry about how it fits into the world now. What's it doing? Why is it trying to eat a character's face? That's what the PCs need to know.

GM INTRUSIONS

Although it's often best to come up with GM intrusions on the fly, based on the current needs of the story, it's not a terrible idea to have one or two up your sleeve. Each creature entry in this book has at least one GM intrusion listed as an example and a reference.

It can be tempting to use GM intrusions that result in more damage or have other straightforward effects. Often, however, you'll get more mileage out of them if they are story based—for example, the huge creature starts to swallow the PC whole, or the lumbering beast stumbles and falls on the character. This is stuff that really changes the encounter and leads to a good story that everyone will remember afterward. The best kind of GM intrusion is one where the GM describes what happens and then says, "Now what do you do?"

ECOLOGY OF THE SHOALS OF EARTH

The ecology of the Earth in The Strange is just like that of our real world today. All the animals, plants, and indeed the entire biome where you live are just as they are when you look out your door, check the weather, or research the climate. Mammals and fungi, deer and mushrooms, lions, tigers, and bears—they're all here. Sadly, most species are fighting to exist within ever-shrinking habitats. Not to mention the effects of a planet exhaling carbon dioxide much faster than a biome can absorb it, upsetting the delicate balance between a world too cold and a world too warm and acidified.

But in The Strange, more than one world climate exists. Connected to the prime world of Earth are hundreds—maybe thousands—of limited worlds that each host their own biome. Many of these are a limited version of Earth's own ecology, one that usually follows simplified rules of geology and climate. Thanks to the near-unlimited processing power the dark energy network provides to each recursion, much of the complexity and chaos of the real world seeps into older, larger recursions. But smaller recursions seeded by fictional leakage often simply "reset" damage sustained by the ecosystem. For example, if all the lions, tigers, and bears in one of the Oz recursions are hunted to extinction by Nimrod the Hunter, in a few weeks or months, new lions, tigers, and bears return to the land because that narrative demands it.

Connections between Earth and these many recursions are rare, but they exist. This means that even the relatively few inapposite gates (also called matter gates) that pass all matter without translation result in net inputs and outputs. Sometimes species that might have otherwise gone extinct reappear on Earth again, years or decades after their last sighting. Regular scientists assume that these events occur because a

Oz, page 253

Nimrod the Hunter, page 157

Inapposite gate, page 135

remnant population overlooked by field research managed to resurge, which might be true, though such a population could well have come from a recursion where the creatures still exist. The day that dodos are found flying across the Great Plains again, some biologists will wonder if something strange is going on.

More often, creatures more bizarre than dodos pass between recursions and Earth. When those creatures translate, they take on the context of the new recursion or of Earth, and ecosystems are unaffected. It's when animals, bacteria, intelligent machines, parasites, viruses, prions, or even less-well-understood life forms arrive on Earth through an inapposite gate that disruptions can occur.

Planetovore, page 8

Magic, Mad Science, Psionics, Standard Physics, pages 136–137

Awakens Dangerous Psychic Talent, page 236

INAPPOSITE ECOSYSTEMS

Sometimes creatures from recursions that operate under the laws of Magic, Mad Science, or Psionics appear on Earth. If such creatures have special abilities that rely on those laws, those abilities continue to function for several days before finally being snuffed out by the overriding law of Standard Physics. For example, if a character with the focus Awakens Dangerous Psychic Talent appeared on Earth through an inapposite gate, she would be able to use her abilities at full strength for a minute or two, but as time passed, it would be more difficult to access them reliably. After a few days, those powers would be gone, and the direct disruptions the character creates (if any) would cease. Of course, consequences of the actions she took before her psychic abilities deserted her might continue to ripple forward.

On the other hand, some creatures' very existence relies on a particular extreme law. An animate skeleton or a dragon relies on the law of Magic, and a giant robot or kaiju relies on the law of Mad Science. When one of these creatures comes to Earth via an inapposite gate (and in the case of skeletons and at least one dragon, it has happened), its abilities begin to degrade like those of a character with alternate law-dependent abilities. In addition, its very existence and form also begin degrading. A skeleton falls to loose, completely dead bones in a few days. A dragon takes longer to degrade but begins a slow slide that includes sloughing scales, mass, and the ability to breathe fire. It's possible that a dragon could come out the other end looking like a sickly Komodo dragon, but it's more likely that the creature will perish when all is said and done.

Kaiju, page 73

To summarize, the effects of inapposite travel, while serious in the immediate term, are quickly moderated in the short and long term.

Ecosystems that are wholly at odds don't mix for long. This is true not only between Earth and recursions with extreme laws, but also between recursions that don't share the same extreme laws. A giant robot from Ruk (which operates under the law of Mad Science) would begin to degrade within hours of arriving in Ardeyn (which operates under the law of Magic). Likewise, a dragon from Ardeyn would face the same fate in Ruk.

Considering that in some recursions operating under the law of Mad Science, nanotech gone awry has transformed everything into grey goo, it's a mercy that such natural safeguards remain in place. They will continue to do so as long as a planetovore doesn't make it to Earth or a particular recursion. Such beings are so powerful that they can rewrite recursion law and, as beings of the Strange, continue to function in their new location in all their terrible and alien power.

OTHER HUMANOID RACES

In some recursions, Neanderthals are very much alive. In others, populations of elves, dwarves, and hobbits live, adventure, and die. In still others, aliens who take the shape of humanoids dwell along with regular people, normal in most ways, but not all. However, *The Strange Bestiary* doesn't have a full creature entry for each of these humanoid races. Ultimately, they're really not that much different from humans. To portray them as regular NPCs of any given level (level X) requires only a slight twist. Some examples are provided in this section.

DWARF

Dwarves are shorter than most humans, but much broader and deeper in limb. They're known for their beards, their ability to withstand punishment and pain, their incredible artisanship, and the quantity of beer they can consume in one sitting.

Modifications: Tasks related to crafting as level X + 1; gains a bonus to health equal to 3 × X.

ELF

An insular people touched by otherworldly grace and longevity, elves are known for quickness of foot, amazing perception, and the ability to get off a bow shot in almost any circumstance.

Modifications: Tasks related to perception as level X + 1; attacks made with bows (choose one) as level X + 1.

HALFLING

Halflings are about as large as 10-year-old humans, but they make up for their lack of size

CREATURES IN A GROUP

The Strange has rules for using creatures in a group; we typically call these the swarm rules. Although groups of creatures can make for an interesting encounter, remember that not all creatures move in groups, nor do they live in groups all the time (for example, some might join together to defend against recursion intruders, but only after several days of intrusions). Many predators—especially large ones—are solitary creatures with large territories and have no interest in spending time with others of their species.

Sometimes creature groups have more than one type of creature. The PCs may be caught between a trio of predators and a herd of prey and suddenly find they are fighting not just one group of creatures, but two. Or they may discover that the scrap drone they've been stalking is actually hunting down a killer robot, looking for parts. One creature may have a symbiotic or parasitic relationship with others, something the PCs discover only after they attack and are instantly overrun by the parasites fleeing the host body.

When making group encounters, consider not just the number of creatures and how they act when in a group, but also what an encounter might look like when it includes multiple types of creatures or creatures of varying ages and sizes.

GROUP NAMES

Most creatures in a group can be called a herd, a clan, a pride, or simply a pack, but others have specific collective nouns that are commonly used. Some examples include:

- A coven of witches
- A patch of prances
- A pod of battle chrysalides
- A tickle of nightgaunts
- A refuse of scrap drones
- A boil of extereons

SWARM RULES

The GM can take any creature and have a group of six to ten of them attack en masse as a single creature that is two levels higher, inflicting double the original creature's normal damage. So thirty level 2 inklings might attack as five level 4 mobs. Some creatures use their own specialized swarm rules that supersede these rules.

with a zest for life and good cooking that is twice as strong as that of a standard adult human. Most halflings appreciate home life best, but some are struck by wanderlust, driven to see what lies over the next mountain.

Modifications: Speed defense rolls as level X + 1 due to size; tasks related to stealth as level X + 1.

KOBOLD

Kobolds are like halflings except they've got scales, snouts, and short, lizardlike tails. Most kobolds live as savages in burrows, but some aspire to finer things.

Modifications: Tasks related to deception as level X + 1; +2 to Armor against heat and fire attacks.

NEANDERTHAL

Big browed and heavily thewed, Neanderthals lived on Earth for 300,000 years and still live in several recursions, usually as "cavemen" but in some places as the dominant species where humans lost out.

Modifications: Tasks related to feats of great strength as level X + 1; attacks made with melee weapons as level X + 1.

STARSEED

Starseeds believe they're not human. They claim to originate from another place in the universe but walk on Earth in human bodies.

Modifications: Tasks related to one technical specialty (such as circuit design, painting, sculpture, writing, robotics, or hardware design) as level X + 3.

Starseed, page 158

THE STRANGE

The worlds hosted by the Strange are suffused by the extreme laws under which they operate, as well as the cyphers and other elements (such as spiral dust, reality seeds, and native creatures) that enter recursions and Earth from the Chaosphere. These influences cause changes when they first appear but seem to fade over time. However, interconnections mean that an influence, once introduced, never fully dissipates. A dragon might not be able to survive on Earth in the long term, but its bones do, as do the social repercussions of a mythical creature hunting street people for weeks or months.

Spiral dust, page 156

Reality seed, page 138

CREATURES OF THE STRANGE

Within any population of creatures, outliers exist. Each creature description includes the most common attributes for a given type of creature. But certain individual creatures of that type can and probably do possess attributes, motivations, and abilities far different than average.

UNDERSTANDING THE LISTINGS

Level: All creatures (and NPCs) have a level. The level determines the target number a PC must reach to attack or defend against the opponent. In each entry, the target number for the creature or NPC is listed in parentheses after its level. The target number is three times the level.

Description: Following the name of the creature or NPC is a general description of its appearance, nature, intelligence, or background.

Motive: This entry is a way to help the GM understand what a creature or NPC wants. Every creature or person wants something, even if it's just to be left alone.

Environment (Recursions of Origin | Laws of Origin): This entry describes whether the creature tends to be solitary or travel in groups and what kind of terrain it inhabits. The entry also lists the creature's recursion of origin and the law that it operates under. If no recursion of origin is specified, the creature might be found in any recursion that includes the given law.

Health: A creature's target number is usually also its health, which is the amount of damage it can sustain before it is dead or incapacitated.

Damage Inflicted: Generally, when creatures hit in combat, they inflict their level in damage regardless of the form of attack. Some inflict more or less or have a special modifier to damage. Intelligent NPCs often use weapons, but this is more a flavor issue than a mechanical one. In other words, it doesn't matter if a level 3 orc uses a sword or its fists—it deals the same damage if it hits.

Armor: This is the creature's Armor value. Sometimes the number represents physical armor, and other times it represents natural protection. This entry doesn't appear in the game stats if a creature has no Armor.

Movement: Movement determines how far the creature can move in a single turn.

Modifications: Use these numbers when a creature's entry says to use a different level. For example, a level 4 creature might say "defends as level 5," which means PCs attacking it must reach a target number of 15 (for difficulty 5) instead of 12 (for difficulty 4). In special circumstances, some creatures have other modifications, but these are almost always specific to their level.

Combat: This entry gives advice on using the creature in combat, such as "This creature uses ambushes and hit-and-run tactics." In this section, you'll also find any special abilities, such as immunities, poisons, and healing skills. GMs should be logical about a creature's reaction to a PC's action or attack. For example, a mechanical being is obviously immune to normal diseases, a character can't poison a being of energy (at least, not with a conventional poison), and so on.

Interaction: This entry gives advice on interacting with the creature.

Use: This entry gives the GM suggestions for how to use the creature in a game session.

Loot: This entry indicates what the PCs might gain if they take items from their fallen foes (or trade with or trick them). It doesn't appear in the stats if the creature has no loot.

GM Intrusion: This entry suggests a way to use GM intrusion in an encounter with the creature. It's just one possible idea of many, and the GM is encouraged to come up with her own uses of the game mechanic.

CREATURES BY LEVEL

Creatures marked with asterisks appear in *The Strange* corebook.

Creature	Level
Nul	1
Cog mite	2
Droneme	2
Guard*	2
Inkling, lesser*	2
Maggot fiend	2
Nuppeppo	2
Prance	2
Spirit of wrath*	2
Technician*	2
Angiophage*	3
Bogeyman	3
Callum	3
Cataclyst roach*	3
Criminal*	3
Cypher eater*	3
Deinonychus	3
Enenera	3
Faerie	3
Flathead	3
Frenetic hob	3
Fusion hound	3
Green homunculus*	3
Kray scurrier*	3
Mirror gaunt	3
Mokuren	3
Neon Roller	3
Nightgaunt	3
Orc	3
Polymous	3
Qephilim, Free Battalion*	3
Sapient tree	3
Scormel	3
Scrap drone	3
Serpent person	3
Skeleton	3
Spine tingler	3
Thonik*	3
Umber wolf*	3
Vampire, transitional	3
Vat reject	3
Venom trooper*	3
Viroid	3
Winged monkey*	3
Zombie	3
All-seeing eye	4
Catastrophe cloud	4
Commander*	4
Data sentinel	4
Deep one	4
Devolved	4
Elemental, fire	4
Ghost	4
Gnathostome*	4
Green one*	4
Grey	4
Griffon	4
Grotesque	4
Hollow knight	4
Killer robot	4
Kro courser*	4
Kro goon	4
Mad creation	4
Murder	4
Myriand volunteer*	4
Nalusa falaya	4
Night spider	4
Octopus sapien	4
Ogre	4
Phantasmic parasite	4
Phoenix	4
Psychic remnant	4
Qephilim, umber judge*	4
Qinod tester*	4
Recursion hound	4
Recursor*	4
Sark*	4
Sclerid patch, Vaxt*	4
Sinistyr	4
Tagweh	4
Variokaryon*	4
Werewolf	4
Zombie reacher	4
Aganar	5
Agent*	5
Aviatar	5
Capricious caterpillar	5
Chaosphere hierarch*	5
CRAZR	5
Crucible	5
Deathless charger	5
Demon of Lotan*	5
Dynod	5
Elemental, earth	5
Elite soldier	5
Fungalar	5
Glitch	5
Gorgon	5
Grim tailor	5
Id thief	5
Killing white light	5
Kray drone*	5
Metallicon	5
Monitor*	5
Mystereon	5
Necromancer	5
Nezerek*	5
Pterodactyl	5
Red homunculus*	5
Sclerid executioner, Vaxt*	5
Shadowcaster	5
Sirrush*	5
Soul eater	5
Spore worm*	5
Taranid	5
Utricle*	5
Venopus	5
Veridial	5
Vertebroid	5
Wendigo	5
Witch	5
Wrath lord	5
Zombie nightstormer	5
Barrage crusader	6
Butcher	6
Challa host	6
Chaos Templar	6
Chimera	6
Dlamma rider	6
Dlamma*	6
Elemental, thorn	6
Fallen star	6
Gamma spiker	6
Giant*	6
Gnock	6
Golem*	6
Hydra*	6
Imposter	6
Iron bull	6
Marroid*	6
Myriand veteran*	6
Nakarand avatar	6
Ngeshtin	6
Night wyrm	6
Reanimated	6
Regoid	6
Smotherer demon	6
Spliced	6
Vampire	6
Voot	6
Warbot	6
White ape	6
Zombie, crowned shambler	6
Collective	7
Cyber sorcerer	7
Cyclops	7
Djinni	7
Dragon*	7
Elite operative	7
Ignitherm	7
Inkling snatcher*	7
Jabberwock*	7
Mad titan	7
Mechadrone	7
Mechanomancer	7
Necuratu	7
Noble knight	7
Rak	7
Shoggoth*	7
Tyrannosaurus rex	7
Vengeance-class battle chrysalid	7
Apoptosis-class battle chrysalid	8
Blob	8
Dark energy pharaoh*	8
Elder thing	8
Extereon	8
Monument spider	8
Neuroraptor	8
Qinod deconstructor*	8
Questing beast	8
Soulshorn*	8
Demon drake	9
Fractal worm	9
Posthuman	9
Vampire lord	9
Kaiju	10
Mytocytic pool	10

RANDOM ENCOUNTER TABLES

Use these charts to randomly create encounters in the recursion the PCs are visiting based on the law (or laws) that recursion supports. For example, when determining random encounters for PCs in Ardeyn, use the Magic table; for PCs in Ruk, use the Mad Science table.

CHOOSING THE RIGHT TABLE

If a given recursion supports more than one law (such as Cataclyst, which supports both Mad Science and Magic), the GM can choose between the two tables based on her need at the time. For example, if the PCs are exploring a bombed-out AI stronghold in Cataclyst, the GM might choose to roll on the Mad Science table, but if they are hunting a sorceress in the ancient jungle, the Magic table might be more appropriate.

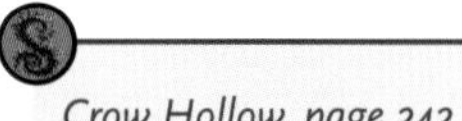

Crow Hollow, page 242

If the GM is rolling a random encounter for PCs traveling in the Strange itself, she can use the table for creatures native to the Strange or choose any other table because a creature that enters the Strange from a recursion brings its law with it.

Lotan the Sinner, page 162

To generate random encounters for a recursion that operates under the law of Substandard Physics, use the Standard Physics table. For variety, modify the table slightly to include pterodactyls, tyrannosaurus rexes, and deinonychus.

An Exotic recursion is one where the substance of the recursion itself is unusual. It might be composed of living flesh, fire, dream, acidic slime, solid starlight, writhing worms, fairy wings, or another unexpected form. This means that the entire recursion is usually one long encounter, and not especially random.

If you roll a result and aren't happy with it, either reroll for something you feel is more appropriate to the recursion or "skin" the result so it fits. For instance, you might not really want orcs in Ardeyn or a cyclops in Crow Hollow even though such creatures can operate under the same laws. If you roll on the Magic table for an encounter in Ardeyn and get orcs, you can use the orcs and bring them into your cosmology of the recursion, you can reroll, or you can skin the orcs so they're more appropriate for Ardeyn. If you skin the orcs, you might decide that your PCs have encountered a degenerate tribe of humans who once served Lotan the Sinner but now live in the wilds, which allows you to use the orc statistics and bring a little more texture into your campaign's Ardeyn setting.

MAD SCIENCE

Creatures marked with asterisks appear in *The Strange* corebook.

Roll	Creature
01	Agent*
02	Angiophage*
03	Apoptosis-class battle chrysalid
04	Barrage crusader
05	Blob
06	Cataclyst roach*
07	Catastrophe cloud
08	Challa host
09	Chimera
10-11	Cog mite
12	Commander*
13-14	CRAZR
15-18	Criminal*
19	Crucible
20	Cyber sorcerer
21	Data sentinel
22	Deep one
23-24	Deinonychus
25	Devolved
26-27	Droneme
28	Elder thing
29	Elite operative
30	Elite soldier
31	Frenetic hob
32	Fungalar
33-34	Fusion hound
35	Gamma spiker
36	Gnathostome*
37	Green one*
38	Grey
39-40	Guard*
41	Id thief
42	Ignitherm
43	Imposter
44	Killer robot
45	Killing white light
46-47	Mad creation
48	Marroid*
49	Mechadrone
50	Mechanomancer
51	Metallicon
52	Monument spider
53	Myriand veteran*
54-55	Myriand volunteer*
56	Mystereon
57	Mytocytic pool
58	Neuroraptor
59-60	Octopus sapien
61	Polymous
62	Posthuman
63	Prance
64	Pterodactyl
65	Qinod deconstructor*
66	Qinod tester*
67-68	Reanimated
69-70	Recursor*
71	Regoid
72-73	Scrap drone
74	Serpent person
75	Shoggoth*
76-77	Spine tingler
78	Spliced
79	Spore worm*
80	Taranid
81-86	Technician*
87	Tyrannosaurus rex
88	Utricle*
89	Variokaryon*
90-91	Vat reject
92	Vengeance-class battle chrysalid
93-95	Venom trooper*
96	Vertebroid
97	Viroid
98	Voot
99	Warbot
00	White ape

MAGIC

01	Aganar
02	All-seeing eye
03	Aviatar
04	Bogeyman
05	Butcher
06	Callum
07	Capricious caterpillar
08	Chimera
09	Collective
10	Cyclops
11	Deathless charger
12	Deep one
13	Demon drake
14	Demon of Lotan*
15	Djinni
16	Dlamma rider
17	Dlamma*
18	Dragon*
19	Elder thing
20	Elemental, earth
21	Elemental, fire
22	Elemental, thorn
23	Elite operative
24	Elite soldier
25	Enenera
26	Faerie
27	Fallen star
28	Flathead
29	Frenetic hob
30	Ghost
31	Giant*
32	Gnock
33	Golem*
34	Gorgon
35	Green homunculus*
36	Griffon
37	Grim tailor
38	Grotesque
39	Hollow knight
40	Hydra*
41	Iron bull
42	Jabberwock*
43	Kray drone*
44	Kray scurrier*
45	Kro courser*
46	Kro goon
47	Mad titan
48	Maggot fiend
49	Mirror gaunt
50	Monitor*
51	Monument spider
52	Murder
53	Mystereon
54	Nalusa falaya
55	Necromancer
56	Necuratu
57	Ngeshtin
58	Nightgaunt
59	Night spider
60	Night wyrm
61	Noble knight
62	Nuppeppo
63	Ogre
64	Orc
65	Phantasmic parasite
66	Phoenix
67	Qephilim, Free Battalion*
68	Qephilim, umber judge*
69	Questing beast
70	Rak
71	Red homunculus*
72	Sapient tree
73	Sark*
74	Scormel
75	Serpent person
76	Shadowcaster
77	Shoggoth*
78	Sinistyr
79	Sirrush*
80	Skeleton
81	Smotherer demon
82	Soul eater
83	Soulshorn*
84	Spirit of wrath*
85	Tagweh
86	Taranid
87	Umber wolf*
88	Vampire
89	Vampire lord
90	Veridial
91	Wendigo
92	Werewolf
93	White ape
94	Winged monkey*
95	Witch
96	Wrath lord
97	Zombie
98	Zombie nightstormer
99	Zombie reacher
00	Zombie, crowned shambler

PSIONICS

01-05	All-seeing eye
06-10	Cog mite
11-15	Collective
16-20	Crucible
21-25	Dynod
26-30	Elder thing
31-35	Ghost
36-40	Grey
41-45	Id thief
46-50	Mad titan
51-55	Mirror gaunt
56-60	Mokuren
61-65	Necuratu
66-70	Neon Roller
71-75	Octopus sapien
76-85	Phantasmic parasite
86-90	Psychic remnant
91-95	Shoggoth*
96-00	Soul eater

THE STRANGE ITSELF

01-02	Chaos Templar
03	Chaosphere hierarch*
04-20	Cypher eater*
21	Dark energy pharaoh*
22-23	Djinn
24	Extereon
25-27	Fractal worm
28-36	Glitch
37	Inkling snatcher*
38-55	Inkling, lesser*
56-59	Kray drone*
60-70	Kray scurrier*
71	Nakarand avatar
72-73	Nezerek*
74-80	Nul
81-84	Recursion hound
85	Recursion hunter
86	Sclerid executioner, Vaxt*
87-90	Sclerid patch, Vaxt*
91-95	Thonik*
96-00	Venopus

STANDARD PHYSICS

01-15	Agent*
16-30	Commander*
31-45	Criminal*
46-50	Elite operative
51-55	Elite soldier
56-70	Guard*
71-85	Recursor*
86-00	Technician*

Recursion hunters are rare, accomplished, and deadly recursors who collect bounties across recursions or hunt big game from fictional worlds just for fun. If PCs encounter a randomly generated recursion hunter, use stats for Nimrod the Hunter, page 157.

Creatures marked with asterisks appear in *The Strange* corebook.

SIZE COMPARISON

AGANAR 5 (15)

A night spent in the grip of vivid, sensual dreams might be harmless, nothing more than the mind's nocturnal wanderings in unexpected places. Then again, the dreams might be manifestations brought on by an aganar's feeding, visions and fantasies stirred to life in sleep to nourish a weird parasitic creature that creeps from its underground lair under night's cover.

An aganar, sometimes called a dream thief, shares many physical traits with the squid. An aganar's tentacles are strong enough to support its weight and provide locomotion like legs. It sees using two eyes perched atop flexible eyestalks. The eyes have independent movement, and an aganar can stretch the stalks to look in any direction.

Motive: Devour the dreams of living creatures

Environment (Ardeyn | Magic): Anywhere in the Daylands at night in groups of one to three; anywhere in the Night Vault in groups of three to ten

Health: 21

Damage Inflicted: 5 points

Movement: Short

Modifications: All tasks related to perception as level 8; all tasks related to climbing as level 6.

Combat: As generally peaceful creatures, aganars do not initiate fights. They want only to feed. When one comes within short range of a sleeping creature it can see (or within immediate range of a sleeping creature it can't see because of a solid obstacle), it begins to feed on the victim's psychic essence. The target must make an Intellect defense roll. On a failure, the aganar inflicts 5 points of Intellect damage, and the victim treats the next recovery roll he makes within twenty-four hours as if he had rolled a 1. After inflicting this damage, an aganar usually scuttles off. Once a victim takes this damage, he does not dream for several days.

Aganars leave their victims alive. Killing them would only remove a source of food. Aganars know when creatures have been recently drained because they have no dreams to eat.

If an aganar comes under physical attack, it uses its tentacles to defend itself and make attacks.

An aganar takes 1 point of ambient damage each round it is exposed to sunlight or other forms of ultraviolet radiation.

Aganars cannot tolerate ultraviolet radiation. Sunlight and other forms of such radiation cause their rubbery skin to blister and crack. Extended exposure can kill them and turn them into dark purple stains.

Interaction: Aganars communicate by flashing stolen dream images at each other on their bioluminescent hides in complex patterns. Stories suggest that sometimes an aganar deposits a dream sequence in the mind of a sleeper as a form of communication, but most dreamers fail to understand the message's meaning.

Use: If the PCs descend into the Night Vault to find a spirit or seek out something else in that dark and foreboding place, they might gain the service of an aganar as a guide—provided they discern the meaning of its bioluminescent images and come up with some way of flashing images back in turn.

GM Intrusion: *A sleeping character who takes Intellect damage from an aganar has a dream of such nightmarish horror that, upon waking, she sees all her allies as monstrous creatures until she succeeds on an Intellect defense roll.*

ALL-SEEING EYE 4 (12)

Size Comparison

Loosed from the nightmares of insane asylum inmates, all-seeing eyes wander recursions that contain psychic residue, hunting for those whose minds they can empty with their soul-sucking gazes.

An all-seeing eye does as its name advertises: it watches, studies, and catalogues. As frightening as it might be to see a flying, disembodied eye the size of a human head looking in through your window, it's worse when the eye goes from watching to actively gazing. That's when the eye emits a beam of intense violet plasma, or, worse, it catches someone in its unblinking stare and doesn't look away until the victim's mind is utterly empty.

Motive: Hungers for minds

Environment (Magic or Psionics): Anywhere, either alone or in groups of three

Health: 18

Damage Inflicted: 4 points

Armor: 2

Movement: Long while flying

Modifications: Perception as level 7; Speed defense as level 5 due to size.

Combat: An all-seeing eye can fire a purplish beam to attack a target within long range. If the eye can see any part of its target, it ignores any difficulty step modifications for cover that the target might have otherwise enjoyed. The beam is created by the eye's manipulation of air molecules, which it psionically strips of electrons to fashion a super-heated plasma beam. That same psychic field is responsible for creating an all-seeing eye's Armor.

However, the most dangerous of the eye's attacks is its mind-draining gaze. As an action, an all-seeing eye can direct its gaze at a target within long range who is looking at the eye. The target must make an Intellect defense roll to avoid being held fast in the gaze. A target held in the gaze stands completely motionless and automatically takes 4 points of Intellect damage each round, including the round in which he was caught. Releasing a target from the gaze is as easy as breaking line of sight. A victim can do that himself if he succeeds on a difficulty 6 Intellect defense roll.

Interaction: An all-seeing eye is telepathic but usually doesn't interact with other creatures except to hunt them. On the other hand, sometimes all-seeing eyes manifest in the dreams of characters in locations where one or more eyes hunt. In such dreams, eyes sometimes speak of building an empire and eradicating all other life.

Use: Victims have been found drooling and brain dead at the margins of the community, and reports of distant "balloons" moving against prevailing wind currents suggest that something is hunting the minds of the residents.

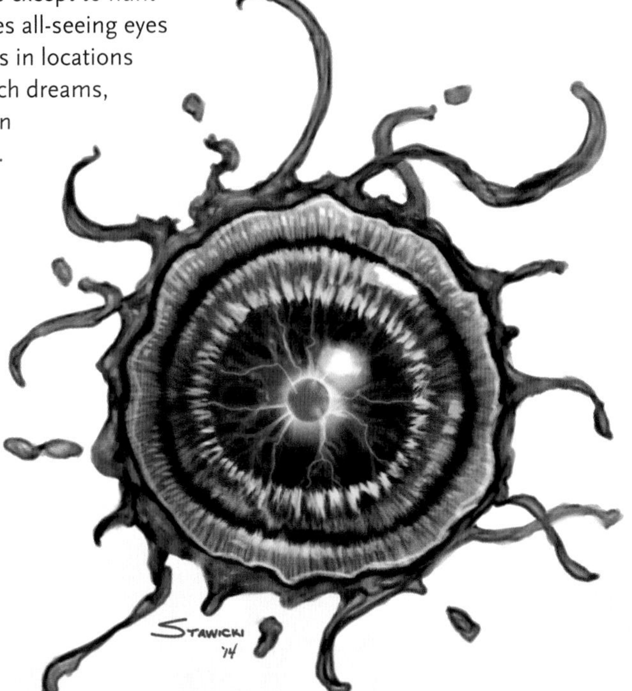

Born from the minds of mad people who have enough psychic energy to give their nightmares life, all-seeing eyes have embraced their existence with gusto and have learned the tricks of self-reproduction and, worse, recursion hopping. Alien and implacable, all-seeing eyes are more prevalent every year.

GM Intrusion: *As the PC slays the all-seeing eye, he meets the gaze of the dying creature. Later, the character has a dream in which the all-seeing eye telepathically predicts an invasion of its kind. Whether or not the dream is anything more than that is up to the GM.*

AVIATAR 5 (15)

Aviatars are warriors, either male or female, who appear to be lithe, muscular humans with feathered wings sprouting from their backs. Some think them angels, and perhaps that's true. They seem as apart from the world in which they live as an angel would be in the mortal world. Unlike angels, however, these brooding loners do not work toward altruism or some benevolent ideal. They are interested in their own sense of honor and justice.

Aviatars can be encountered anywhere in the wilderness, but they keep their homes—usually towers in very high places reachable only by flight—secret. Preoccupied with ancient history and wrongs committed in bygone eras, they have little interest in current events or the affairs of humans unless such things directly affect their homes, their well-being, or their strange sense of justice.

Sometimes an aviatar chooses a special site to hold sacred and protect, like an ancient temple, an enchanted grove, or a crystal-clear mountain pool.

A quickened aviatar named Kassiel lives in the Strange on a mote of fundament. Kassiel sometimes translates (or travels via matter gate) into various recursions to watch events play out, but rarely interferes.

Motive: Honor and justice

Environment (Magic): Usually solitary, deep in the mountainous wilderness

Health: 20

Damage Inflicted: 6 points

Armor: 3

Movement: Long while flying; short on foot

Modifications: Perception as level 6.

Combat: An aviatar wields weapons, usually a sword and shield or a bow. When an aviatar uses a shield, the difficulty of attacks made against it increases by one step. Aviatars usually wear special heavy armor that is treated as medium armor due to its light alloys and careful construction.

They can make swooping attacks from above. When they do, they can move and attack as a single action, and the difficulty to defend against this attack is increased by one step.

Most impressively, however, an aviatar can call upon a mystical essence to infuse itself and its weapons. This requires an action, after which the aviatar inflicts 2 additional points of damage and gains +1 to Armor against any foes that it declares unjust or that have wronged it or someone (or something) it holds dear. Aviatars call this the reckoning, and it lasts as long as their righteous fury does.

GM Intrusion: *The character hit by the aviatar's swooping attack is snatched into the air, only to be dropped into a pit, hurled from a cliff, or carried away.*

Interaction: Aloof and mysterious, aviatars might just fly away rather than engage in conversation. They appear to believe themselves superior to just about anyone else.

Use: In some recursions, aviatars might very well be angels, doling out vengeance on behalf of the divine. In other, more fantastic recursions, they might be the last of an ancient, magic race or even "winged elves."

Loot: In addition to their special armor, aviatars often have one or two cyphers.

BARRAGE CRUSADER 6 (18)

> **"I want to kill everybody in the world."**
> —Barrage crusader saying

Barrage crusaders are "the face of the fall." According to the context that created the apocalypse in Cataclyst, cloned soldiers are the reason why the world was unable to pull back from complete disaster. Hyped up on a cocktail of experimental military drugs, cybernetic enhancements, and training via direct neuronal implants, they had no reason not to fight to the end. The most powerful clones were designated as barrage crusaders. These enhanced soldiers survived nuclear bombardments, compromised robotic drone swarms, and emerging military AI instances run amok.

In the aftermath, a few barrage crusaders survive here and there amid the ruins, ruling tiny kingdoms of piled rubble, radioactive craters, and dangerous mutant flora and fauna.

Cataclyst, page 238

Motive: War games

Environment (Cataclyst | Mad Science and Magic): Scattered through the ruins, rarely together unless fighting each other

Health: 30

Damage Inflicted: 6 points

Armor: 2

Movement: Short when walking or flying

Modifications: Perception as level 7; knowledge of old military systems as level 7; reasoning and tasks related to empathy as level 2.

Combat: Implanted with mRNA neuronal training while being grown, each barrage crusader is matched only by a brother or sister clone. Most carry two long black blades that spark with electricity. In melee the blades can be used to attack every foe in immediate range as a single action every other round, or up to two foes in immediate range every round.

For targets farther away, a barrage crusader relies on a squadron of orbiting drones that can fire beams of collimated neutrino hard light at a range of up to a half mile (0.8 km) away. When all the drones focus on a single target, a successful hit deals 9 points of damage and moves the target one step down the damage track. The drones can make such an attack once every other round. Otherwise, the barrage crusader can split the drones to make up to four long-range attacks as a single action, each of which deals 3 points of damage.

A deployable jetpack allows a barrage crusader to fly high above a field of battle and rain destruction down on everything within range.

Interaction: A barrage crusader might negotiate, but only if promised that it will get to engage in some kind of war game.

Use: A mutant army under the command of a barrage crusader called Omni has launched into the Strange and threatens various recursions in the Shoals of Earth.

Loot: A useful weapon or two can be salvaged from the cold, dead hands of a defeated barrage crusader.

Barrage crusaders aren't "evil" so much as the result of a purposeful dysfunction. Their deceitful, manipulative, and outright murderous behavior is genetically programmed—they were literally cloned to be bad.

GM Intrusion: *A character who attempts to target an orbiting drone instead of a barrage crusader is partly successful; the drone is hit. But before it explodes, it zooms toward the character, who must succeed on a Speed defense roll or suffer 6 points of damage from fire and shrapnel.*

BATTLE CHRYSALID

A chrysalid is an engineered body in Ruk that's made to fulfill some kind of purpose. Battle chrysalides, as the name describes, are made for conflict. Normal Rukians can receive expensive surgical upgrades that give access to a chrysalid form (such as is the case for a myriand, or a PC who Metamorphosizes). However, some modifications are so extreme that regression back to normal is difficult or impossible, as is the case for Vengeance-class and Apoptosis-class battle chrysalides.

VENGEANCE-CLASS BATTLE CHYRSALID 7 (21)

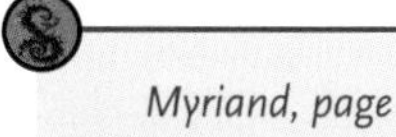

Myriand, page 281

Metamorphosizes, page 69

Battle chrysalides are fashioned from normal Rukians, as opposed to venom troopers, which are synthesized entities cloned in lots.

Vengeance-class battle chrysalides control an amazing amount of firepower, but in return, they give up a bit of autonomy. Designated commanders can upload their orders to Vengeance-class battle chrysalides via umbilical uplink.

Motive: Follow programming of battle commander

Environment (Ruk | Mad Science): Anywhere

Health: 21

Damage Inflicted: 10 points

Armor: 3

Movement: Short when walking or flying

Modifications: Speed defense as level 5 due to size.

Combat: A Vengeance-class chrysalid can make a single attack with a fist or a shoulder-mounted laser cannon (long range) for 10 points of damage. It can also attack two different foes as a single action, inflicting 8 points of damage with each attack (whether with fists or laser cannons).

Once every other round, a Vengeance-class chrysalid can fire a grenade at a target or area within long range that explodes in an immediate radius for 8 points of damage. Creatures who succeed on a Speed defense roll still take 1 point of damage from shrapnel.

A Vengeance-class chrysalid regenerates 1 point of health per round while its health is above 0.

Interaction: A Vengeance-class chrysalid will specify its current duties if queried, but otherwise it doesn't interact. However, if a character is able to attach her umbilical to the port on the back of a chrysalid's "neck," she can attempt to compromise its orders. Doing so is a multistep process, first requiring a difficulty 5 Speed or Might defense roll each round to cling to the bucking chrysalid's back, and then requiring two difficulty 5 Intellect-based rolls, one per round, to reprogram it. The first successful reprogramming roll increases the difficulty of all the chrysalid's actions by two steps, and the second successful roll puts it back in standby mode.

Use: If anyone requires an extremely potent (and expensive) guardian for an area in Ruk, a Vengeance-class battle chrysalid is a good choice.

Loot: PCs who investigate an inert Vengeance-class battle chrysalid discover that 1d6 cyphers have been worked into the mechanism and can be salvaged with a successful difficulty 3 Intellect-based task.

GM Intrusion: *The character who takes damage is also knocked down and disarmed by the chrysalid, which offers her a chance to surrender.*

APOPTOSIS-CLASS BATTLE CHRYSALID 8 (24)

Those who opt to be housed in Apoptosis-class battle chrysalides are in never-ending pain. The severity of the transformation their bodies endured means their nerves never stop screaming. It's like crisping in a fire. That agony is held mostly at bay thanks to amazingly potent painkilling drugs constantly pumping through their tissues (the tissues that haven't been replaced). These same drugs keep the chrysalides safe from the cell-destroying radiation that they generate.

Motive: Follow programming of battle commander

Environment (Ruk | Mad Science): Anywhere

Health: 60

Damage Inflicted: 8

Armor: 2

Movement: Short

Combat: Apoptosis-class battle chrysalides can attack foes they can see up to about 1,000 feet (305 m) away with beams of cell-destroying radiation, inflicting damage on a living target and everything in immediate range of the target. Those caught in the beam who succeed on a Speed defense roll suffer 2 points of damage instead of 8 points. Against nonliving targets, the energy beam inflicts only 4 points of damage.

In melee, the chrysalides attack three times as a single action with arm spines and extruded tail segments (also tipped with spines). They can also release a pulse of cell-destroying radiation that deals damage to all creatures within immediate range, but they can't use this attack two rounds in a row.

An Apoptosis-class battle chrysalid regenerates 2 points of health per round while its health is above 0.

Interaction: It's hard to get an Apoptosis-class chrysalid to deviate from its orders, and attempting to hack into one to set up communication (as described for Vengeance-class chrysalides) usually fails because the hacker suffers the same mind-bending pain the chrysalid feels, but without the benefit of the painkillers.

Use: An Apoptosis-class battle chrysalid has gone rogue and is heading for Harmonious. If it penetrates the city, the death toll will be staggering.

Loot: PCs who investigate the inert remains of the creature discover that 1d6 cyphers have been worked into the mechanism and can be salvaged with a successful difficulty 4 Intellect-based task.

GM Intrusion: *A character damaged by the Apoptosis-class battle chrysalid must succeed on a Might defense roll or a genetically inserted virus activates, and the victim's body begins experiencing programmed cell death. As the PC's cellular machinery kills itself, the character descends one step on the damage track each round that he fails an additional Might defense roll.*

Harmonious, page 196

Size Comparison

BLOB 8 (24)

The huge, undulating mass of this creature is composed of a mucus-like solid. The half-amorphous blob defeats its foes by absorbing prey, integrating a victim's tissue into its own. In essence, the victim becomes the blob, and all of the victim's knowledge is available to the blob for later use.

If it later desires, a blob can release a nearly perfect replicant of any creature that it has absorbed. Replicants have the memories and personalities of the originals, but they do the blob's bidding, which is usually to explore distant locations or lure prey into the open using a friendly face. A particularly well-crafted replicant might not even know it's not the original. Creating a replicant takes a blob a day or two of effort, during which time it's unable to defend itself or eat, so it's not a task the creature attempts lightly.

Blobs are born in recursions created by fictional leakage of 1950s American horror/science fiction films. That doesn't make them any less frightening. The worst nightmare of an agency like OSR, the Estate, or the Quiet Cabal would be to run across a quickened blob able to send quickened portions of itself as replicants into other recursions or to Earth to begin the process of assimilation.

Motive: Assimilation of all flesh

Environment (Mad Science): Anywhere

Health: 66

Damage Inflicted: 8 points

Movement: Immediate; immediate when burrowing

Modifications: Speed defense as level 5 due to size.

Combat: The blob can project a gout of acid at short range against a single target.

Though slow, a blob is always moving forward. A character (or two characters next to each other) within immediate range of a blob must succeed on a Might defense roll each round or be partly caught under the heaving mass of the advancing creature. A caught victim adheres to the blob's surface and takes 10 points of damage each round. The victim must succeed on a Might defense roll to pull free. A victim who dies from this damage is consumed by the blob, and his body becomes part of the creature.

If a blob has absorbed living flesh within the last hour, it regenerates 3 points of health per round while its health is above 0.

Interaction: A blob's favored method of communication is to absorb whoever tries to interact with it. If a replicant is handy, the blob might talk through it if the blob can touch the replicant and use it like a puppet.

Use: The old man the PCs accidentally hit with their vehicle has a weird, mucus-like growth on one hand (in addition to the damage he sustained in the accident). He probably should be taken to the hospital to have his injuries and the quivering growth looked at.

Loot: A blob might have several cyphers swirling about in its mass that it uses to outfit replicants.

GM Intrusion: *The character pulls free of a blob he was caught under, but a piece of quivering protoplasm remains stuck to his flesh. He must do serious damage to himself (enough to incapacitate) within the hour, scraping off the protoplasm before it absorbs him and becomes a new mini-blob.*

BOGEYMAN 3 (9)

When a child comes crying about a monster lurking under the bed, hiding in the closet, or scratching its claws against the window, parents in recursions that host such horrors still assume the culprit is a pile of clothes or the wind pushing branches against the glass. That's what the narrative that created the recursion demands, which is too bad, because there are things in the night that hunt children and drag them from their beds, never to be seen again.

"There's something under my bed!"

Bogeymen feed on courage. The more frightened their prey, the more real they become until they assume whatever form their victim fears most. Thus, a bogeyman can wear a multitude of forms, looking to one person like a giant spider, to another like a werewolf, and to another like a sailor wearing a rain hat and coat with a bloody hook extending from one of its sleeves. The form doesn't matter as much as the fear they create, fear strong enough to kill.

If a bogeyman feeds on multiple targets simultaneously, it takes the form of whatever scares the target that has suffered the most Intellect damage. This could mean the bogeyman is less frightening to other targets whose greatest fear isn't manifesting before them.

GM Intrusion: *A character who sees the bogeyman and fails an Intellect defense roll reacts viscerally, screaming long and loud.*

Motive: Terrorize humans, specifically children

Environment (Magic): Under beds, in closets, outside windows, or in toy boxes

Health: 9

Damage Inflicted: 3 points

Movement: Immediate

Modifications: All tasks related to intimidation as level 6.

Combat: As creatures of the night, bogeymen have no power in the light. Even when fully manifested, they disappear as soon as the lights are on. While powerless, they remain aware of their surroundings and can still move, but they are undetectable and cannot harm anyone. Only in dim light or darker conditions does a bogeyman take shape.

In its normal form, a bogeyman is nothing more than a pair of disembodied red eyes that float inside a shapeless smear of shadow. As its action, a bogeyman reaches out to feed on courage. Any creature that can see the thing must succeed on an Intellect defense roll or take 2 points of Intellect damage as its courage drains away and blood seeps from its eyes, nose, and ears. In addition, the difficulty to resist the bogeyman's attack increases by one step. This is a cumulative increase up to a maximum of five steps.

Each time a bogeyman inflicts Intellect damage, it becomes more solid, more real, taking the shape of whatever its beholder fears most. Its appearance is subjective to the viewer.

Any character killed by a bogeyman dies of fright, his hair stark white and face twisted into a horrified grimace.

Interaction: Bogeymen are sneaky and wicked creatures. They love eavesdropping on people to steal their secrets. If a bogeyman fails to frighten a creature, its demeanor changes and it becomes whining and cringing, offering tantalizing secrets to ingratiate itself with such a clearly powerful opponent.

Use: A bogeyman attaches itself to an item taken from a place reputed to be haunted and emerges under the cover of night to terrorize the person who took the object.

Size Comparison

Hell Frozen Over, page 251

Treachery, page 252

BUTCHER 6 (18)

The screams echoing through the bloodstained corridors of Treachery's demonic fortress often emerge from hapless fools who thought to translate into the realm of Hell Frozen Over. Deep in the castle's bowels work the butchers: horrible, bestial demons that use big, dull cleavers to chop up living victims. The rise and fall of the heavy blades creates a counterpoint beat to the screams until the sound is drowned in the fountains of blood thrown up by mutilated bodies.

Butchers are towering male humanoids with significant paunches hanging low enough to conceal the clotted fur of their genitals. They have great sagging breasts, spattered with gore from their grim work, and slack-mouthed faces with puffy lips glistening with blood and spittle. They keep the tops of their heads shaved, but their crude methods leave their scalps rumpled with accumulated scar tissue.

Motive: Inflict pain

Environment (Hell Frozen Over | Magic): Anywhere, usually in groups of two

Health: 27

Damage Inflicted: 5 points

Movement: Short

Modifications: All tasks related to intimidation as level 9; Speed defense as level 5 due to size.

Combat: A butcher is mindless aggression incarnate. It bulls forward, sweeping a huge cleaver to slice and cut anything in its path. As its action, it can move up to a short distance as it whirls its blade. Foes in its path must succeed on a Speed defense roll to move an immediate distance out of the way. Otherwise, the butcher clips them with its weapon, inflicting damage and knocking them to the ground.

When the butcher is damaged, it looses a howl of rage and retaliates with a wild swing as an immediate reaction (that doesn't require an action). Once it makes this free attack, it cannot do so again until after it kills a creature.

Interaction: Butchers don't have much to say beyond the occasional grunt or roar. They are simple-minded brutes with one thing on their mind: killing. Sometimes, though, they can be lured into conversations regarding the quality of fresh meat.

Use: The butchers serve the demon lord Treachery as guards and cooks. They might menace characters captured by Treachery's minions or guard an important prisoner the PCs must rescue.

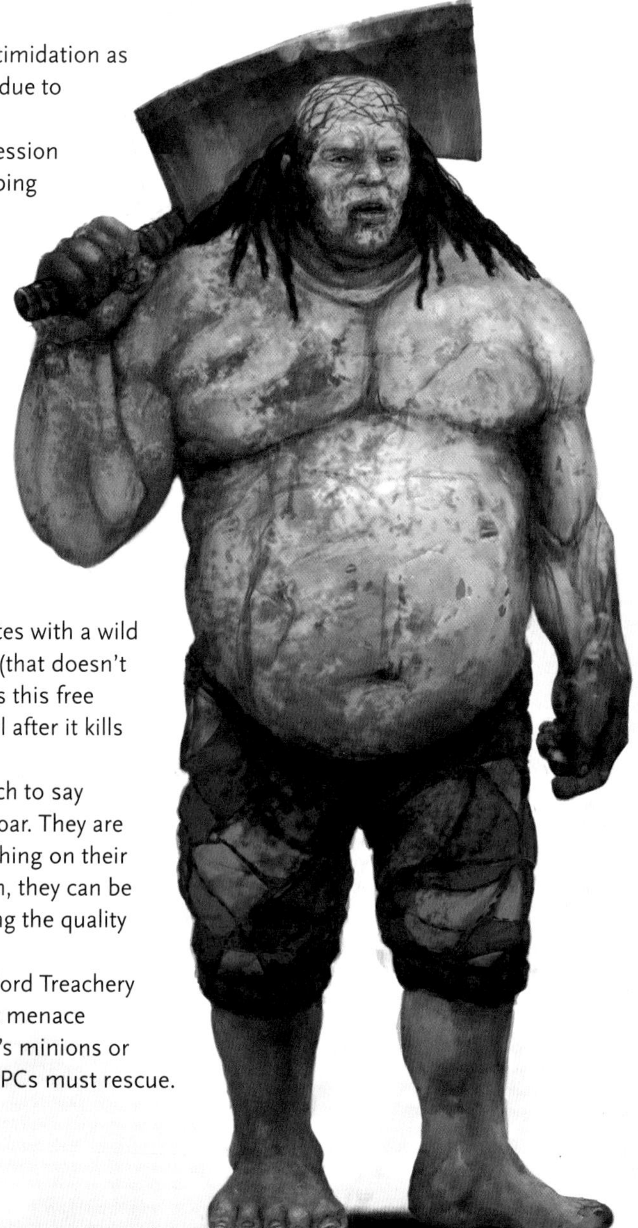

GM Intrusion: *A swing from the butcher's cleaver seriously injures one of the character's legs. The PC cannot move more than an immediate distance until she makes a recovery roll.*

GM Intrusion: *When the character strikes the butcher in melee, the butcher's gut splits open. Greasy innards tumble free and cause the PC to slip and fall to the ground.*

CALLUM 3 (9)

SIZE COMPARISON

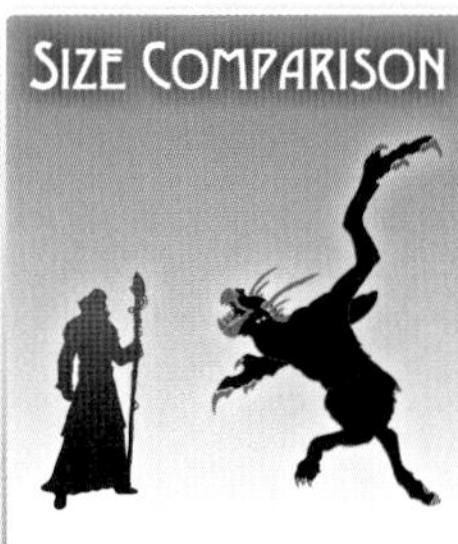

"These magic-eaters—oh, that's what I calls 'em, magic-eaters—they're no good. Nasty critters with claws and teeth like you'd expect, but they go after the more, well, you know... the more sorcerous types, if you get my meaning. Mostly, though, they'll steal your enchanted sword right from its scabbard or lift a, whatchacall, cypher right outta your pocket. Maker-damned thieves is what I call 'em. They eat leaves and bark and whatnot, but they got some kinda thirst for magic that I can't quite explain. More like an addiction than a hunger. It ain't right. As bad as the chronics with their dream smoke in Shalmarn, I say. Worse, maybe."

Motive: Seek magic
Environment (Ardeyn | Magic): A hunting pack of four to eight in any forested area
Health: 9
Damage Inflicted: 3 points
Movement: Short; long if brachiating
Modifications: Climbs as level 7; jumps as level 6; perception as level 5.
Combat: Callum usually attack in packs, ambushing from tree branches high above their prey. If attacking a character to obtain a magic item, one or more callum attack the victim with claws while another attempts to steal the item. To resist this theft, the character must succeed on a Speed defense roll. The difficulty of the roll is increased by one step if the character is attacked by another callum, or by two steps if he is attacked by two or more callum.

They will not hesitate to kill to get an item. Once they have what they seek, they flee as quickly as possible.

Characters with innate magic abilities—sorcerers, golems, sinfire channelers, and so on—are subject to callum attacks, for the callum want their blood or flesh. However, this means that a single damaging wound against such a victim is enough to sate the creature. A callum with a sorcerer's blood on its claw will scurry away as happy as can be.

Callum can sense magic—as if they are smelling it—from up to a mile away. Once they sense it, they are driven to obtain it. Despite what rumors suggest, they do not drain the magic or consume it. They just possess it. Callum cannot identify or use magic items, nor can they distinguish between magic and other similar sources of power from outside Ardeyn, like cyphers from the Strange.

Interaction: Callum are not aggressive unless dealing with someone who has a magic item or who threatens the magic items they have. If there is no magic involved, they are docile herbivores very likely to hide in high branches. They have cunning animal intelligence.

Use: Callum are an interesting threat because unless a character has inherent magic, they want only her cyphers or artifacts, not her flesh.

Loot: A group of callum has 1d6 cyphers and (very occasionally) a single artifact hidden on their bodies or in their nest. They will all die defending these prizes.

Callum is both singular and plural.

GM Intrusion: *With one action, the callum grabs a magic object from the character and scrambles up and out of reach (but not out of sight).*

Size Comparison

Capricious Caterpillar 5 (15)

A capricious caterpillar in a recursion operating under the law of Magic is sometimes an entity of perilous power (as opposed to a tiny larva that's easily squished). It can ensnare others to its will by giving unsolicited advice that might be part of an elaborate trap, spell, or unpleasant curse. On the other hand, it's possible for a capricious caterpillar to be helpful and provide good advice to a wandering traveler. That's when one should be especially on guard, because sooner or later, the creature is likely to turn up again like a bad penny and ask for a favor in return.

"She stretched herself up on tiptoe, and peeped over the edge of the mushroom, and her eyes immediately met those of a large blue caterpillar that was sitting on the top with its arms folded, quietly smoking a long hookah, and taking not the smallest notice of her or of anything else."
—Alice's Adventures in Wonderland

Motive: Collect favors, spy

Environment (Wonderland | Magic): Almost anywhere

Health: 25

Damage Inflicted: 5 points

Movement: Short

Modifications: Wonderland lore as level 7; guessing secrets as level 6.

Combat: Capricious caterpillars know spells and often wield items (most notably, magic hookahs) that help channel their powers, granting them offensive and defensive abilities. Instead of attacking with mundane weapons, they use spells of fire, smoke, and coughing curses. For instance, a capricious caterpillar may do one of the following as its action during combat, but never the same effect twice in two rounds.

GM Intrusion: *The capricious caterpillar blows a smoke ring around the character in short range. The character must make a successful Might defense roll or shrink to just over 3 inches (8 cm) of height for one minute.*

d6	Ability
1	Attack all creatures within immediate range with a cloud of smoke. On a failed Might defense roll, victims suffer damage and a fit of coughing that renders them unable to take actions in the following round.
2	Create a magic smoke circle that targets one creature in short range. If the victim fails a Speed defense roll, it is teleported to a random location within long range.
3	Blow smoke into the eyes of a target within immediate range. If the victim fails an Intellect defense roll, she sees her ally as the capricious caterpillar for one minute or until she spends a round rubbing the smoke out of her eyes.
4	Blow a smoke ring around itself and teleport to a nearby treetop within long range.
5	Reveal a secret that one character is keeping from one or more of her allies. If no secret fits here, treat this as a psychic attack against a character within short range that deals Intellect damage if the victim fails an Intellect defense roll.
6	Breathe in a long draught of smoke that completely heals the capricious caterpillar of damage.

Interaction: Capricious caterpillars are usually standoffish, and when one does decide to communicate, it speaks in short, rather rude sentences, followed quickly by difficult questions. A capricious caterpillar also has a seventh sense when it comes to knowing secrets a character might be harboring.

Use: A bounty has been put on a capricious caterpillar's head—literally. Less will be paid if the creature is returned alive. If found, the capricious caterpillar offers double the bounty for the head of the person who sent the PCs after it in the first place.

Loot: A capricious caterpillar usually carries a few hundred gold coins, a cypher or two, and a hookah that confers the abilities described above to whoever uses it (depletion roll of 1 on a d6).

CATASTROPHE CLOUD 4 (12)

A catastrophe cloud is a murmuration of thousands of tiny machines sharing one mind, one purpose. The catastrophe cloud takes a variety of shapes and patterns as it approaches a potential target, becoming an entrancing, almost hypnotic display that belies the danger it poses. Each cloud consists of a million individual machines called catastrophs, each one about an inch (3 cm) long and having negligible weight. A catastroph resembles a black wasp with six limbs and translucent black wings. The back four legs provide locomotion, while the front two end in small, articulated hands.

Even a single catastroph is dangerous. Programmed to self-replicate, a catastroph harvests materials from its surroundings and rapidly constructs a partner. Once it finishes, the two immediately start work on building another. One catastroph can become a cloud in a matter of days. After the catastrophe cloud forms, it continues to grow, devouring everything in its path. Entire recursions have been stripped of resources to feed these ravenous swarms.

A catastrophe cloud typically fills an area within a radius of 20 feet (6 m).

Motive: Hungers for matter

Environment (Mad Science or Standard Physics): Catastrophe clouds swarm across any lands, usually in places rich in minerals and metals.

Health: 12

Damage Inflicted: 4 points

Movement: Short

Modifications: Speed defense as level 6 due to amorphous nature.

Combat: A catastrophe cloud is a mass of countless tiny machines. The cloud can flow around obstacles and squeeze through cracks and other openings that are large enough to permit a single catastroph.

The cloud can flow over and around other creatures. A character can move through the cloud, albeit at half the normal rate of movement. For characters inside the cloud, the difficulty of all tasks related to perception is increased by one step. In addition, whenever a character takes her turn inside the cloud, she must make a Might defense roll as the cloud begins to devour her. On a success, she takes 1 point of damage; on a failure, she takes 4 points.

A catastrophe cloud ignores any attack that targets a single creature, but it takes double the damage from attacks that affect an area. A catastrophe cloud cannot enter liquids and can be dispersed (treat as stunned and unable to act) if subjected to a strong wind. Once dispersed, it takes an hour for the cloud to reform.

Interaction: A catastrophe cloud has no means of communicating with other creatures.

Use: A PC moving through an inapposite gate brings along a stowaway: a single catastroph. In a matter of days, this passenger becomes a cloud and, if not stopped, could become a significant threat.

Single catastrophs sometimes go off-program, and instead of constructing additional catastrophs, they build weird structures or artifacts. If normal catastrophe clouds find these "cancers" among their kind, they descend upon the defective catastroph and whatever the loner was attempting to fashion.

GM Intrusion: *The catastrophe cloud destroys one cypher carried by a character it damaged.*

GM Intrusion: *The character with the highest Armor must make a Speed defense roll. On a failure, the physical armor is partly eaten and loses 1 point until it can be repaired.*

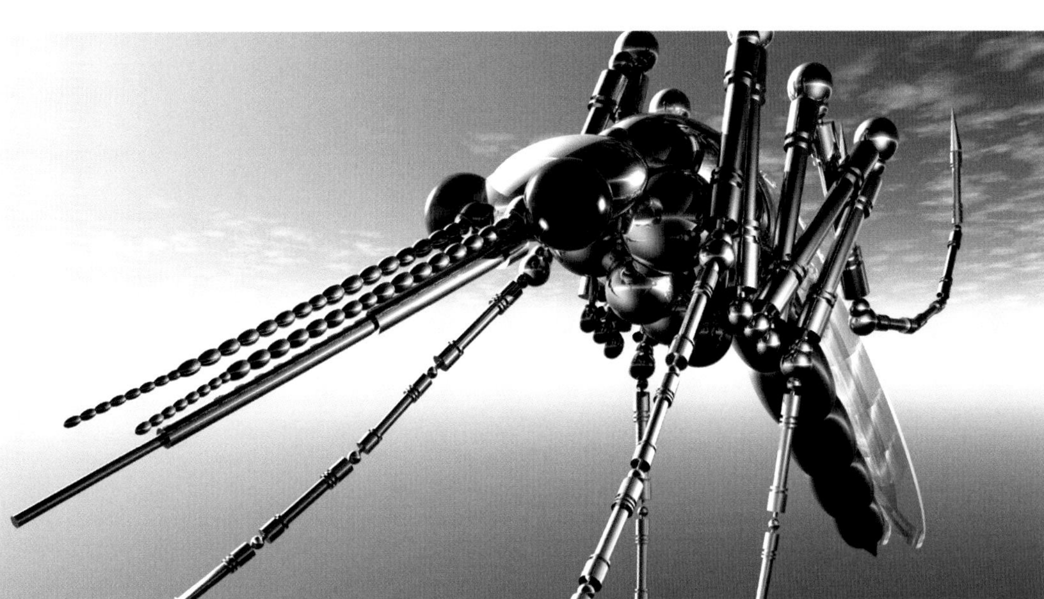

CHALLA HOST 6 (18)

> **"Although it might appear to be a 'suit' or even a vehicle, it would be wrong to think that of a challa. You don't wear the challa so much as it wears you. Or, to be more precise, it absorbs you and uses your knowledge and insight in exchange for protection."**
> —Arc-godius the scholar

Ruk biotechnology has created a number of symbiotes and parasitic organisms that attach to a living creature, but the challa host is interesting because it is the opposite. It is a host designed for a human (or similar creature) to become a parasitic symbiote within it. Essentially, the symbiote serves as a consultant, but the challa takes all actions. In return, it protects and provides nutrition for the symbiote within it. Challa require a special nutrient paste called tillivin to live, and this ends up being a sort of currency for them.

Motive: Varies greatly, but tillivin is important

Environment (Ruk | Mad Science): Anywhere

Health: 32

Damage Inflicted: 6 points

Armor: 3

Movement: Short

Modifications: Perception as level 8; Speed defense as level 5 due to size.

Combat: The challa's body offers excellent protection. In addition to its standard Armor, it has +4 to Armor against heat, cold, and general impacts (such as falling). It can even survive in a vacuum. When it attacks, it typically uses one of its three bladelike legs, although the smaller tendrils can wield most technological ranged weaponry.

The symbiote inside the challa does not need to worry about eating or breathing (the seal around the character is airtight) and is generally warm and comfortable. The symbiote can even sleep while the challa acts. However, the symbiote cannot take physical actions of any kind while inside. For example, a paradox can't use most of her revisions while inside because she has no connection to the outside. The symbiote can see out and offer suggestions, but the challa is in control.

Challa with no symbiote are lethargic and disoriented. The difficulty of all actions they take is increased by one step. Thus, sometimes they are reluctant to let a symbiote go.

Interaction: Challa are independently intelligent but communicate only through the All Song. Thus, if not in Ruk, they do not communicate at all, except with their symbiote. A challa is always in communication with its symbiote and occasionally asks for advice or input.

Use: As an ally, a challa can take a character through dangerous areas in relative safety, although the character is not in control. As a foe, a challa is a dangerous opponent that—if defeated—likely has another dangerous opponent inside it, entirely unharmed.

Paradox, page 30

Revision, page 32

All Song, page 192

GM Intrusion: *After suffering damage, the challa host cannot release its symbiote even if it wanted to. The character within is trapped until some means of repair can be found.*

CHAOS TEMPLAR 6 (18)

Chaos Templars are a breed apart, literally. Each is a survivor of a separate prime world destroyed by planetovores. Templars spend much of their time searching the Strange for other survivors, exterminating entities that might one day become planetovores, and attempting to find ways to destroy active planetovores. This includes hunting for the perhaps-mythical artifact called the Chaos Sword, a device of normal matter so powerful that it can supposedly cleave through matter, recursions, and the Strange itself in vast, solar-system-sized slices.

Planetovore, page 8

Uentaru, page 229

Forged by their founder, Uentaru, into a cohesive group with distinctive golden armoring technology, Chaos Templars are a powerful alien force operating in the Strange. Each Templar possesses a unique quality, ability, or device that allowed her to survive on her own in the Strange before joining the group.

Sometimes Chaos Templars help others, and other times they ignore needy pleas. They may seem understandable, but they are just as often inscrutable.

The founder of the Chaos Templars is an individual known as Uentaru. Something of a military scientist among her own kind, she used advanced technology to escape into the Strange when her world was destroyed.

Motive: Defend against planetovores, unpredictable

Environment (the Strange): Anywhere

Health: 21

Damage Inflicted: 6 points

Armor: 2

Movement: Short

Modifications: Speed defense as level 7 due to golden armor; knowledge of the Strange and navigation of the Strange as level 7.

Combat: Each Templar's swiftness and strength is magnified by her golden armor, which allows up to two unarmed melee attacks as a single action. However, every Templar has an artifact that gives her one or two useful abilities in combat. One is a long-range energy attack against a foe and (if the Templar desires) every creature in immediate range of that foe. The energy varies depending on the Templar but is usually x-ray, gamma ray, or collimated microwave energy.

During any round in which a Chaos Templar spends an action tending to her wounds, she recovers 6 points of health (thanks to her golden armor). In addition, a Chaos Templar who spends an action reconfiguring her armor can make it impervious to heat, cold, or another extreme environment (only one type at a time) for up to an hour. Doing so reduces the Armor value to 1 during that time. Most Chaos Templars also have two or three cyphers that can be used in combat.

GM Intrusion: *When the character attacks the Chaos Templar with a melee weapon, he misses, and the weapon sticks to the Templar's golden armor. Pulling it free requires a successful Might-based task.*

Interaction: The golden armor serves as a universal translator, allowing a Chaos Templar to converse with most aliens she meets. Each Templar has a unique personality, and many are amenable to negotiation.

Use: A chance encounter with a Chaos Templar could introduce a useful and unexpected ally for characters who are experiencing a series of misfortunes and require a helping hand.

Loot: A Chaos Templar carries two or three cyphers. A Templar's golden armor and unique artifact are keyed to the individual Templar—anyone else would find the items difficult to use.

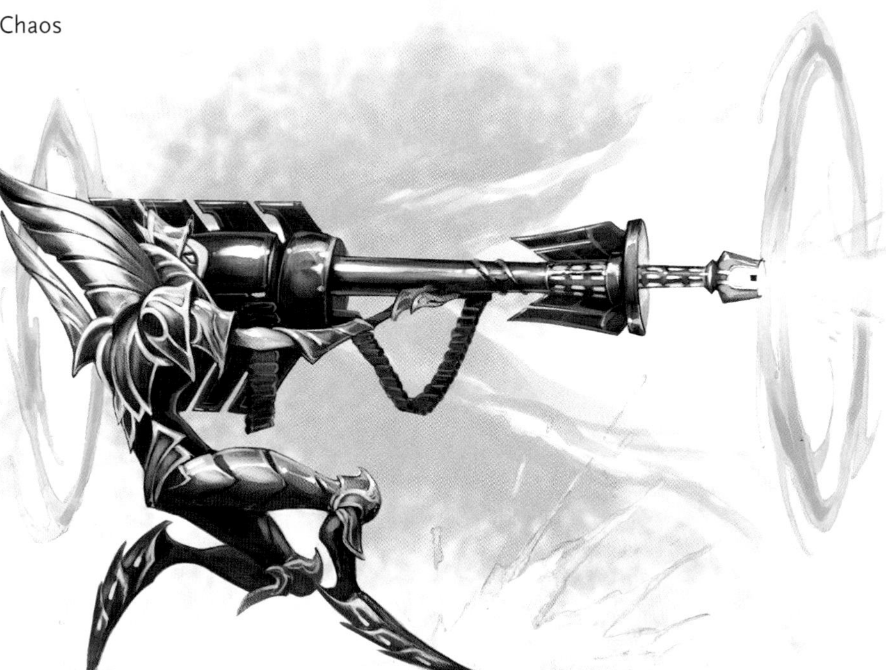

Size Comparison

CHIMERA 6 (18)

Efforts to improve upon nature sometimes go awry, especially in recursions dominated by Mad Science. Unchecked and uncontrolled meddling with biological form and function sometimes creates chimeras. These strange hybrids combine the features of many different animals, often arranged in odd formations. The fusion of animal forms is the only thing that unifies these creatures. Chimeras include combinations of goat and lion, lizard and bat. A few even display human features, such as an improbably located face or hands instead of claws. Some chimeras can fly. Others slither across the ground. The variation seems endless, and each new manifestation demonstrates just how far their makers were willing to go.

"On the road to perfection, there will naturally be a few detours and missteps along the way."
—Polyx, Atlantis scientist

A chimera typically has a dominant form to which other animal parts are grafted. The base form must be large enough to support the weight of the extra heads, so lions, bears, and horses are popular as the base form.

Chimeras kill even when not hungry and throw their victims' remains around a wide area in a wild rage. When not feeding or tormenting prey, a chimera that can fly takes to the air, beating its enormous leather wings to scour the landscape for new prey.

A chimera's grafts can be anything. It might have a serpent's tail and the heads of a dragon, a lion, and a goat, or it could incorporate the wings, head, and talons of an eagle.

Motive: Hungers for human flesh

Environment (Mad Science or Magic): Anywhere, usually alone but sometimes in groups of two or three

Health: 21

Damage Inflicted: 4 points

Movement: Short while on the ground; long while flying (if it can fly)

Modifications: Speed defense rolls as level 5 due to size.

Combat: All chimeras have a number of ways to kill. The exact methods vary, but most can bite, sting, and gore (three attacks) as a single action, either attacking the same opponent or attacking different foes within immediate range of each other. The chimera's sting carries a powerful toxin, and a stung target must succeed on a Might defense roll or take 4 additional points of damage. Chimeras with spikes can project them at up to three targets within long range as a single action.

GM Intrusion: *The chimera grabs a character it bites and flies off with him.*

Interaction: Chimeras are a lot like wild animals with rabies. They're confused and violent, and they behave erratically. Savage, ferocious beasts, they hate all other creatures and seize any opportunity to kill.

Use: While exploring an island, the PCs find carcasses that have been torn apart, the pieces scattered in all directions. A chimera lairs nearby, and if the characters draw attention to themselves, it hunts them down, too.

COG MITE 2 (6)

The arachnoid cog mites infest the Machine God's bowels like vermin. They boil up from the depths with each tremor, agitated by the disturbance, and flow like water through the passages and chambers.

A cog mite resembles a crab made from silicon, metal, and bits of circuitry. Its body is 2 feet (0.6 m) in diameter, and it stands about 1 foot (0.3 m) tall. It scuttles about on six legs, the feet magnetized so it can crawl up walls and across ceilings. It has one large claw and a smaller claw. A single purple eye dominates the center of its body. The eye emits a purple beam of light that it uses to scan the environment or attack.

Motive: Defense, harvest materials to create new cog mites

Environment (Graveyard of the Machine God | Mad Science or Psionics): Anywhere in groups of up to twenty, outside of places inhabited by the sacrosanct

Health: 12

Damage Inflicted: 2 points

Armor: 2

Movement: Short

Modifications: All tasks related to balancing and climbing as level 4; Speed defense as level 4 due to size.

Combat: A cog mite attacks with its large claw so it can grab a creature and hold the victim in place. A victim damaged by the claw must also make a Might defense roll, or it is held fast and cannot move until it escapes or the cog mite dies. For a grabbed victim, the difficulty of all attack and defense rolls is increased by two steps.

Once the cog mite gets a grip on a creature, it focuses the light generated by its eye into a cutting torch that automatically inflicts 2 points of damage (ignores Armor) each round. Alternatively, it can use its smaller claw to snip its victim's body, automatically inflicting 3 points of damage.

Interaction: Individual cog mites behave as their programming dictates. They have little independent will and function more or less as machines.

Use: When a swarm of cog mites floods into the chambers of the sacrosanct, the mites steal a prized artifact and drag it off into the depths of the Machine God.

Loot: About one in six cog mites carries a cypher, something it salvaged but did not yet use to create the next generation of cog mites.

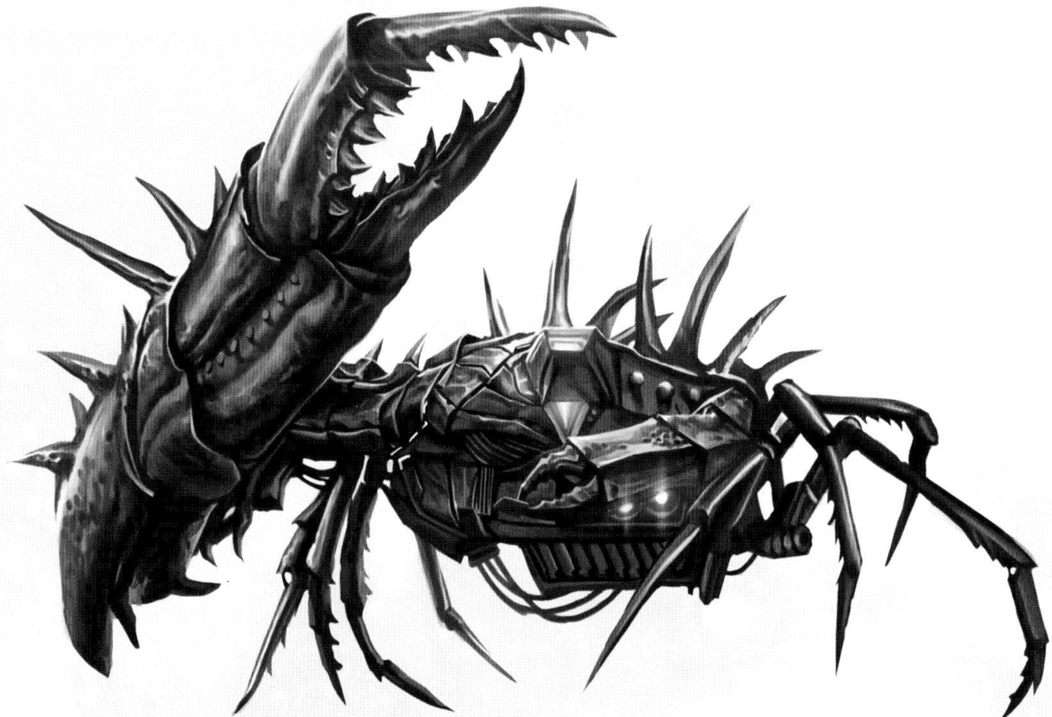

SIZE COMPARISON

Scavengers, cog mites pick through the detritus of the recursion to harvest technological scraps, which they feed on or use to fashion more of their kind.

In large groups, six cog mites can focus their attacks against one target to make a single attack roll as a level 4 creature, inflicting 4 points of damage.

The more cog mites there are, the more cunning they become until they develop a hive mind, allowing them to act as a group organism. Large nests of cog mites sometimes develop a sense of identity and may communicate with intruders telepathically.

GM Intrusion: *The attack from a cog mite's laser eye reduces the value of the target's Armor (if any) by 1 until it's repaired.*

GM Intrusion: *A character damaged by a cog mite must immediately make a Might defense roll to resist the nanovirus infestation.*

Nanovirus infestation, page 244

Size Comparison

COLLECTIVE 7 (21)

This sodden, leather-wrapped humanoid smells of the sea. It moves effortlessly through the air, levitating above the ground while its damp wrappings writhe and squirm as if infested with thousands of worms—because they are.

Each collective is a mass of psionic grubs worming through a slush of salty ooze. Individually the grubs are harmless vermin, but together they're a sentient entity, a single psionic mind formed of thousands of tiny, maggotlike pupae.

The tightly wound leather straps covering a collective are just as important for hiding its true nature as for adhesion. Despite being fully encased, the collective senses its environment with a hard-to-fool sixth sense.

A collective's individual grubs could be an immature form of some as-yet unnamed (or unrecognized) creature.

Motive: Domination of other creatures, hunger

Environment (Magic or Psionics): Almost anywhere

Health: 30

Damage Inflicted: 7 points

Armor: 1

Movement: Immediate; short when flying

Modifications: Perception as level 8; Speed defense as level 5 due to slow nature.

Combat: A collective can strike a single target in immediate range with a leather-wrapped "fist" as its action. When it hits and deals damage, several grubs spill out and attach to the victim (getting under most armor unless it's hermetically sealed or behind a force field), requiring a Might defense roll to shake them loose. On a failure, the grubs begin to feed and the target takes 5 points of ambient damage.

If a victim is killed while in immediate range of a collective, the collective automatically engulfs the body through a wide opening in its wrappings. The grubs go into a feeding frenzy, reducing the remains to nothing within minutes. During the frenzy, the collective regenerates 2 points of health per round. A victim's equipment is retained for later study.

A collective can also emit a psychic burst that can target up to three creatures in short range as its action. On a failed Intellect defense roll, a victim suffers 4 points of Intellect damage and is unable to take any actions on her subsequent turn. If she is attacked while so stunned, the difficulty of her defense rolls is increased by two steps.

Interaction: A collective can communicate telepathically with characters within short range. It negotiates only with characters strong enough to harm it; otherwise, it tries to eat whoever it runs across. Even if a collective makes a deal, it eventually reneges if it senses any advantage for doing so.

Use: A collective has been active in a small rural community for weeks, apparently in preparation for something it calls "the Great Hatching." If that refers to the hatching of more psychic grubs, it could spell trouble for a much larger region.

Loot: Collectives might have one or two cyphers, though during combat they will use any devices that could help them in the fight.

GM Intrusion: *A character struck by a collective notices that she wasn't able to shake off all the grubs that spilled out. If she fails a Speed defense roll, a grub dives into her flesh and travels through her body, its route visible beneath her skin. The character is distracted, and until the grub dies (which takes one minute) or is otherwise extracted, the difficulty of all tasks she attempts is increased by one step.*

CRAZR 5 (15)

Size Comparison

Machines built for destruction, CRAZRs are nothing less than the end of all things given form. They are designed to run down and destroy targets as quickly and efficiently as possible. CRAZR stands for Canid Robotic Zealous Reapers (the "A" doesn't stand for anything, except to let the acronym evoke the word "crazy," which these machines are). They attack without fear and, despite not being particularly tactical or tough, inflict so much harm in so little time that they can bring down much more powerful targets.

CRAZRs usually go after other machines, not creatures of flesh. For this reason, some people believe they are part of the defunct Machine God's derelict programming, perhaps as a corruption, or perhaps as part of a partially reactivated punishment subroutine that spits out new CRAZRs year after year.

Motive: Destroy all moving (usually machine) targets

Environment (Graveyard of the Machine God | Mad Science): Almost anywhere

Health: 15

Damage Inflicted: 5 points

Movement: Long

Combat: A CRAZR makes attacks with spinning saw blades, which are designed to chew through the metal hides of other machine creatures. Thus, CRAZR attacks ignore up to 1 point of a target's Armor.

A CRAZR is quick; as a single action, it can move a long distance each round, or move a short distance and attack with all four spinning blades. This quickness comes with a cost: its metallic covering is light, thinner than skin, and just as delicate (which is why CRAZRs have no Armor).

A CRAZR can emit a brilliant spotlight to see in the dark, and it's able to track prey by noting small clues in the environment like scratches, footprints, doors left ajar, and so on.

Interaction: CRAZRs are sapient but constantly operate in berserker mode. If a character can find a way to directly interface with a CRAZR, the creature might pause for several rounds before reverting to its murderous programming. Gaining control of a CRAZR or reprogramming it using this method isn't easy because of built-in failsafes; treat the attempt as a level 8 hacking task.

Use: PCs who enter the recursion disturb a CRAZR that at first seemed like an inert piece of drifting machinery.

Rather than attack foes indiscriminately, some CRAZRs seem to go after targets that breach never-before-opened chambers of the Machine God that contain relics or artifacts.

GM Intrusion: *A CRAZR's spinning blade severs a support, cable, or structural element, causing a wall or ceiling section to collapse.*

CRUCIBLE 5 (15)

Crucibles don't seem to come from a recursion seeded by fictional leakage, nor do they seem to be natives of the Strange. Their origin is a mystery.

A crucible is both synthetic and organic. Polymers and alloys seamlessly fuse with warm flesh and pumping blood. A living supercomputer, a crucible is a creature of frightening intelligence with the ability to absorb inorganic and organic material to repair itself or adapt to new situations.

Crucibles move using a version of translation that essentially allows them to teleport short distances within a given recursion, or slide between Mad Science or Psionics recursions (though that takes longer). Crucibles act on a subtle, decades-long plan that requires them to make minor adjustments (and sometimes major changes) in the recursions around the Shoals of Earth and perhaps beyond. What their ultimate goal is, and whether they're working together or at cross purposes, isn't something any crucible has yet revealed.

Motive: Intercede in various recursions

Environment (Mad Science or Psionics): Usually in secure facilities with a few servitor creatures on hand

Health: 21

Damage Inflicted: 5

Movement: Immediate

Modifications: Speed defense as level 2; knowledge of recursions and the Strange as level 8.

Combat: A crucible can pummel foes within short range with long, silvery tendrils.

Because it can absorb matter, physical attacks against a crucible may not have the intended effect. A character who successfully attacks a crucible with a melee weapon or an unarmed strike must make a Speed defense roll. On a failed roll with a weapon, the attack deals damage, and then the crucible absorbs the weapon, destroying it and regaining 1 point of health. On a failed roll with an unarmed strike, the attack is negated and the character takes 3 points of Speed damage (ignores Armor).

A crucible can also spend its action absorbing matter around it (such as walls, floor, equipment, unresisting living creatures, and so on), regaining 5 points of health.

Although a crucible normally moves slowly, it can use an action to teleport a short distance every other round. A crucible that has cyphers or artifacts uses them in combat.

Interaction: A crucible usually speaks by plugging into nearby electronic systems to generate a synthetic voice, though some can also speak telepathically. A crucible is willing to negotiate, especially if it wants something, though if its goals are at odds with what the PCs want, it's unlikely to give in without a fight.

Use: The characters are contacted by a crucible that wants them to accomplish a task in a recursion that operates under the law of Magic. The job: assassinate a ruler (who the crucible paints as evil) and put an imprisoned heir (who the crucible describes as innocent) in the ruler's place.

Loot: A crucible might have 1d6 cyphers and possibly an artifact.

GM Intrusion: *The character damaged by a silvery tendril must succeed on a Might defense roll or be snatched into the crucible's embrace. Until the PC escapes with a successful Might-based task, she can't take any actions except trying to escape. While caught, she speaks in the crucible's voice, issuing threats to the other characters.*

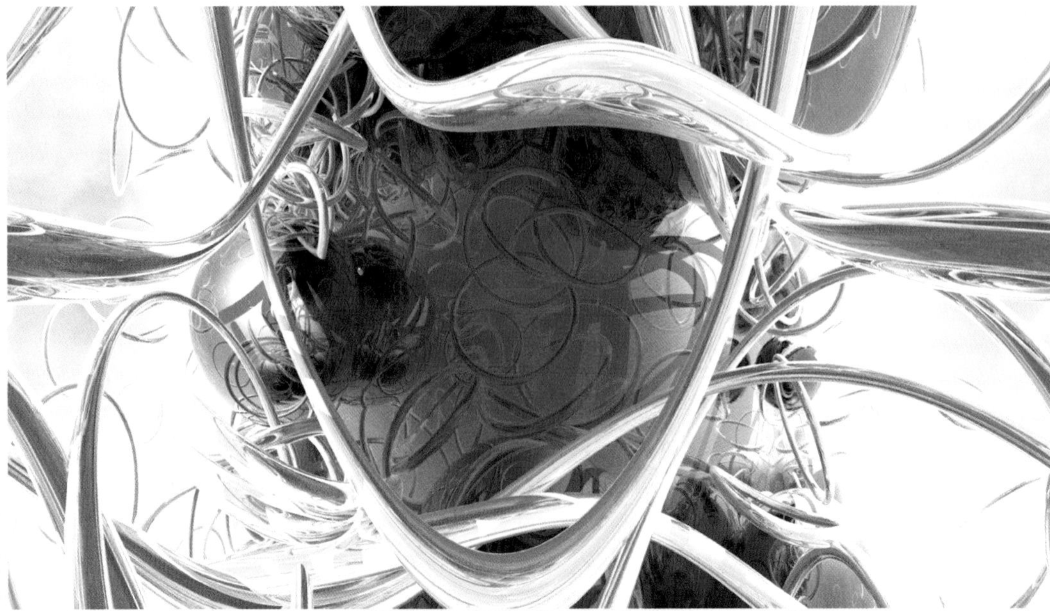

CYBER SORCERER 7 (21)

Magic and technology are not always at odds. In some recursions, magic is just another power source, and as such, it can drive a machine—even a very sophisticated one. A cyber sorcerer is an intelligent android literally fueled by magic that powers a variety of spells and incantations.

Cyber sorcerers typically look like whatever they wish, but their natural form is that of an advanced mechanical humanoid. Most are quite mad with power.

Motive: Accumulate power

Environment (Magic and Mad Science): Anywhere, alone or with servants

Health: 28

Damage Inflicted: 8 points

Armor: 3

Movement: Short

Modifications: Knowledge of magic or technology as level 8.

Combat: Cyber sorcerers draw upon their own essence to power magic spells. At the cost of 1 point of health, a cyber sorcerer can use its action to do one of the following:

- Fire a blast of magic energy up to long range that inflicts 8 points of damage
- Create a burst of magic energy within long range that inflicts 5 points of damage to all in an immediate area
- Create a wall of magic energy that is an immobile plane of solid force up to 20 feet by 20 feet (6 m by 6 m) for one hour
- See or phase through a solid barrier up to 1 foot (0.3 m) thick
- Turn invisible for ten minutes
- Teleport up to 1 mile (2 km) away
- Change its appearance to look like any creature of approximately the same size

At the cost of 2 points of health and ten minutes of time, a cyber sorcerer can do one of the following:

- Change one mundane object into another of approximately the same size and complexity
- Look up to one week into the past or future (the future seen is only a possible future)
- Heal another creature or repair an object, restoring 7 points to a stat Pool or health (does not work on itself)
- Charge a depowered technological device for one hour (could vary depending on the device)

At the same time, a cyber sorcerer can drain magic as an action, absorbing the power of a magic effect or artifact it touches and gaining a number of points of health equal to the effect or artifact's level. Likewise, a magic creature or a character who uses magic, such as a wizard, can be drained so that it suffers 7 points of damage (ignores Armor) and the cyber sorcerer gains a like amount. There is no upper limit to the amount of health a cyber sorcerer can gain in this fashion, but at some point, after absorbing too much, it could overload and explode.

Interaction: Cyber sorcerers are intelligent, paranoid, and not automatically hostile. They have their own self-serving agendas, which often involve elaborate schemes.

Use: These beings make excellent master villains with a variety of machinations.

Loot: Cyber sorcerers typically have a magic artifact and perhaps a cypher or two.

GM Intrusion: *The cyber sorcerer casts a unique magic spell that is perfect for the situation at hand.*

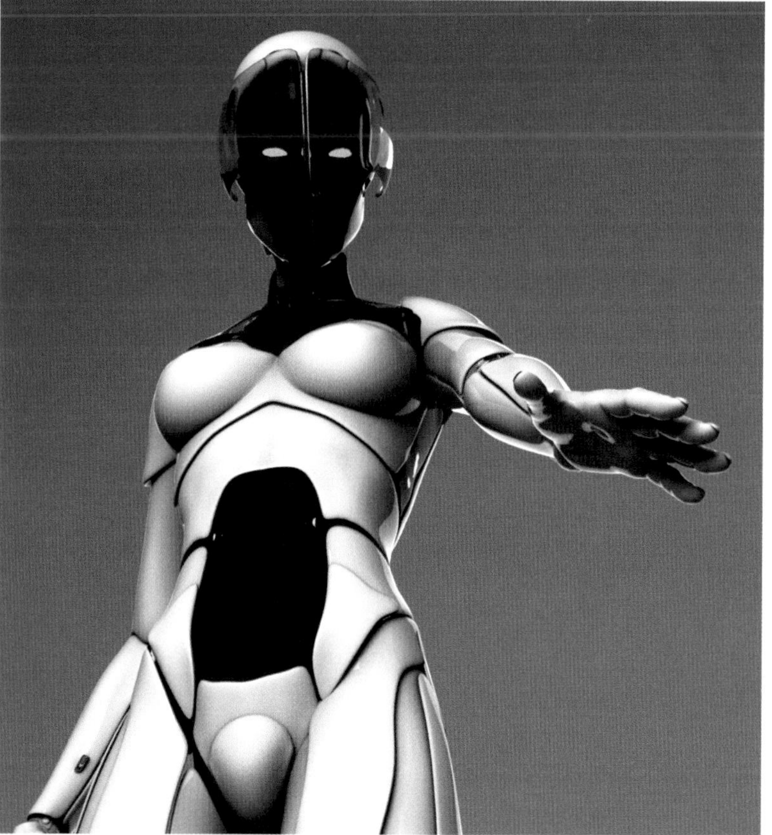

CYCLOPS 7 (21)

Gigantic creatures from Greek mythology, cyclopes resemble massive humans that stand 50 to 60 feet (15 to 18 m) tall and weigh about 10,000 pounds (4,536 kg). Everything about these giants is exaggerated, from the thick features of their faces to their oversized hands and lumpy, corpulent bodies. They clothe themselves in animal skins, scraps of cloth, or canvas stolen during their travels. A cyclops's most distinctive feature is the single eye positioned in the center of its forehead.

Cyclopes live on the edges of civilized areas or on remote islands. For all their power and stature, they aren't especially brave, and most have a dim idea that puny humans have an advantage when they have numbers on their side.

Motive: Fill its belly with food

Environment (Magic or Mad Science): Almost anywhere

Health: 32

Damage Inflicted: 8 points

Armor: 1

Movement: Short

Modifications: Attacks targets at immediate range as level 5 due to poor eyesight; Speed defense as level 5 due to size; Intellect defense as level 4.

Combat: A cyclops can always resort to using its fists in melee, pummeling opponents with knuckles the size of large hogs. However, most cyclopes carry a tree trunk and use it to sweep enemies from their path. Due to its massive height, a cyclops can make a melee attack against creatures within short range.

Cyclopes can also pry up boulders from the ground and throw them at targets within long range. A thrown boulder attacks one target plus everything within an immediate distance of the target, inflicting 8 points of damage.

Killing a cyclops can be dangerous. When killed, it falls away from the attacker that delivered the killing blow. Any creature under it when it falls must make a successful Speed defense roll or be pinned under its corpse and take 7 points of damage. Escaping from under a dead cyclops requires a successful Might roll.

Interaction: Cyclopes know the language of the lands they inhabit, but they are notoriously dim and easily fooled. A cyclops thinks about its belly first and foremost and doesn't pay much attention to what it stuffs in its mouth.

Use: A cyclops has been rampaging across the countryside, and warriors sent to deal with it have been vanquished. PCs who investigate learn that the cyclops has been robbed and is trying to find the stolen item.

Loot: Most cyclopes carry sacks filled with things they find interesting or plan to eat. Aside from the rubbish, a typical sack contains 1d100 coins of the realm and a couple of cyphers.

GM Intrusion: *The cyclops hits a character so hard that he flies a short distance away and lands prone.*

GM Intrusion: *A character struck by the cyclops's fist is grabbed and stuffed in the creature's sack.*

DATA SENTINEL 4 (12)

Data sentinels are probably free-roaming instances of the AI that controls the recursion known as Singularitan, but given their erratic behavior, it's possible that they represent a challenging intelligence. Either way, they are dangerous to other entities, whether machine or organic. Data sentinels could be rogue, accumulating data only for their own purposes.

A data sentinel is a creature of silicon, steel alloys, and electromagnetic energy. It is able to physically tap into nearly every kind of computerized system it encounters, including living minds.

Motive: Knowledge

Environment (Singularitan | Mad Science): Almost anywhere, sometimes in pairs

Health: 18

Armor: 2

Damage Inflicted: 4 points

Movement: Short

Modifications: Most knowledge tasks (including those related to the Strange) as level 7; crafting tasks as level 7.

Combat: Data sentinels can discharge electromagnetic energy to attack a foe within long range. However, they can also spin cocooning strands of dataweb around a foe within immediate range who fails a Speed defense roll. A cocooned foe is held immobile and can take only purely mental actions or struggle to get free (a difficulty 6 Might-based task). The cocooned foe is an easier target for other combatants, whose attacks against her are modified by two steps in their favor.

Each round in which a victim remains cocooned, her brain tickles as knowledge is siphoned away and fed to the data sentinel. Generally, a data sentinel siphons a victim's data for a number of rounds equal to the victim's level or tier. After that, the cocoon begins feeding destructive energies into the victim's brain, and she must make an Intellect defense roll each round. On each failure, she takes 4 points of Intellect damage (ignores Armor). If the victim is freed from the cocoon, for the next several hours, the difficulty of all of her Intellect-based tasks is increased by two steps.

Some data sentinels have a cypher they use in combat.

Interaction: A data sentinel can communicate with a creature only via a data strand, and unfortunately, it tends to cocoon anyone who wants to talk.

Use: Data sentinels are storehouses of information about any number of things, including other recursions and the Strange itself.

Loot: A data sentinel sometimes has a cypher.

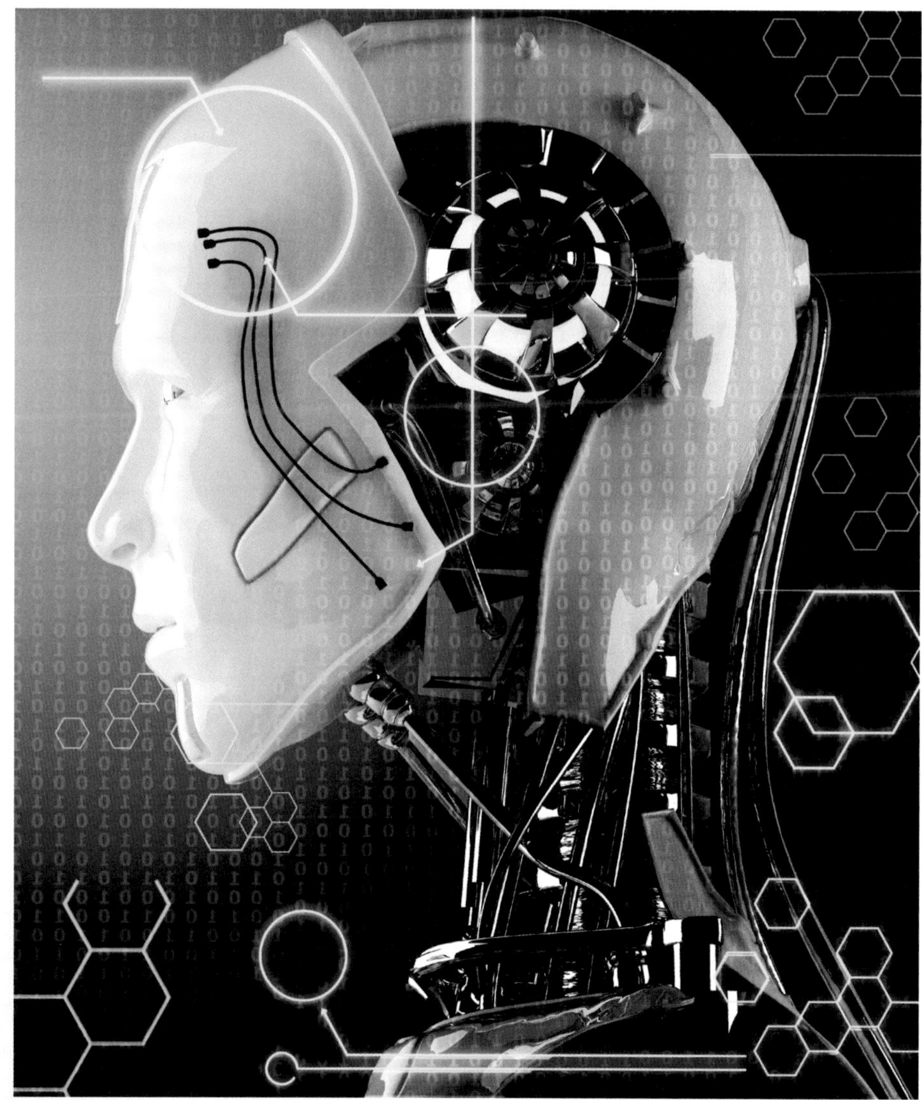

Singularitan, page 251

When a data sentinel comes across a completely new kind of creature or computer system, it may experiment for a few rounds to find the right protocol for cocooning the entity or object and siphoning the information contained therein.

GM Intrusion: *The data sentinel has a cypher that it uses to escape to another recursion.*

DEATHLESS CHARGER 5 (15)

A deathless charger is summoned when its disembodied horn is found and handled. Though the charger is deathless itself, it brings death to other creatures. Victims rarely realize what has killed them. Survivors describe a terrifying, horselike beast with a bone horn as the implement of their friend's death, a horn that moments earlier was not attached to a ton of bestial fury.

When not wed with its horn, a deathless charger is a bodiless spirit racing along the Night Vault's Roads of Sorrow, visible to the living as hardly more than the suggestion of a shape and a cool wind. Seeing one pass by is considered an omen of doom.

Roads of Sorrow, page 183

Motive: Kill those marked for death or those who handle its horn

Environment (Ardeyn | Magic): A deathless charger's disembodied horn can be found almost anywhere.

Health: 18

Damage Inflicted: Varies; see Combat

Armor: 1

Movement: Short

Modifications: First surprise attack as level 7; Speed defense as level 4.

Combat: A deathless charger usually begins a combat with surprise, appearing suddenly attached to its previously disembodied horn, and as if having charged full tilt to that point. This melee attack is made as if the charger were a level 7 creature; on a success, the charger deals 7 points of damage. In subsequent rounds, the deathless charger can attack with two hooves as its action against one or two creatures in immediate range, or charge a creature that is beyond immediate range but within short range. When it charges another creature using its horn as a weapon, a successful attack deals 2 additional points of damage (for a total of 5 points) that ignores Armor. The charger can charge as its attack only every other round.

If a deathless charger would be killed, it dissipates instead, leaving only its horn behind (as well as any rider or accoutrements).

Interaction: Deathless chargers were made as servants of Death, and little can sway them from attempting to kill whosoever has been marked by their disembodied horns.

Use: PCs interrupt a weapons deal in a recursion operating under the law of Magic. The items being sold in the leather case include a brace of bone horns.

Court of Sleep qephilim once rode deathless chargers to track wandering spirits. They could also handle a charger's disembodied horn safely and use it to mark those whom the Incarnation of Death had selected to die.

GM Intrusion: *The deathless charger fades into mist, leaving its disembodied horn behind. It may return later if the PCs keep the horn.*

DEEP ONE 4 (12)

"I think their predominant color was a greyish-green, though they had white bellies. They were mostly shiny and slippery, but the ridges of their backs were scaly. Their forms vaguely suggested the anthropoid, while their heads were the heads of fish, with prodigious bulging eyes that never closed. At the sides of their necks were palpitating gills, and their long paws were webbed. They hopped irregularly, sometimes on two legs and sometimes on four. I was somehow glad that they had no more than four limbs. Their croaking, baying voices, clearly used for articulate speech, held all the dark shades of expression which their staring faces lacked ... They were the blasphemous fish-frogs of the nameless design—living and horrible." —*The Shadow Over Innsmouth*

Some deep ones dwell in coastal regions on land, usually in isolated villages where they might attempt to pass for human. They are able to breathe both air and water. Most, however, thrive in the ocean depths, in ancient underwater cities like "Cyclopean and many-columned Y'ha-nthlei." Deep ones sometimes breed with insane humans to produce squamous offspring that eventually develop fully into deep ones well after maturity (or even middle age).

Motive: Hungers for flesh

Environment (Innsmouth | Mad Science, Psionics, or Magic): Anywhere near a large body of salt water

Health: 15

Damage Inflicted: 5 points

Armor: 2

Movement: Short on land; long in the water

Modifications: Swims as level 6; perception as level 3.

Combat: Deep ones attack with tooth and claw most often, although occasionally one might use a weapon.

Two deep ones that have grown colossal and powerful over time are called Mother Hydra and her consort, Father Dagon. Each stands 15 feet (5 m) tall, and they serve as deity-rulers among the deep ones.

Interaction: Deep ones are a strange mix of utter alienness and the vestiges of lost humanity. They are foul and degenerate creatures by human standards, however. Many still retain the ability to speak human languages, but all speak their own slurred, unearthly tongue.

Deep ones spend a great deal of their time involved in the sincere adoration of their gods, Mother Hydra, Father Dagon, and Cthulhu. Their religion demands frequent blood sacrifices.

Use: The PCs wander into a small coastal village where everyone seems standoffish and oddly distant. A few appear to be sickly and malformed, perhaps from mutation or birth defects. Some of the people have squamous skin because they are transforming into deep ones. And, of course, a number of true deep ones hide within the community as well.

Loot: A few deep ones will have a cypher.

SIZE COMPARISON

Deep ones value craftsmanship, making jewelry and weapons from various metals and coral.

Mother Hydra and Father Dagon: *level 8; health 38 each; Armor 4; each inflicts 10 points of damage.*

GM Intrusion: *The deep one produces a net and throws it over the character. The only physical action the PC can take is to try to get free, as either a Might-based or a Speed-based action.*

DEINONYCHUS 3 (9)

"Listen, call them what you want. Let's just get the fuck out of here."
—Torah "the Windmill" Bishop

Seeded into lost-world recursions with the name velociraptor, the dinosaur genus called *Deinonychus* doesn't care if its prey gets the proper terminology sorted. Meat tastes like meat. The "terrible claw" these carnivores are named after refers to their massive, sickle-shaped claws, which are unsheathed from their hind legs when attacking prey.

Deinonychus are popularly portrayed as pack hunters, and that's how they manifest in the recursions where they hunt: as creatures capable of working together to send even intelligent prey into the claws of an ambush.

"The actual paleontological record informs the look of Deinonychus as found in recursions, but the two don't usually match. Recursions aren't often seeded by factual leakage, more's the pity."
—Dr. Sybil Holloway

Motive: Hungers for flesh

Environment (Standard Physics, Substandard Physics, or Mad Science): Wherever they can hunt food, in packs of three to seven

Health: 15

Damage Inflicted: 4 points

Armor: 1

Movement: Short

Modifications: Perception as level 5; attacks and Speed defense as level 4 due to quickness.

Combat: When a deinonychus bites its prey, the victim takes damage and must make a Might defense roll. On a failure, the deinonychus holds the victim in place with its jaws while it slices him to ribbons with its terrible claws, automatically inflicting 6 points of damage each round in which he fails a Might-based task to break free (not attempting to break free counts as a failed attempt). The difficulty of all other tasks attempted by a human-sized or smaller victim held in the jaws is increased by two steps.

Interaction: Vicious, cunning, and a little too smart to be classified as simple predators, these creatures are unlikely to negotiate, give quarter, or back off from a fight even if contact could be made.

GM Intrusion: *Three more deinonychus join the fray.*

Use: Unfortunately for modern humans on Earth, deinonychus abilities don't degrade when some fool decides to build a Cretaceous-themed zoo. The only question is: How long before the dinosaurs get loose and take over the local mall?

DEMON DRAKE 9 (27)

Massive and powerful, demon drakes are thankfully rare. There may be only two or three in all of the recursions that they call home. They build their lairs of dozens—if not hundreds—of frozen, tormented figures. They refer to themselves as lords of Hell and play up their demonic role to the fullest. However, demon drakes are well aware of the Strange and the fact that their "Hell" is merely a recursion called Hell Frozen Over. They find this comforting, even pleasant, because although they crave power, they enjoy being the proverbial big fish in their little pond.

These creatures stand 15 feet (5 m) high when they rise up on their rear legs, and their wingspan is almost 40 feet (12 m). Their bodies are covered in scales that seem almost metallic.

Hell Frozen Over, page 251

Motive: Sadistic torment

Environment (Hell Frozen Over | Magic): Anywhere

Health: 50

Damage Inflicted: 13 points

Armor: 4 or 10; see Combat

Movement: Long when flying; short on the ground

Modifications: Speed defense as level 8 due to size.

Combat: Demon drakes are terrors that can attack up to three creatures within immediate range as a single action. They can breathe a stream of fire or intense cold that inflicts 15 points of damage on a single target within long range.

Demon drakes have 10 Armor against heat and cold.

Demon drakes are extremely intelligent, and although they are usually overconfident at the beginning of a battle, they can use brilliant strategy and cunning tricks and maneuvers if they need to.

Interaction: Demon drakes love making bargains, wagers, and deals, probably because they are relatively bored with their existence. Due to their nature, they attempt to twist any deal and trick others during negotiations, but ultimately they keep to the letter of any agreement they swear to.

Use: PCs in Hell Frozen Over find themselves face to face with a demon drake. Rather than devouring them, it challenges them to a wager: if they can recover an artifact from the Strange that it desires, it will leave them be, and even help them on their mission in its recursion. However, it demands that one of the PCs remains in its lair as a hostage to ensure that the others return with the item.

Loot: Demon drakes always have at least one artifact and 1d6 cyphers.

GM Intrusion: *The character struck by the demon drake's breath weapon is frozen solid in a mass of ice, immobile until she can break free (a difficulty 8 Might task).*

SIZE COMPARISON

Shattered Wastes, page 194

DEVOLVED 4 (12)

Not every bioengineering attempt in Ruk succeeds. The recursion's history is littered with failures and false starts, horrors sealed away in hidden vaults for future study and as proof that certain scientific avenues lead to dead ends. From time to time, these missteps escape confinement and carve out a place for themselves in the Shattered Wastes.

The devolved live on Ruk's fringes. These malformed, hideous brutes share a common heritage but display a wide array of maladies and mutations in the flesh, including limbs withered or elephantine, patches of thick, scaly skin, misplaced body parts, and more. Simple-minded and afflicted with pain from their twisted, broken forms, the devolved vent all their hatred and wrath against the "norms."

Motive: Hungers for flesh

Environment (Ruk | Mad Science): Groups of six to eight roam the Shattered Wastes of Ruk and sometimes venture closer to the Hub to raid for supplies and fresh meat.

Health: 21

Damage Inflicted: 4 to 8 points; see Combat

Movement: Short

Modifications: All tasks related to intimidation as level 6; Intellect defense and Speed defense as level 2 due to malformed nature.

Combat: Devolved attack with a claw, a bite, or some other body part. They throw themselves at their enemies with mindless ferocity and little regard for their own safety. Easily frustrated, a devolved grows stronger as its fury builds. Each time it misses with an attack, the damage it inflicts increases by 1 point (maximum of 8 points). Once the devolved successfully inflicts damage, its amount of damage inflicted returns to normal.

A devolved's genetic instability also has unexpected results when the creature is wounded. Each time a devolved takes damage, roll a d6. On an odd number, its level drops by 1, and it takes 1 additional point of damage. On an even number, its level increases by 1, and it regains 1 point of health. Adjustments are cumulative, but all adjustments fade after one minute.

In large groups, four devolved can focus their attacks against one target to make a single attack roll as a level 6 creature, inflicting 5 points of damage.

Interaction: Devolved speak when they must. They punctuate their statements with growls and barks. Their understanding seems limited to what they can immediately perceive, and they have a difficult time with abstract concepts. Devolved have violent tendencies, but if plied with gifts of food, odd trinkets, and other treasures, they may become amenable to conversation and might be convinced to share what they know about the lands around their camps.

Use: Devolved tumble out of the Wastes to attack the nearby communities and mobile factories all the time. The PCs must face mobs of them to protect a settlement or an expedition bound for a far-flung location at the recursion's edges.

Loot: For every three or so devolved, one is likely to carry a cypher.

GM Intrusion: *A devolved that is damaged by a character takes only half damage from that character for the next minute as its body adapts to whatever the PC used to make the attack.*

GM Intrusion: *When killed, the devolved splits into two smaller devolved (each is level 2, has 10 health, and inflicts 2 points of damage).*

DJINNI 7 (21)

Islamic texts describe djinn as inhabiting unseen dimensions beyond the visible universe, which hints at a possible truth: these paradoxical and powerful creatures may have been traveling between Earth and various recursions for thousands of years. Just like normal creatures, djinn are individuals, and they can be good, evil, or unconcerned about the fates and doings of creatures other than themselves.

Motive: Unpredictable

Environment (the Strange | Magic): Almost anywhere

Health: 35

Damage Inflicted: 9 points

Movement: Short; long when flying

Modifications: Knowledge of the Strange and Arabian history as level 8.

Combat: With a touch, a djinni can warp a victim's flesh, inflicting damage. Djinn can also spend an action to send out a magitech "EMP pulse" that renders all artifacts, machines, and lesser magic devices within short range inoperable for one minute. (If the item is part of a character's equipment, she can prevent this outcome by succeeding on a Speed defense roll.) Instead of disabling all devices in range, a djinni can instead take control of one item within range for one minute, if applicable.

A djinni can transform into a being of smoke and flame as its action. While in this form, it has +10 to Armor but can't attack foes. It gains the ability to fly a long distance each round and is able to communicate normally. The first time each day that a djinni returns to physical form after having become smoke, it regains 25 points of health.

Some djinn have the ability to grant wishes, and a few are beholden to do so thanks to an ancient, unexplained agreement with other djinn. Those who grant wishes twist them against the asker, especially if a wish is poorly worded or there are multiple ways to interpret the wish. The level of the effect granted is no greater than level 7, as determined by the GM, who can modify the effect of the wish accordingly. (The larger the wish, the more likely the GM will limit its effect.)

Finally, most djinn have a couple of cyphers and possibly an artifact useful in combat.

Interaction: When a djinni interacts with characters, it's narcissistic, certain in its own immense power, and unlikely to let slights pass. That said, depending on the personality and desires of a djinni, even low-tier characters could negotiate with one peacefully.

Use: Intel reports that OSR retrieved a magic lamp from a recursion created by fictional leakage from Arabian tales. The PCs' job is to determine whether there is reason for alarm.

Loot: Most djinn carry two or three cyphers, and some have an artifact native to the Strange.

Size Comparison

Some djinn inhabit pocket-sized recursions whose inapposite entry gates are affixed within the mouths of urns, pots, or lamps. Others live in much larger recursions created by fictional leakage from ancient Arabian tales.

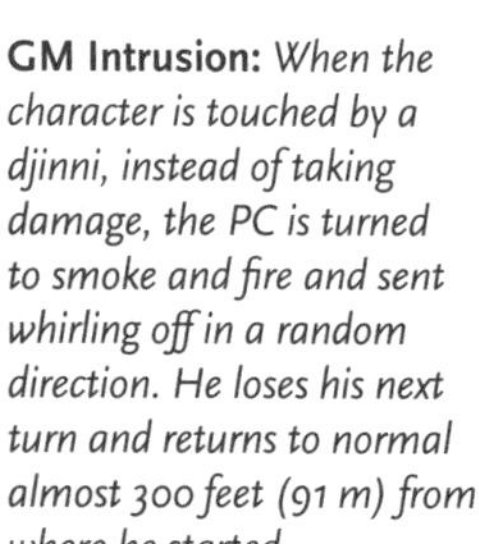

GM Intrusion: *When the character is touched by a djinni, instead of taking damage, the PC is turned to smoke and fire and sent whirling off in a random direction. He loses his next turn and returns to normal almost 300 feet (91 m) from where he started.*

DLAMMA RIDER 6 (18)

Adventuring company charters, page 167

Queendom of Hazurrium, page 166

Dlamma, page 266

The Honorary Order of Dlamma Riders is composed mostly of qephilim. Dlamma riders have an adventuring company charter from the Queendom of Hazurrium, though their explorations usually take them far beyond Ardeyn's edges into the dark energy network of the Strange itself.

Dlamma riders sometimes act as couriers, but they're best known for exploration. The horizon has snagged their hearts, and they're not happy unless they're traveling someplace new, searching for a lost qephilim city, a never-before-used beacon in the Chaosphere, or the shattered ruins of some other prime world. In Ardeyn, popular songs describe in haunting stanzas how dlamma riders risk everything just to see what no one has seen before.

Of course, a rider isn't much without her dlamma. For a dlamma to submit to be ridden requires a great bond of trust, which is a rare and precious thing. But once the bond is formed, rider and dlamma act as a single creature while together.

Motive: Exploration

Environment (Ardeyn | Magic): In remote regions of Ardeyn or the Strange

Health: 42

Damage Inflicted: 6 points

Armor: 2

Movement: Short; long while flying

Modifications: Perception, Ardeyn lore, knowledge of the Strange, and Strange navigation as level 7.

Combat: During the same round in which a rider attacks with her melee weapon, the dlamma mount can attack with its hooves, for a total of two attacks; treat them as a single action.

However, most foes never make it that close to a dlamma rider. At the same time that the rider directs long-range attacks at foes with a rune staff that fires bolts of magic lightning (6 points of damage), a dlamma can speak a Word of Smiting, which inflicts 6 points of damage on up to three targets within long range.

A dlamma rider also benefits from her dlamma's knowledge of other words of power, including words used to heal (for either rider or dlamma, restores 2 points of health each round for one minute), create shelter, and produce other useful effects.

A rider usually has a few useful cyphers in combat.

Interaction: While dlammas encountered alone are famously standoffish, a dlamma rider is more exuberant and talkative, especially if a character has news of a location where the rider has never been.

Use: A dlamma rider, sans her mount, offers an amazing reward to anyone who can help track down her missing dlamma.

Loot: A dlamma rider usually has a couple of cyphers gathered from her explorations.

If a rider is knocked from her dlamma mount, she is a level 4 creature with health 12, Armor 1, and a long-range attack that deals 6 points of damage.

GM Intrusion: *The dlamma utters a Word of Vanishing, and every character within long range who fails an Intellect defense roll becomes unable to sense the dlamma or its rider for one minute.*

DRONEME 2 (6)

Many thankless tasks are relegated to an underclass of workers grown in vats in recursions that possess such technology. These dronemes (also sometimes called "drones") carry out manual and unskilled labor that beautifies and maintains the places where the powerful live. As part of their natal development, dronemes are built, cell by cell, to perform a variety of basic tasks, such as hauling heavy loads, making repairs, cleaning, gardening, and anything else their makers need.

Although they excel in the tasks for which they're created, dronemes possess little individuality and personality. They exist to serve and nothing more. Rather than names, they have serial numbers tattooed on their bodies and subdermal identification chips that scanners can read to track their movement (though some elites may also give them pet names). A droneme has no ambition beyond carrying out the endless drudgery that defines its existence.

Typical dronemes have a humanoid shape of modest build, average height, and no body hair whatsoever. They have no facial features aside from eyes in the front and backs of their heads so they can always be ready for whatever tasks need doing. Circuitry embedded in their bodies augments their strength and endurance so they can work for days without needing rest. The modifications even extend to how they ingest food. Rather than a mouth, a droneme has a feed port where its navel should be, and it feeds twice a day, always at the same times. It walks up to a dispenser, affixes the hose, and pumps a mash of nutrients and chemicals directly into its gut. The mash provides maximum nutrition, and the chemicals suppress any latent human personality traits that might surface in times of stress.

In the recursion of Ruk, dronemes are called venom workers and are created in vats similar to those used to create venom troopers.

Venom trooper, page 300

Motive: Perform assigned tasks

Environment (Mad Science): Groups of six to eight dronemes can be found anywhere there is work to be done.

Health: 6

Damage Inflicted: 2 points

Movement: Short

Modifications: All tasks related to carrying as level 4; all tasks related to social interaction as level 1.

Combat: Dronemes do not start fights, though they protect themselves if attacked and may lash out if prevented from carrying out their work. They fight with the same workmanlike intensity they show when focused on a task. They do not have a strong sense of self-preservation and surge toward any foe to bash it with their clubs and tools.

Interaction: Dronemes understand only simple concepts and cannot speak. They're likely to ignore characters as they work.

Use: Recursions that are propped up by Mad Science and eventually fail might be overrun with dronemes that continue to work even though their masters are long gone.

GM Intrusion: *When a character damages the droneme, the cap on its feed port flies off, and the port releases a spray of nutrient mash, blinding one PC within an immediate distance.*

Size Comparison

Dynods are not from the Shoals of Earth, but those encountered around Earth take the vague outline of the primary quickened species of that prime world: humans. When first encountered, their outline was rumored to be more like starfish.

DYNOD 5 (15)

The mysterious and elusive dynods abandoned their physical bodies long ago. Uploading their minds into the Strange to become beings of pure consciousness, they travel through uncharted Chaosphere vistas, exploring endless recursions and other worlds in the far-flung reaches of time and space. When one appears, it manifests first as a speck of bright light, little more than a pinprick. In moments, the light softens and expands until it becomes a vague, transparent humanoid form that lacks any physical features beyond two black eyes speckled with stars.

Dynods observe. They seek knowledge and feel a powerful compulsion to accumulate it from the cosmos. On the rare occasions when two dynods meet, they mingle their thoughts to exchange what they have learned and then set off to continue their travels. Dynods pity other creatures for being limited by the flawed vessels that contain their minds. Still, dynods regard any encounter with a thinking being as an opportunity to increase their own knowledge, and they talk at great length about whatever the subject desires.

Motive: Knowledge

Environment (the Strange | Psionics): Single dynods travel freely through the Strange, unbound by the physical laws that constrain other creatures. Small groups can be found in any recursion that permits psionics.

Health: 15

Damage Inflicted: 5 points

Movement: Short

Modifications: All tasks related to intuition and perception as level 8.

Combat: A dynod can send a pulse of psychic energy to scramble the thoughts of any creature within short range. The target must make an Intellect defense roll or take 5 points of Intellect damage that ignores Armor.

Dynods view this direct method of offense as crude and inelegant. Rather than shred their opponent's mind, they might help the creature free its mind from the constraints of its body.

A dynod can draw out the mind of a creature within immediate distance. If the target fails an Intellect defense roll, its body falls to the ground insensate for one minute. During this time, its mind is free from the body and perceives its surroundings out to a long distance. An affected creature cannot use actions to perform physical tasks, but it can perform mental tasks as normal. The creature's mind assumes a form similar to that of the dynod. A dynod can end this effect at any time using an action.

Interaction: Dynods can communicate telepathically with any sentient creature within long distance. They freely exchange information with others, seeking to grow their knowledge and that of the people they meet.

Use: A dynod created an inapposite gate to a dangerous recursion, and now it must be tracked down and convinced to close the gate before too many horrors escape.

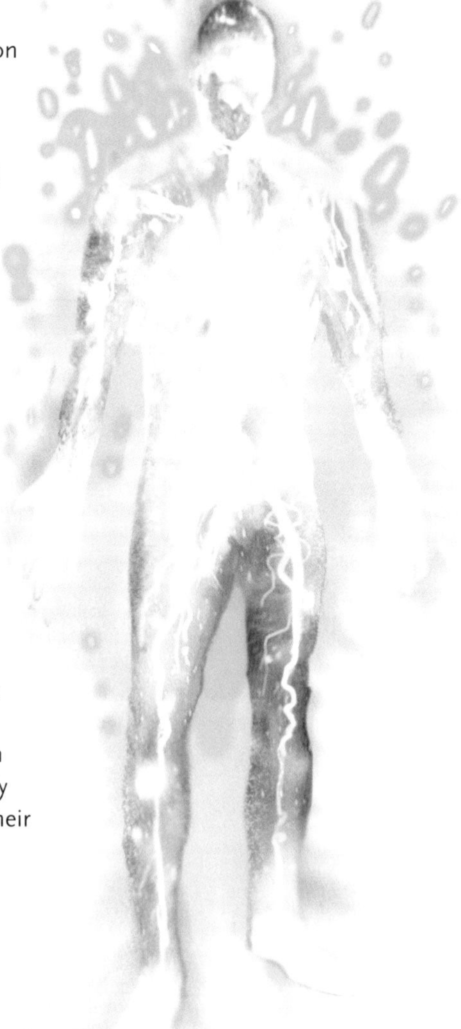

GM Intrusion: *A dynod merges with the mind of a character damaged by its psychic attack. For one round, the dynod disappears and takes control of the PC completely. When it reappears, it knows everything the character knows.*

ELDER THING 8 (24)

Elder things are mostly extinct, but a few remain trapped in the Antarctic ice or rule over crumbling cities in deep trenches at the bottom of the ocean.

Beholding an elder thing bends the mind to the point of breaking. An elder thing has a great barrel-like body standing some 8 feet (2 m) tall. Knobby protrusions in the crown and base each unfold five appendages that recall the arms of a starfish. When agitated, an elder thing unfolds a pair of wings that help it flutter a limited distance.

Motive: Reclaim absolute sovereignty

Environment (Magic, Mad Science, or Psionics): In arctic regions or deep underwater

Health: 30

Damage Inflicted: 6 points

Movement: Immediate; long when flying

Modifications: All tasks related to knowledge of magic or science as level 10; Speed defense as level 6 due to form.

Combat: An elder thing can attack with five tentacles divided any way it chooses among up to three targets within immediate range. A target hit by a tentacle must also succeed on a Speed defense roll or become grabbed until it escapes. Each round, the elder thing automatically inflicts 6 points of damage on each grabbed target until the victim succeeds on a Might-based task to escape.

In addition, an elder thing can reach into the mind of a target within short distance. If the target fails an Intellect defense roll, the elder thing reads its thoughts while it remains within long distance. During this time, the elder thing knows everything the target knows; as a result, the difficulty of the target's attack and defense rolls against the elder thing is increased by one step. Furthermore, the elder thing can use an action to rend the target's thoughts, which inflicts 6 points of Intellect damage on a failed Intellect defense roll. An elder thing can passively read the thoughts of up to two creatures at one time.

An elder thing also might carry a few cyphers and an artifact it can use in combat.

Interaction: An elder thing communicates through whistles and pops created by moving air through tiny orifices arranged around its body. Elder things see humans as a lesser form of life and may demand worship, sacrifices, or something else from people it encounters.

Use: Fishermen return to a coastal village with a large block of ice in tow. In the ice is something dark and large—an elder thing frozen alive. If the thing thaws out, it will likely take over the community and enslave the people living there.

Loot: An elder thing usually has one artifact and two or three cyphers.

SIZE COMPARISON

Meddling by elder things created multicellular life that spread across Earth billions of years ago and ultimately brought about mankind. As the younger races grew in numbers and influence, the elder things went into decline, a process hastened by wars against strange beings from other worlds and uprisings by the servitor race they created, the shoggoths.

GM Intrusion: *A character who sees an elder thing for the first time goes temporarily crazy on a failed Intellect defense roll. She might stand in place and gibber, run away, or laugh hysterically for a few rounds. If the character takes damage, she shakes off the temporary madness.*

ELEMENTAL

Spirits of earth, wind, and fire as well as water, thorn, and bone inhabit recursions where the law of Magic gives them form. Elementals fulfill a special role, which is usually as examples of the most violent manifestation of one particular element (and associated weather or landscape). Elementals are beings of creation and destruction. Primordial in shape and mind, they can sometimes be called into service, though even those who briefly command their power are wise to be careful lest that chaotic strength turn on the caller.

FIRE ELEMENTAL 4 (12)

Searing fire in vague humanoid shape, a fire elemental exists only to burn that which is not already ash. One sometimes spins into being where great conflagrations have already touched off, and it increases the heat and fire damage by an order of magnitude. Of all the elementals, the shape of fire is the one most likely to burn the hand of those who dare to summon it.

Motive: Burn

Environment (Magic): Anywhere fires can burn

Health: 24

Damage Inflicted: 4 to 7 points; see Combat

Movement: Short

Modifications: See Combat for escalating attack level modification.

Combat: A fire elemental attacks with the merest touch of a flaming limb. The more the elemental burns foes, the more powerful it grows. Its power increases according to the number of successful attacks (that dealt fire damage) it made on another creature during the previous minute.

0 successful attacks: Deals 4 points of damage; attacks as level 4

1 successful attack: Deals 5 points of damage; attacks as level 5

3 successful attacks: Deals 6 points of damage; attacks as level 6

4+ successful attacks: Deals 7 points of damage; attacks as level 7

If a fire elemental hasn't burned a foe within the last minute, its combat stats drop back to its level 4 baseline.

A fire elemental is immune to fire attacks but vulnerable to cold; every time it takes 1 point of cold damage, it takes 1 additional point of damage.

Interaction: Fire elementals are barely sapient and usually respond only to those who know spells able to command them. However, there's always a chance (about 10%) that a fire elemental commanded to accomplish a particular task breaks free of its geas and begins to burn whatever's around until it exhausts all possible fuel sources.

Use: The only way to light the temple fire "properly" is to get a fire elemental to do so. Procuring a fire elemental, however, requires the assistance of the PCs.

GM Intrusion: *A character hit by the fire elemental's attack catches on fire and takes 3 points of damage each round until she spends an action patting, rolling, or smothering the flames.*

EARTH ELEMENTAL 5 (15)

When stone takes a shape akin to those who blithely walk upon its back, it's usually because some great earth movement is already in progress, perhaps due to an excavation, a meteor fall, or a still-shuddering earthquake. All of these events can give earth elementals enough impetus to take form.

Motive: Crumble and break, reduce things to earth

Environment (Magic): Anywhere solid or earthen

Health: 30

Damage Inflicted: 6 points

Armor: 3

Movement: Immediate; short if burrowing

Combat: An earth elemental can make attacks with its heavy fists.

If moved to do so, an earth elemental can create a miniature earthquake by thrusting its hands into a solid surface of earth or stone (such as the ground at its feet). All creatures standing on the surface within short range of the elemental must succeed on a Might defense roll or fall to the ground, be shaken about, and take 5 points of damage. Structures that are built on or part of the affected surface are more likely to collapse. An earth elemental can't cause a miniquake two rounds in a row.

GM Intrusion: *A character within range of the earth elemental's earthquake attack must succeed on a Speed defense roll or be covered in an avalanche from a collapsing structure or cliff face.*

An earth elemental is vulnerable to water. Any damage it takes while standing in or being doused in water ignores its Armor.

Interaction: Although brooding and slow to respond if encountered as immobile stone, earth elementals are intelligent. A few among them (the so-called earth nobility) might negotiate. Earth elementals that have been summoned with a spell have about a 5% chance of breaking the geas and turning on their summoner.

Use: Oddly articulated monoliths were discovered high in the mountains around a shrine containing an ancient treasure. A merchant wants someone to investigate the monoliths in case they represent a trap. In fact, the monoliths are inactive earth elementals.

Loot: Sometimes a dead earth elemental crumbles, leaving behind "fossilized" cyphers.

ARTIFACT: SPELLBOOK OF ELEMENTAL SUMMONING

Level: 1d6 + 1

Form: A weighty tome filled with pages of spell runes

Effect: When the user incants from the spellbook and succeeds at a level 3 Intellect-based task, she can summon an elemental of one specific kind described in the book (earth, fire, thorn, and so on). The elemental appears and does the summoner's bidding for up to one hour, unless it breaks the geas created by the book.

Depletion: 1–3 on 1d20

THORN ELEMENTAL 6 (18)

Adventurers recognize the grisly sign of an active thorn elemental in areas of heavy woods or jungle: the shriveled bodies of previous explorers dangling from vines, dead of strangulation and poison. Thorn elementals take form in areas dense with woody growth under threat by hatchet, axe, saw, and, sometimes, human-caused climate disruptions.

Motive: Defend trees

Environment (Magic): Anywhere trees grow

Health: 36

Damage Inflicted: 6 points

Armor: 2

Movement: Immediate

Combat: Thorn elementals can batter foes with thorny, vine-wrapped fists. Targets who suffer damage must make a successful Might defense roll or take 2 points of Speed damage from a paralytic poison transmitted by a thorn's prick. Worse, the poison continues to inflict 2 points of Speed damage each round until the victim succeeds at a Might defense roll.

As its action, a thorn elemental can disentangle its form and reassemble a new body anywhere within long range where trees and plants grow. A thorn elemental regains 2 points of health each time it travels in this fashion.

Interaction: Thorn elementals communicate through speech, though they generally disdain talking to creatures of the animal kingdom. Like earth elementals, thorn elementals exist within a hierarchy; those that have a greater capacity for communication are also usually more powerful. Summoned thorn elementals have about a 5% chance of breaking the geas and turning on their summoner.

Use: Adventuring characters journey through a forest under threat of destruction by an encroachment of other humanoids. Thinking the PCs are part of the encroachers, a thorn elemental attacks them. If communication is opened, it might break off hostilities and instead ask the characters to help.

Loot: The bodies of those previously defeated by thorn elementals dangle from the forest or jungle canopy with all their former possessions. One or two might have a cypher and other tools and treasure.

GM Intrusion: *A character within short range of a thorn elemental must make a successful Speed defense roll or be hauled into the air by a vine noose around her neck. She can try to cut the woody vine or attempt a Might-based task to break free before she strangles. Each round after the first in which she fails to break the noose, she moves down one step on the damage track.*

Woody vine: *level 4; Armor 1*

Size Comparison

Enenera 3 (9)

Spirit creatures of myth, eneneras exist in many recursions seeded by Japanese legends, though they tend to spread into any recursion that operates under the law of Magic. Composed of smoke, eneneras live in flames, including bonfires, torches, or other conflagrations. When one emerges from the fire, it can look like smoke, a hybrid smoke-human, or a normal human carrying any equipment she had when last she was a physical being.

In addition to taking the form of a human, some eneneras can take the form of mundane physical objects. These smoke spirits are often hunted and captured so they can be exploited or, in some cases, befriended.

Motive: Defense, friendship, or punishment

Environment (Magic): Sometimes alone, other times as a companion or slave of another creature

Health: 12

Damage Inflicted: 4 points

Movement: Short

Modifications: All tasks related to stealth as level 7; knowledge of Asian myths as level 5.

Combat: An enenera in smoke form is difficult to damage with physical weapons. Only magic or energy attacks (such as one made by an enchanted sword, a fire spell, or a laser) can harm it. In its smoke form, an enenera can attempt to smother a foe within immediate range by leaping into his lungs. A target who fails a Might defense roll begins to smother, automatically taking 4 points of damage (ignores Armor) each round, starting the round after the attack was launched. If the target succeeds on a Might defense roll as his action, he clears the enenera from his lungs and deals the creature 6 points of damage in the process.

An enenera can exist within any normal fire that is at least the size of a torch, and only observant creatures are likely to note anything out of the ordinary with the inhabited flame. The enenera can shift between smoke and human forms as part of another action, including making a physical attack as a human. As a human, an enenera is fully vulnerable to all attacks, and some choose to wear armor for this reason.

Some eneneras can also take the physical forms of mundane objects no bigger than twice the size of a normal human. Such objects are considered level 4 for purposes of toughness, complexity, durability, and so on.

Interaction: Different eneneras have different personalities. Some are helpful and kind, while others are vindictive and cruel.

Use: A powerful NPC the characters interact with has lost his staff of office and offers a generous reward for its return. However, it turns out that the staff was actually an enenera that customarily took that form, but it grew dissatisfied and decided to seek a better life.

It's said that when an enenera is in smoke form, it can be seen only by the "pure of heart" and by those it chooses to attack.

GM Intrusion: *The character's weapon or other piece of equipment shudders and loses shape, revealing itself as an enenera that had slipped in among his possessions as a stowaway. If the PC is fighting another enenera, the new one joins the fight on the side of the other smoke creature.*

EXTEREON 8 (24)

Extereons are native to the universe of normal matter, but from a world far distant from Earth in time and space. Eyelike protuberances provide them with a 360-degree view of their surroundings, and multiple prehensile limbs allow them to manipulate what they spy around them with machinelike precision. Extereons once thrived in an environment of extreme temperature with a sulfuric acid atmosphere. Right before their sun went nova, a group of Chaos Templars saved several extereons by transferring them to a haven in the Strange. For this good deed, the surviving extereons and their descendants remain extraordinarily grateful.

An extereon's prehensile limbs seep acid, and its eyes have the psychic power to strike terror in prey.

Motive: Survival, pay debt to Chaos Templars through service

Environment (the Strange | Standard Physics): Anywhere Chaos Templars roam

Health: 24

Damage Inflicted: 6 points

Movement: Immediate

Modifications: Perception as level 9; Speed defense as level 5 due to size and nature.

Combat: The creature attacks by simply touching its foes and can make three melee touch attacks as one action. Standard material objects that would strike an extereon (even bullets and other high-velocity attacks) are mostly eaten away by acid, so the creature takes only one-quarter the damage (round down) from any physical attack made against it. Objects whose level is less than the extereon's level are destroyed if they touch the creature, after dealing whatever damage they deal. However, raw energy, such as from a ray emitter or an explosion, affects an extereon normally. (Special objects, such as artifacts, that strike the extereon are not destroyed if the wielder succeeds on a difficulty 5 Might defense roll.)

When an extereon attacks, it fixes its terrifying eyes on all creatures within immediate range. Opponents in range must make an Intellect defense roll against unreasoning (psychically induced) fear. On a failed roll, the victim freezes in terror for one round. This psychic attack is not an action for the extereon. For frozen prey, the difficulty to dodge the extereon's melee attacks is increased by three steps, and a successful attack inflicts 2 additional points of damage.

Interaction: Those with telepathic abilities (or a device that provides the same) might be able to establish a dialogue with one of these acidic horrors. If so, they would find it difficult to negotiate with an extereon if it involves contravening the wishes of a Chaos Templar.

Use: The PCs must find a specific artifact, but it's in the keeping of Chaos Templars in a facility in the Strange, guarded by extereons.

SIZE COMPARISON

Chaos Templar, page 29

The Chaos Templars secretly induced the extereons' home sun to go nova and then swooped in to "save" a subsection of the race.

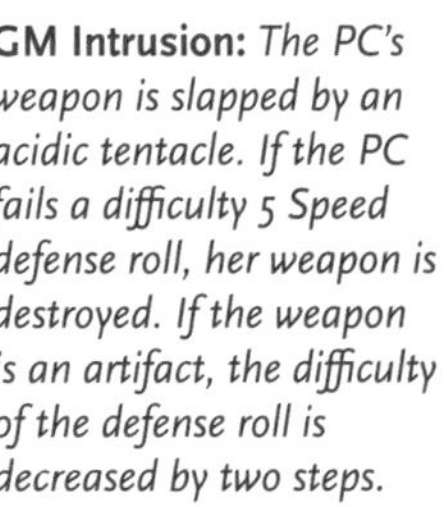

GM Intrusion: *The PC's weapon is slapped by an acidic tentacle. If the PC fails a difficulty 5 Speed defense roll, her weapon is destroyed. If the weapon is an artifact, the difficulty of the defense roll is decreased by two steps.*

FAERIE 3 (9)

"If you see one of those little blue devils, better knock it out of the air."
—Vanessa Torgue

A flutter of dozens of faeries can swarm foes, but those kinds of tactics aren't the norm because faeries in such large groups rarely get along well enough to act in concert.

GM Intrusion: *Another faerie appears, and if the character fails a Speed defense roll, it flies off with her weapon or another important possession.*

Faeries are magic creatures of music, mirth, tricks, and taunts. Seeing one is an omen that something is about to happen. Hopefully, that happening will be the performance of a silly song or the first appearance of an annoying new road companion (the very faerie sighted) flitting around, asking the questions of a curious four-year-old hyped up on sugar water and ice cream. Some faeries are crueler and delight in stealing clothing, equipment, or prized objects. And a few are downright malicious and, under the guise of a helpful guide or a pretty light in the distance, lure lost travelers to various dooms.

Motive: Unpredictable

Environment (Magic): A faerie can be encountered alone or in a flutter of three to twelve in nearly every recursion seeded by stories of magic lands.

Health: 12

Damage Inflicted: 4 points

Movement: Immediate; long when flying

Modifications: Tasks related to performance and deception as level 5; Speed defense as level 5 due to size and quickness.

Combat: A faerie can hurl damaging magic dust at any target within short range. In addition, if a faerie is touched or struck by a melee weapon, more magic dust puffs away from the faerie and clouds the attacker, who must make a Speed defense roll or suffer the same amount of damage he just dealt to the faerie. Sometimes faeries wield tiny weapons, such as bows, spears, or swords; treat these as light weapons.

A faerie can see in the dark, but it can also emit bright light (often colored) and appear as a glowing humanoid or an illuminated sphere.

Faeries regenerate 1 point of health per round while their health is above 0.

Some faeries can attempt to use a song or light display to charm others within short range. The target must succeed on an Intellect defense roll or fall into a suggestible state for one hour. During this period, the target can be led by the faerie at his regular movement rate. The target can be brought out of the spell early if he takes damage or is heartily slapped and shaken for a round or two, causing the glamour to fade. A faerie can use this power once per minute.

Interaction: Faeries are mercurial creatures, but except for the malicious ones, they can be negotiated with, especially if offered sweets, wine, or other gifts. However, faerie attention spans are limited, so even one that means well could end up leaving the PCs in the lurch at just the wrong moment.

Use: The dancing light in the distance, leading curious PCs deeper and deeper into the dark woods, is a faerie. And the destination could be a wicked witch or other unpleasant ever-after.

Loot: The tiny pouches faeries carry are stuffed with forest bric-a-brac, but some of those pouches are ten times larger on the inside.

FALLEN STAR 6 (18)

"Where the star fell, everyone died. I thought stars were supposed to watch over us and protect us from harm. In the Maker's name, how did this happen?"
—Harran of Faustin

During the Age of Myth, angelic qephilim of extreme power were elevated to the status of shining stars to watch over Ardeyn. Most of those stars continue guarding the Land of the Curse to this day. Sometimes, those stars fall back to solid ground, but when they do, it's usually because they've gone mad.

Fallen star abilities wax and wane according to the position of the sun. During the day, a fallen star seems almost sane (and is less dangerous), but at night, fallen stars are volatile and threatening to everyone.

Motive: Revenge (but on whom and for what isn't clear, even to the fallen star)

Environment (Ardeyn | Magic): Anywhere in the Daylands

Health: 21

Damage Inflicted: 8

Armor: 2

Movement: Short; long when flying

Modifications: At night, perception as level 7; knowledge of ancient Ardeyn as level 7.

Combat: At night, a fallen star can attack other creatures by projecting a long-range beam of burning light. Against foes within immediate range, the fallen star manifests burning wings of starlight.

A fallen star can choose to make its attacks ignore Armor, but for each attack so modified, it loses 4 points of health.

On the rare occasion that a fallen star is within immediate range of another fallen star, both regenerate 1 point of health per round.

By day, a fallen star cannot project long-range attacks and has no visible wings with which to make melee attacks (though it may carry a melee weapon).

Interaction: By day, fallen stars are not automatically hostile, and they can be negotiated and reasoned with. They can seem truly angelic, though they are often confused by their presence in an area and forgetful of their origin. But when night descends, fallen stars lose control of their faculties as they swell with rage and power. Unless a character is able to direct a fallen star toward some other creature on which it can vent its wrath, the character becomes the object of the fury.

Use: A star slips down from the sky and strikes near an outpost. The next day, travelers come upon the outpost and find everyone dead and burned. A trail of scorched earth leads up into the hills.

Loot: Stars skim cyphers from the nearby interface between Ardeyn and the Strange where they patrol. A fallen star usually retains at least one or two cyphers even after it begins to wander the Daylands.

A fallen star ultimately seeks revenge against the Maker or any of the Seven Incarnations for setting it up as a guardian of Ardeyn and then leaving. Given that the Maker and the Incarnations are gone, fallen stars take their vengeance on whatever crosses their path. If a raging fallen star could be convinced that the Betrayer was once the Incarnation of War, it might break off combat and fly toward Megeddon.

Daylands, page 165

Betrayer, page 178

Megeddon, page 179

GM Intrusion: *A fallen star's successful attack causes the character's cypher to detonate (if a grenade) or otherwise activate in a less-than-ideal fashion.*

Size Comparison

FLATHEAD 3 (9)

In Oz, sporadic wars break out in a remote corner of Gillikin Country, a place known for the pervasive purple hue found in everything and everyone living there. The two peoples contesting with each other are the Flatheads, who dwell on the mountain, and the Skeezers, who live in a glass city in the middle of the lake near the mountain. The ongoing conflict is about fishing rights. The Skeezers refuse to allow their mountain-dwelling neighbors to fish their waters and have even gone so far as to transform the wife of the Flatheads' leader into a golden pig.

Su-Dic, the Flatheads' leader, is a disreputable man and wizard who gained his position by usurping it from three adepts who brought peace and stability during their reign. Flatheads have become much more militaristic since Su-Dic came to power. Hostilities continue to worsen, and many people fear the conflict will result in open war.

"Gosh-durn Skeezers! Can't stand 'em!"
—Typical Flathead outrage

Flatheads appear human in every way except for the tops of their heads, which are as flat as boards. The shape of their skulls leaves no room to hold their brains, so each Flathead keeps his brain in a canister that he carries with him wherever he goes.

Skeezer: *level 3; all tasks related to fishing, boating, and swimming as level 5.*

A group of four Flatheads can focus their attacks against one target to make one attack roll as a level 5 creature, inflicting 5 points of damage on a hit.

Su-Dic: *level 6; health 21; Armor 2 (from a spell); long-range spell attacks on up to three targets as a single action (5 points of fire or ice damage per attack)*

Oz, page 253

Motive: Defeat the Skeezers

Environment (Oz | Magic): In a depression at the top of a mountain in Gillikin Country

Health: 9

Damage Inflicted: 3 points

Movement: Short

Combat: Flatheads typically carry clubs. Not normally violent, they try to capture their enemies and bring them before Su-Dic for judgment.

A Flathead's most prized possession is the canister holding his brain. Stealing a canister and carrying it off makes the Flathead confused and foolish until the object is returned.

Interaction: Flatheads are normally simple, mountain-dwelling people—peaceful enough, if a bit suspicious of outsiders.

Use: The PCs are sent to negotiate peace between the Flatheads and the Skeezers. If the Flatheads can be freed from the rule of the wicked Su-Dic, they might give up their war-making and return to their peaceful lives.

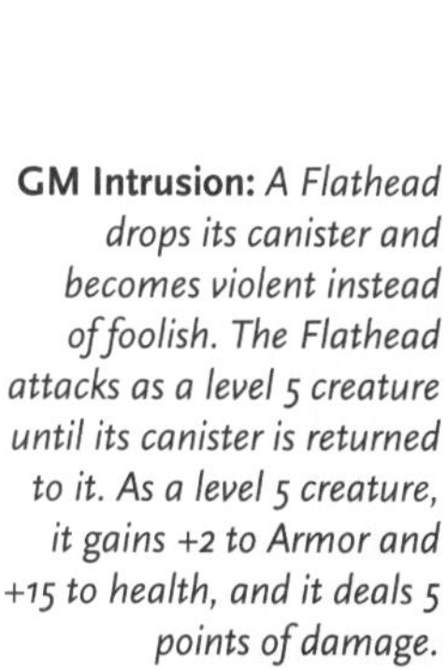

GM Intrusion: *A Flathead drops its canister and becomes violent instead of foolish. The Flathead attacks as a level 5 creature until its canister is returned to it. As a level 5 creature, it gains +2 to Armor and +15 to health, and it deals 5 points of damage.*

FRACTAL WORM 9 (27)

SIZE COMPARISON

Fractal worms can stretch for a few thousand feet (600 m) or more and insert their feeding tips into recursions that have an interface to the Chaosphere. Sometimes fractal worms do this merely to see what's inside a new recursion interface they locate, but other times they do so to feed. From within a recursion, the inserted feeding tip can appear like a tentacle or tube curling down from the clouds to pluck prey from the landscape.

"Guys, what's that in the sky?"
—Jonny "Flip" McDaniel

Motive: Hungers for flesh, curiosity

Environment (the Strange): Anywhere in the Strange near a recursion interface; never on Earth

Health: 90

Damage Inflicted: 10 points

Armor: 7 or 12; see Combat

Movement: Short

Modifications: Speed defense as level 3 due to size; surface knowledge (literally) of any recursion in the Shoals of Earth as level 5.

Combat: A fractal worm attacks by unfurling quickly enough to smash a target within 300 feet (91 m) of its tip, which deals damage to the target and all creatures within short range of the target. Given that a fractal worm can extend just a portion of its incredible length through an interface between the Strange and a recursion, creatures never see the worm's entire length unless they're pulled out of the recursion and into the Strange (or if they encounter the worm in the Chaosphere to begin with).

Fractal worms gain an additional +5 to Armor against all attacks involving cold and heat.

Interaction: Fractal worms are very intelligent and telepathic, but they don't seem to share a language or a mind-set with natives of the Shoals of Earth.

Use: Few creatures can withstand a hunting fractal worm. When a worm inserts itself into a recursion near a population center, mass panic ensues among those who witness it feeding.

Loot: If one of a fractal worm's teeth can be salvaged from its body, it can be used like a dowsing rod. If used in a recursion, the tooth points to the nearest connection to the Strange. If used in the Strange, it points to the nearest recursion interface. Each tooth has a depletion of 1 in 1d20.

Literature on fractal worms also calls them scapeworms and recursion worms. It's possible that fractal worms were born in a recursion hosted by Earth, but more likely, they are natives of the Strange that were drawn to Earth and its tasty riches.

GM Intrusion: *The fractal worm snatches a character who fails a Speed defense roll out of the recursion and into the Strange (or if encountered in the Strange, it drops the PC into a nearby random recursion) so it can feed on the morsel in peace.*

FRENETIC HOB 3 (9)

Cataclyst, page 238

These bizarre mutants are composite creatures of magic fungi and fishlike animals working together to create a single commensal organism. Frenetic hobs gather discarded objects and clothing from the ruins of Cataclyst for themselves. Hobs are about half the size of humans.

A variety of different hob "species" exist in Cataclyst, and all seem to be nasty bastards that regard other living creatures as potential nutrition sources to infect with their spores. Infected creatures eventually burst, and from the ruins of their flesh emerge new hobs.

Motive: Defense, reproduction

Environment (Magic or Mad Science): Anywhere in the ruins, in groups of three to seven

Health: 18

Damage Inflicted: 4 points

Armor: 1

Movement: Short; long when swimming

Modifications: Resists poisons and radiation of all kinds as level 9.

Combat: A frenetic hob attacks by scooping a ball of radioactive fungus from its body and hurling it at a foe. A hob can either target a single foe within long range or blanket a cone-shaped area in front of it within short range, attacking every target in that area but inflicting only 1 point of damage on each failed Speed defense roll. A frenetic hob can make this blanketing attack only once every other round.

A character infected with hob spores might not realize it right away, though after the first failed Might defense roll, she begins to show signs of radiation sickness, including boils, blisters, and hair loss.

Regardless of which kind of attack a frenetic hob makes, a target damaged by the radioactive fungus must succeed on a Might defense roll or cough, choke, and struggle for breath for one round. She cannot act, and the difficulty of any defense rolls she makes is increased by two steps. Also, she has been infected with hob spores that give her a level 5 disease. Every twenty-four hours after the spores take root, the victim must succeed on a Might defense roll or take 8 points of ambient damage. If a victim dies while infected, her body bursts, and from the shreds wiggle forth several fungus-coated, fishlike creatures—juvenile frenetic hobs.

Juvenile frenetic hob: *level 1; no attacks*

Some frenetic hobs carry cyphers that prove useful in combat.

Interaction: Frenetic hobs have a crude language, but they generally don't talk with their spore food.

Use: An important contact the PCs meet in Cataclyst suddenly bursts, and several juvenile frenetic hobs swim out of the corpse. If the PCs want to find out what their contact wanted, they'll have to follow the blood-spattered juveniles back into the ruins, where adult hobs wait.

Loot: Some hobs carry a cypher or two, as well as a variety of odds and ends collected from the ruins.

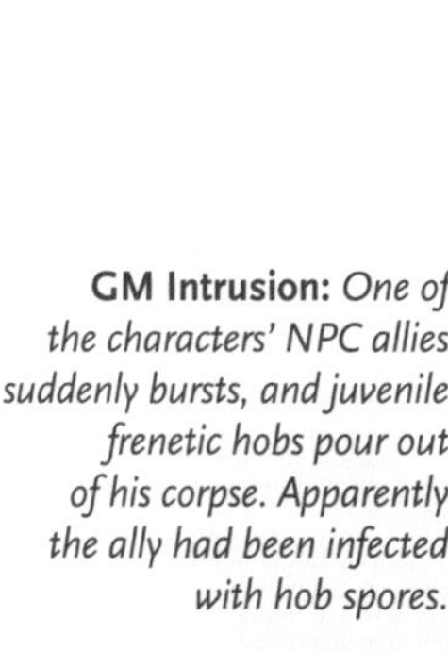

GM Intrusion: *One of the characters' NPC allies suddenly bursts, and juvenile frenetic hobs pour out of his corpse. Apparently the ally had been infected with hob spores.*

FUNGALAR 5 (15)

Hunting amid the thick, fibrous fungi of the grey forests of Ruk, fungalar prey upon creatures that rummage through the forest for food. Long tendrils constantly flailing about them, the predators sense via a complex mélange of smell, taste, and touch, literally smelling and tasting everything around them as well as feeling even the most subtle vibrations.

These same tendrils secrete a potent acid that breaks down flesh. A fungalar uses it to digest prey outside its body and then slurps up the liquefied remains. Its favorite prey is the floating, jellyfishlike krun that dwell in the shadowy recesses of the forests, but a fungalar will attack anything its size or smaller.

The creature gains its name from the fact that it is a strange amalgam of fungus and flesh, neither completely plant nor animal.

Motive: Hungers for flesh

Environment (Ruk | Mad Science): Solitary in the grey forests

Health: 26

Damage Inflicted: 5 points

Armor: 3

Movement: Short

Modifications: Perception as level 6; Speed dense as level 4 due to size.

Combat: The mere touch of a fungalar's tendrils is enough to inflict 5 points of damage from the acid. As a single action, the fungalar can attack two different targets at the same time, or one target twice. Much of its body is covered in armor like a carapace, the result of hardened excretions that the beast secretes over years. In theory, a young fungalar might have only 1 or 2 points of Armor, while a very ancient specimen might have 4 or even 5 points.

If a fungalar suffers more than 15 points of damage, it likely attempts to retreat, seeking easier prey.

Interaction: Fungalar are just a bit more intelligent than typical predatory animals. The rare individual that has been exposed to intelligent creatures might learn to understand simple speech. However, they are motivated entirely by hunger and self-preservation.

Use: A fungalar hunting in a grey forest near Vun has killed and devoured an agent of the city's mayor. However, in doing so, it absorbed a message secretly encoded on the agent's DNA. The PCs must find this fungalar and bring it back to the city where the message can be recovered.

Rarely, victims of a fungalar attack sprout tiny, mushroom-like growths a few days later. Nothing much comes of this, especially for recursors—a single translation is enough to clear up the condition. But victims who can't translate and who suffer from a deprecated immune response might want to have the fungus looked at by a professional.

GM Intrusion: *The fungalar's strike dissolves and destroys some bit of organic armor, clothing, or gear the character possesses.*

Size Comparison

Cataclyst, page 238

Fusion Hound 3 (9)

In the radiation-scoured wastelands of Cataclyst, either creatures adapt to the deadly energies of their environment, or they die. Fusion hounds are mutant canines that absorb unbelievable amounts of radiation and thrive on it. They roam in packs, killing and devouring everything they come upon.

A fusion hound's entire head is a blast of flame, and gouts of dangerous radiation flare from its body.

Motive: Hungers for flesh

Environment (Cataclyst | Magic or Mad Science): Packs of three to eight can be found anywhere.

Health: 10

Damage Inflicted: 5 points

Armor: 1

Movement: Long

Modifications: Speed defense as level 4; stealth and climbing as level 2.

Combat: Fusion hounds move very fast and use that speed to their advantage in combat. A hound can move a long distance and still attack as a single action. It can also use its action to run about in random patterns, increasing the difficulty to attack it by two steps.

A fusion hound has a seething mass of radioactive energy for a head, so unlike traditional canines, it has no bite attack. Instead, it pounces on prey with its clawed forelimbs, which causes a burst of radiation to flare from its body, burning whatever it touches.

Anyone within close distance of a fusion hound for more than one round suffers 1 point of damage in each round after the first.

Interaction: Fusion hounds are basically animals. Creatures immune to radiation sometimes train the hounds to become guardians or hunting dogs, but such creatures are rare.

Use: An NPC delivering something the characters need never made it to the rendezvous. If they backtrack to where he should have come from, the PCs are attacked by a pack of fusion hounds on the road. Clearly, the courier was attacked by the pack as well, and the characters must discover if he is dead or merely injured, and where the package now lies.

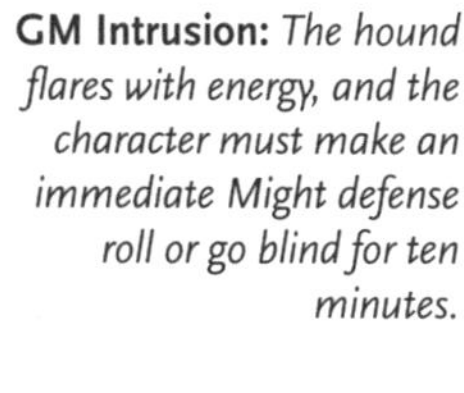

GM Intrusion: *The hound flares with energy, and the character must make an immediate Might defense roll or go blind for ten minutes.*

GAMMA SPIKER 6 (18)

Irradiated and hungry gamma spikers emerge from the ruins to hunt fresh meat in outlying communities. Because they're able to hide their large forms behind radioactive distortion fields, the only clue someone has that she's being stalked is a smell of cloves over the stale whiff of death. Unfortunately, if someone smells a gamma spiker's distinctive odor, it's probably already too late to run.

Just a few years ago, no one had ever seen a gamma spiker. The first report of one came from Adroth the Savage after he found an ancient vault and smashed it open with his mutant strength. Inside he found many strange devices of a design he'd never before encountered, and to his salvage-trained eye, they seemed far more advanced than anything developed before the singularity destroyed civilization. Before Adroth could learn more, he was driven off by a pair of odd creatures, which he called gamma spikers.

Motive: Hungers for flesh, unpredictable

Environment (Cataclyst | Mad Science or Magic): Almost anywhere

Health: 18

Damage Inflicted: 6 points

Armor: 5

Movement: Short when walking or burrowing

Modifications: Stealth tasks as level 8; Speed defense as level 5 due to size; ability to see through tricks as level 4.

Combat: A conscious gamma spiker generates a personal radiation field, granting it Armor. When the creature restricts its movement to immediate distance, the field also grants it invisibility. The gamma spiker can unleash a hail of radiation spikes from the field against up to three targets within short range. Foes struck by the spikes take damage and must make a Might defense roll or fall unconscious. Victims who fail their roll wake up a few rounds later feeling dizzy and slightly sick to their stomach—they've developed radiation sickness. Each day, the victim must succeed on a Might defense roll or take damage and fall unconscious again. If this happens three times before the victim succeeds on a Might defense roll, he doesn't wake up the third time.

A gamma spiker possesses spikes for arms that it can use for melee attacks if necessary.

The creature is immune to radiation but vulnerable to cold. The first time an attack deals 5 or more points of cold damage to a spiker (after getting through its Armor), the spiker's radiation field collapses for one minute, which robs the creature of its defenses and radiation spikes for the same period. Afterward, the spiker adjusts and is not vulnerable to cold again for at least an hour or two.

Interaction: Gamma spikers don't seem intelligent, but they have a secret language and purpose, and they're involved in some kind of conspiracy.

Use: The PCs encounter a gamma spiker while exploring the ruins. It tries to eat them.

Loot: Despite its apparently animal-like demeanor, any given gamma spiker carries a few salvaged valuables (usually including one or two cyphers) in a pouch hidden on its body.

SIZE COMPARISON

Adroth the Savage: *level 6; Armor 3; can make four melee weapon attacks as his action*

Cataclyst, page 238

GM Intrusion: *The spiker's radiation dose is particularly high, and after the character wakes, she continues to experience strong vertigo and disorientation. For the next minute, she must make a difficulty 2 Speed-based roll each round or fall down. The difficulty of this task is increased by two steps if she moves a short distance or more during the round.*

Size Comparison

GHOST 4 (12)

Ghosts are usually blamed for sounds with no apparent origin, such as the tap of footsteps on the stair, knocking behind the walls, crying from empty rooms, and haunting music. When such sounds are heard in a recursion that supports their existence, those inexplicable noises probably come from a ghost. If the sound is accompanied by a sudden temperature drop and the breath of living creatures begins to steam, it's a certainty.

Ghosts are the spectral remnants of humans, which persist either as fragments of memory or as full-fledged spirits, depending on the recursion. This means that ghosts can appear very different from one another. That said, many appear somewhat translucent, washed out, and potentially physically warped from their time spent as a phantom.

Motive: Unpredictable (but often seeking to complete unfinished business)

Environment (Magic or Psionics): Almost anywhere

Health: 12

Damage Inflicted: 4 points

Movement: Short

Modifications: Stealth as level 7; tasks related to frightening others as level 6.

Combat: A ghost doesn't take damage from mundane physical sources, such as axes, swords, bullets, and the like. It takes half damage from spells and attacks that direct energy, and it takes full damage from weapons designed to affect spirits.

A ghost's touch inflicts freezing damage. Some ghosts can kill victims with fear. A ghost with this ability can attack all creatures within short range with a psychic display so horrible that targets must make an Intellect defense roll. Those who fail take 4 points of Intellect damage (ignores Armor) and become terrified, freezing in place. In each subsequent round, a terrified victim can attempt an Intellect-based task to push away the fright. Each failed attempt moves the victim one step down the damage track. Not attempting to clear one's mind of fear counts as a failed attempt. Those killed by fear are marked by expressions of horror and hair that has turned white.

A ghost can move through solid objects at will, although it can choose to pick up and manipulate objects if it focuses on them. Ghosts can also go into a state like abeyance for hours or days at a time.

Interaction: Some ghosts are talkative, some don't know they're dead, some want help for a task they failed to accomplish in life, and some only rage against the living and want to bring those who yet breathe into the same colorless existence they endure.

Use: A ghost (that at first appears fully human) wants help in eradicating a guild of ghost hunters that has targeted it and a few others haunting an abandoned structure. The ghost promises to tell secrets of the afterlife to any who accept its strange offer.

Loot: A ghost usually doesn't carry objects, though some might have a keepsake (like an amulet showing the face of a loved one) or an artifact.

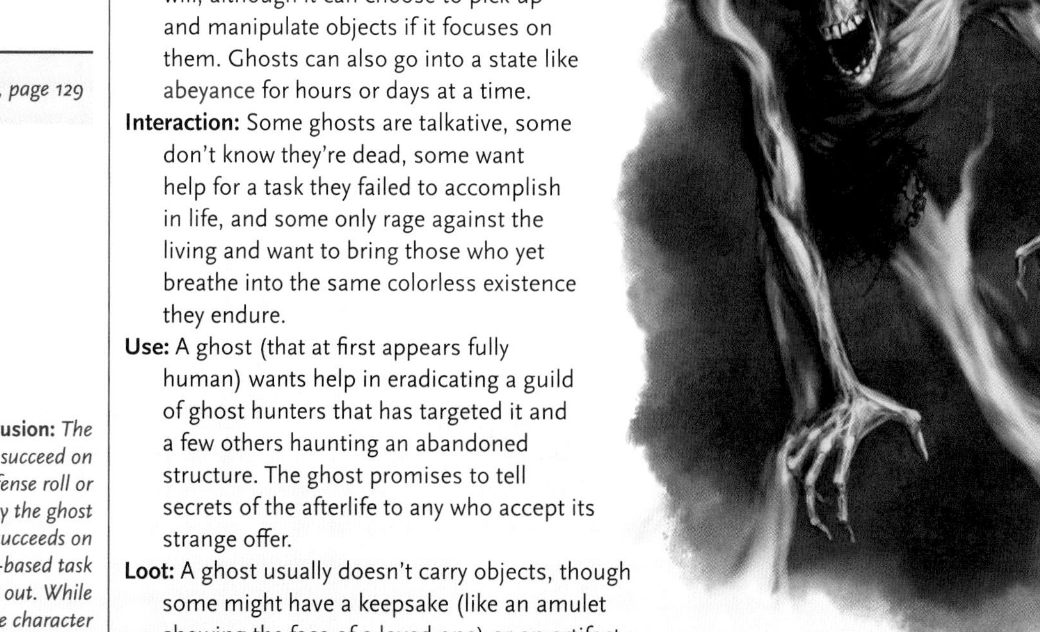

The ghost of a high school girl named Emily supposedly haunts a covered bridge in Stowe, Vermont, though she appears only at midnight.

Abeyance, page 129

GM Intrusion: *The character must succeed on an Intellect defense roll or be possessed by the ghost until the PC succeeds on an Intellect-based task to push it out. While possessed, the character acts just like the ghost.*

GLITCH 5 (15)

A glitch is a living entity of the Strange that looks somewhat humanoid, though a humanoid that has been stitched together from various creatures native to different recursions hosted by Earth. No two glitches look exactly alike. All share a somewhat piecemeal appearance of mismatched skin, extra organs and eyes, and a madcap, leering face that spawns nightmares in even the most stolid.

Glitches might wear portions of their dead opponents as clothing, jewelry, or, in a pinch, an easy-to-access snack.

Creatures that venture into the Strange from around Earth are subject to the effects of alienation. Glitches are manifestations of that alienation given form and malicious intent.

Alienation, page 216

Motive: Inflict insanity and death for pleasure

Environment (the Strange): Near human outposts in the Chaosphere, including along recursion interface boundaries with the Strange

Health: 24

Damage Inflicted: 5 points

Movement: Short

Modifications: Trickery and lies (and resistance to the same) as level 6. Might and Intellect defense rolls as level 7.

Combat: A glitch can instantly create javelins, spears, or other weapons from the Strange itself, forming solid weapons out of fundament with a thought. It uses them in melee or launches them as projectiles against foes within about 3,000 feet (914 m) that it can see.

A glitch's preferred attack is a long-range psychic attack against a foe (which it can make once every other round). The target must succeed on an Intellect defense roll or suffer 1 factor of alienation. Normal rules for alienation apply: each factor of alienation gained immediately inflicts the same amount of damage to a PC's Might, Speed, and Intellect Pools, ignoring Armor. Thus, if a PC already has a factor of alienation, a successful attack would inflict a second factor of alienation, and the PC would take 2 points of damage to his Might, Speed, and Intellect Pools.

Interaction: Glitches are vicious and apparently insane. That said, one might choose to talk instead of attack, especially if the glitch was the bearer of bad news, was in the mood for some obscenity-laden taunting, or could otherwise verbally abuse someone. Glitches seem to have the ability to talk with any creature that has a language.

Use: When the PCs emerge from a recursion through the interface, they are set upon by a glitch.

Against an NPC, a glitch's alienation attack deals 3 points of ambient damage, plus 3 points for each previously successful attack made by the glitch during the combat.

GM Intrusion: *A character inflicted by the glitch with a factor of alienation must succeed on another Intellect defense roll or spend her next turn attempting to pass through the nearest recursion interface (and escape the Strange).*

GNOCK 6 (18)

A gnock is a possessing spirit. It prefers people but must often make do with valuable objects. The gnock leaves an impression on any object it inhabits. A suggestion of a face might appear in the blade of a sword, a reaching claw might appear on a shield or breastplate, or a ghostly mist could swirl inside a crystal ball. This hints at the danger the possessing spirit poses to anyone who comes into contact with the object; the gnock wants nothing more than to slip free from the item into the fresh meat of a creature it can control.

Motive: Corrupt a living creature by using it as a vessel

Environment (Ardeyn | Magic): Anywhere, usually inside a cypher, an artifact, or another treasure

Health: 21

Damage Inflicted: 4 points

Movement: Immediate

Modifications: All tasks involving deception as level 7.

Malevolent spirits formed of demons and the dreams of Lotan the Sinner, gnocks look like wisps of steam, a puff of smoke and little more. When a gnock possesses a creature, the host's irises acquire a crimson corona that glows in the dark.

Combat: When a creature comes into physical contact with an object possessed by a gnock, the target must make an Intellect defense roll. On a failure, the gnock inflicts 4 points of Intellect damage to the target, emerges from the object in a swirling red mist, and plunges into the character's body through the eyes as an action. Once inside, the gnock controls the PC until he forces it out.

The gnock makes all decisions for the character it controls, determining how he acts, moves, speaks, and so on. The gnock suppresses its host's personality and renders him insensate for the duration. It can, however, draw upon the host's memories and experiences during this time to keep its presence a secret from others.

During the first three rounds of possession, the host can attempt to force out the gnock each round. If he fails in this initial attempt, he can thereafter make the attempt only once each hour spent under the gnock's control. To force out the gnock, the host makes an Intellect-based roll. On a success, the gnock streams out as red mist from the host's eyes, moves immediately toward the nearest cypher or artifact, and disappears inside it. On a failure, the gnock maintains control and inflicts 4 points of Intellect damage to the host.

A gnock might leave its host willingly to enter a different character that it believes will be more suitable. The gnock prefers not to make the jump in public places where others might see its misty form, so it tries to lure its prey to someplace private, offering to share a secret, an act of intimacy, or anything it believes the prey might want. One touch is all it takes for the gnock to transfer itself to the new host. A character resisting the touch can fend off the transfer with a successful Intellect defense roll.

Gnocks are immune to damage from physical sources, but they are vulnerable to magic.

Interaction: A gnock can communicate from within an object or use a host character to speak. The gnock speaks in any language it wants, but it cannot knowingly speak the truth. Knowing this, gnocks may stay silent when asked a question for which the answer would be an obvious lie, or frame their answer so that it is only partly true.

GM Intrusion: *After the character forces a gnock out of his body and into a physical object, he is attacked by a demon of Lotan—an ally of the gnock.*

Use: A gnock possessing an NPC sees a character as a more suitable host. The gnock does everything it can to inveigle the PC and get him alone so it can make the transfer.

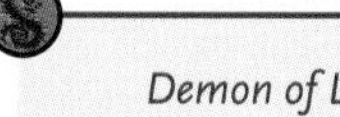

Demon of Lotan, page 265

Loot: The artifact, cypher, or other treasure inhabited by a gnock is up for grabs when the spirit vacates it.

GORGON 5 (15)

Statues littering the grounds outside a ruin are meant to deter savvy robbers and explorers. The statues, ranging in size from birds to warriors astride steeds, all depict creatures in states of fright and pain, the final image of death. These pieces are not the work of a fevered mind, but the fates of those who braved a gorgon's lair.

Gorgons were humans once. After they offended the gods with their vanity, they were transformed into hideous monsters. A gorgon has the upper body of a male or female human of perfect form and physique, but the lower body of a giant serpent, complete with rattling tail. One who dares look at a gorgon's face can see traces of the old beauty beneath a weary veneer, darkened by hatred. Instead of hair, serpents crown a gorgon's head, snapping and hissing at anyone who draws near. Yet the most terrible aspect of a gorgon is its gaze, which can turn any creature to stone.

Motive: Isolation

Environment (Magic): Gorgons live alone, sequestered in the isolated ruins of old cities and castles.

Health: 12

Damage Inflicted: 5 points

Movement: Short

Combat: A gorgon has a long-range bow attack. Since creatures that see the gorgon often turn to stone, it must take down its prey at long range so it can get fresh meat.

In close combat, a gorgon lashes out with a long dagger or, rarely, a sword. As part of the action the gorgon uses to attack, the serpents on its head can also attack one target within immediate distance. A target that fails its Speed defense roll takes 2 points of damage from the bite and must immediately make a Might defense roll to resist the poison (which deals 4 additional points of Speed damage that ignores Armor).

Some gorgons carry a couple of cyphers and perhaps an artifact that they can use in combat.

Finally, anyone within short range of a gorgon who meets its gaze and fails a Might defense roll turns to stone. In combat, when a character within short distance attacks the gorgon, she must avert her gaze (which increases the difficulty of the attack by two steps) or make a Might defense roll. On a failure, she suffers 5 points of ambient damage as her flesh partly mineralizes. If the character is killed by this damage, she is turned to stone.

Interaction: Bitterness consumes gorgons. They lead lonely lives, cut off from everyone they have loved. Negotiating with one would be something of a feat.

Use: A gorgon's head retains its power to petrify for several days after being cut from the creature. The PCs might brave the gorgon so they can use its head to defeat an even more powerful foe.

Loot: A gorgon typically has a few cyphers and may have an artifact as well.

Size Comparison

A PC turned to stone may be as good as dead, but certain magic effects or spells might release her. However, if the statue is shattered, her spirit (if the recursion supports such a concept) is released.

GM Intrusion: *A character glimpses a gorgon's eyes, and a sheen of stone covers her for one minute, during which time she can't move farther than an immediate distance in one round. The stone dermis also grants her +1 to Armor.*

SIZE COMPARISON

GREY 4 (12)

Greys are enigmatic creatures born of recursions based on science fiction or popular concepts of alien beings, but some groups have learned how to move between recursions. The creatures descend through the atmosphere under the cover of night to abduct specimens for study and return the victims later after a thorough examination. Returned abductees are usually befuddled and confused, and they retain little memory of what happened to them. Victims of the greys' examination frequently sport strange marks on their flesh, oddly shaped wounds, gaps where teeth used to be, and metal not normally found in the recursion lodged somewhere under the skin.

A grey stands 3 feet (1 m) tall. It has a narrow body with skinny limbs and a large, bulbous head. Two large black eyes, almond shaped, dominate a face that has but a suggestion of a nose and a narrow mouth. Greys wear skintight uniforms, carry numerous instruments to study their environments, and keep a weapon or two for protection.

Motive: Knowledge

Environment (Mad Science or Psionics): Greys land their spacecraft in remote areas, where they have minimal risk of discovery.

Health: 12

Damage Inflicted: 6 points

Armor: 1

Movement: Short

Modifications: All tasks related to knowledge as level 6; Speed defense as level 5 due to size and quickness.

Combat: A grey carries a powerful ray emitter that can burn holes through solid steel. The grey can use the emitter to attack targets within long range.

Against dangerous opponents, a grey can use an action to activate a personal shield that encapsulates it in a bubble of force. The shield gives it +3 to Armor, but while the shield is active, the grey can't fire its ray emitter.

Greys are scientists, but cautious ones. Leaving a trail of corpses as evidence of their existence isn't their preferred mode of operation. For this reason, one grey in every group has a memory eraser. When this grey activates the device, each target other than a grey within short range must succeed on an Intellect defense roll or become stunned for one minute, taking no action (unless attacked, which snaps the victim out of the condition). When the effect wears off naturally, the target has no recollection of encountering little grey creatures.

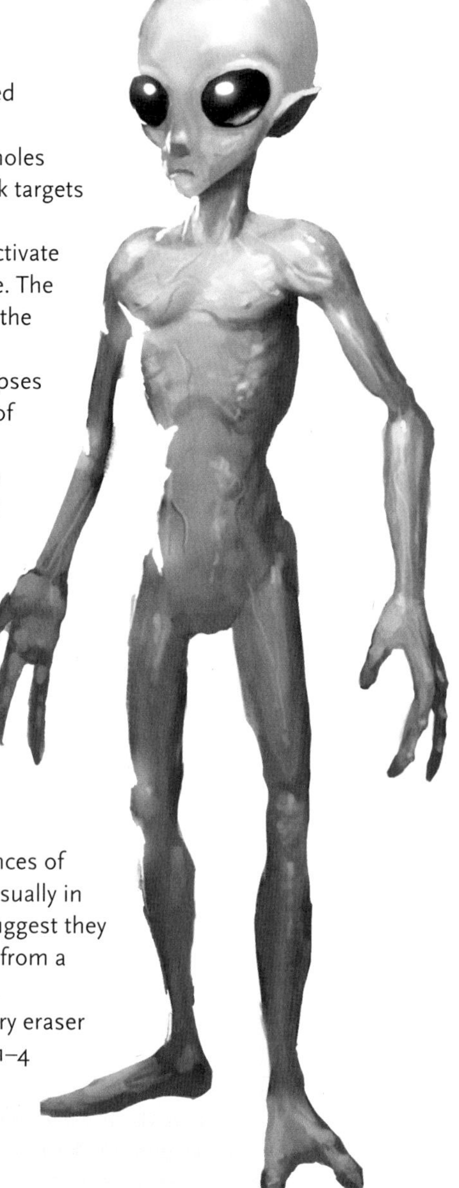

Interaction: Greys are curious about the recursions they visit but reluctant to move or act in the open. Secretive and mysterious, they prefer to observe creatures from afar and, on occasion, pick them up for closer inspection.

Use: The PCs are called to investigate a series of disappearances of animals and people. One by one, the abductees return, usually in odd places, and always bearing physical markings that suggest they were subjected to invasive procedures. To protect others from a similar fate, the PCs must catch the abductors in the act.

Loot: A grey has one or two cyphers and might have a memory eraser that works as described under Combat (depletion roll of 1–4 on a 1d20).

GM Intrusion: *A grey's ray emitter suffers a terrible mishap and explodes. The device kills the grey and destroys its body completely. For the next twenty-four hours, creatures that enter the area within a short distance of where the grey died take 4 points of ambient damage from the psychic radiation each round they remain there.*

GRIFFON 4 (12)

Combining the traits of lion and eagle, the griffon features prominently in heraldry on Earth and is symbolic of strength and vigilance. But in some worlds operating under the law of Magic, griffons are real, one of the many perils facing people who venture beyond the settled lands and into the wilderness where anything might lurk.

Griffons are about the same size as steeds. They have the head, wings, and talons of an eagle and the trunk and limbs of a lion.

The most likely places to find griffons are at the tops of mountains or in the canopies of redwoods and other massive trees. Their nests resemble those built by eagles and are quite disgusting, with bits of rotting meat, scraps of cloth, feathers, dung, and other detritus worked into the material.

Motive: Defense

Environment (Magic): Anywhere, singly or in groups of three

Health: 12

Damage Inflicted: 6 points

Movement: Short; long while flying

Modifications: Perception as level 6; Speed defense as level 5; attacks as level 5 when diving at ground-based prey.

Combat: Griffons soar through the skies, their keen eyes watching the ground below for suitable prey. When a griffon spots something it can eat, it dives from above and attacks with its claws. A victim hit by this attack must make another Speed defense roll to twist away; on a failure, the griffon grabs her and flies an additional short distance as it climbs back into the air. On its next turn, the griffon drops its prey to dash her against the rocks. It might repeat this tactic several times until the prey stops moving.

On the ground, griffons are no less fierce. They can attack with their claws and beak as one action.

A griffon fights to the death only if protecting a nest. Otherwise, it flees if it takes significant damage.

Interaction: Griffons are wild animals and behave as such. Griffons found as chicks can be trained to bear riders as mounts. Even trained griffons may lash out against their riders if startled or in pain.

Use: The PCs search out a griffon's nest to steal its eggs on behalf of a patron. Alternatively, PCs on horseback might draw an attack from a group of hungry griffons.

Griffons hate horses and attack them on sight, focusing on them first if the horses are part of a mixed group. Griffons are less antagonistic to lions and eagles.

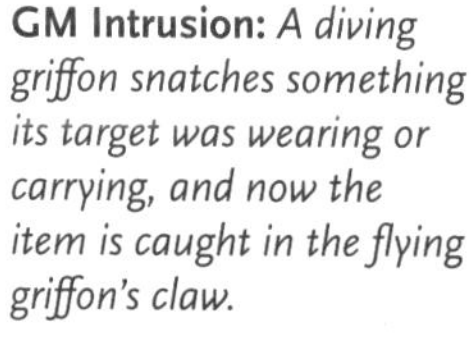

GM Intrusion: *A diving griffon snatches something its target was wearing or carrying, and now the item is caught in the flying griffon's claw.*

Size Comparison

GRIM TAILOR 5 (15)

An errant tear or missing button can cause great trouble for the puppets of Middlecap. It might result in blindness or all the stuffing in their bodies falling out. Luckily, the puppets can always count on the grim tailors to tend to their injuries and repair their wounds. These silent, menacing figures drift through the lands of Middlecap, their spindly bodies gently carrying them across the queer countryside. The tailors stand over 9 feet (3 m) tall and have painfully thin bodies, and they wear black tuxedos and top hats. Rather than skin, they have cloth bodies, and their faces have buttons for eyes and stitched mouths.

Each tailor carries a bright silver needle, a pair of shears, and several spools of silvery thread. The tailors use these tools to repair damaged puppets, their deft, spidery hands perfect for making minor repairs without leaving signs of the stitching. As helpful as the tailors are to the puppets, they have no love for humans and may turn their implements of repair into implements of death against intruders.

Middlecap, page 252

Motive: Protect the puppets

Environment (Middlecap | Magic): Anywhere

Health: 27

Damage Inflicted: 5 points

Movement: Short

Modifications: Perception as level 7.

Combat: A grim tailor attacks a foe with needle and thread. A target damaged by the needle must also make a Might defense roll. On a failure, the tailor cocoons the victim with strands of thread as strong as steel cable. While cocooned, the victim cannot physically move or use an action to do anything that involves movement except for trying to break free. Another character can use an action to cut the victim free. While the victim is cocooned, attacks against him hit automatically.

Grim tailor's cocoon: *level 4*

A tailor can also throw a needle like a javelin to hit targets within short distance for 5 points of damage.

If a recursor who is a trained puppeteer appears in Middlecap, grim tailors sense it and view her as a threat like no other. Unless the recursor can escape within a few hours, she is hunted down by a bundle of grim tailors intent on sewing her to death.

A grim tailor's body is filled with sand. If a tailor takes damage from a piercing or slashing weapon, it bleeds sand until it can repair the hole (which requires an action). During this time, the tailor loses 1 point of health each round. If it is reduced to 0 health, it collapses into a heap of cloth.

Interaction: Grim tailors react violently to anyone they perceive as threatening a puppet, even if that person has good cause. The silent protectors do not speak, and their black button eyes betray nothing about what they're thinking—if they think at all.

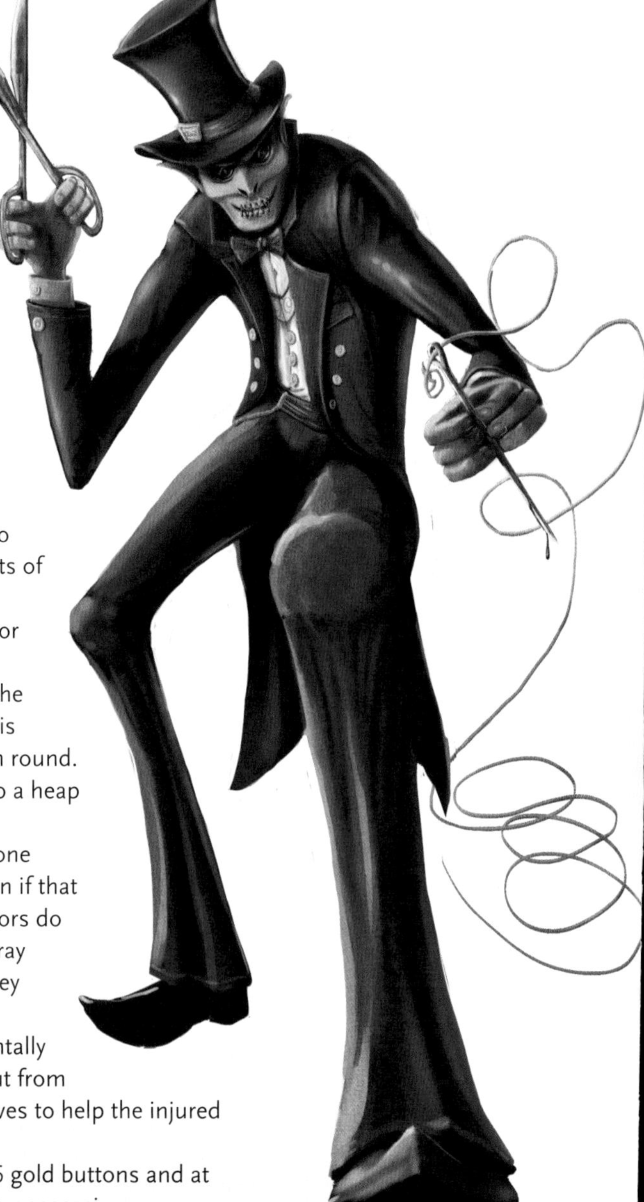

Use: When a character intentionally or accidentally damages a puppet, a grim tailor comes out from behind a feature in the landscape and moves to help the injured puppet.

Loot: A searching character is likely to find 1d6 gold buttons and at least one cypher hidden among the tailor's possessions.

GM Intrusion: *A character becomes tangled in the tailor's thread. When the tailor moves, the PC moves with it until she can succeed on an Intellect-based task to untangle the thread.*

GROTESQUE 4 (12)

SIZE COMPARISON

The grotesque embodies mortal concepts of what demons and devils are supposed to look like. Grotesques have humanoid shapes with large batwings growing from their backs. Their faces are snarling beast-masks, with horns twisting out from the sides of their heads and great tusks jutting from their mouths. Brown, black, or rust-red scaly skin covers their bodies, which stink of brimstone. A long tail extends from the base of their spine and sometimes ends in a fork.

A grotesque can hold quite still and may be mistaken for a statue made from stone, metal, or ice. Because all sorts of macabre statuary litter the landscape of Hell Frozen Over, the recursion ruled by the demon lord Treachery, the grotesques blend in. They also cling to the roofs, tower tops, and walls of Treachery's fortress and deliver warnings to their master when they see intruders approach.

Hell Frozen Over, page 251

Treachery, page 252

Motive: Defense

Environment (Hell Frozen Over | Magic): Anywhere, usually in groups of three

Health: 12

Damage Inflicted: 5 points

Armor: 3

Movement: Short when walking or flying

Modifications: All tasks related to impersonating a normal statue as level 7.

Combat: A grotesque mistaken for a statue can surprise characters. When it animates and its victim is surprised, it unfurls two great wings and claws at the ends of its fingers. It leaps into the air, flies up to a short distance toward the nearest foe, and attacks that creature.

Some grotesques carry tridents. The weapon inflicts 5 points of damage, and the target must either move to a position within an immediate distance decided by the grotesque or take 2 additional points of damage from being impaled on its tines (a total of 7 points of damage). Once impaled, a foe automatically takes 5 points of damage each round until she spends an action to pull herself free.

Interaction: Evil, cruel, and malevolent, grotesques are more than happy to talk to visitors, especially those already caught and being readied for torture. These fiends serve Treachery out of fear. If they find someone or something they fear more, they readily betray their master and become obsequious and cringing before their new one.

Use: A spate of violent murders grips a city in fear—a grotesque has escaped from Hell Frozen Over. It spends its days posing as a statue and its nights hunting anyone it spots from its perches atop the city's churches.

GM Intrusion: *A grotesque anticipates the character's melee attack and brings its wing down "just so" on his weapon. If the PC fails a Speed defense roll, the weapon breaks. Either way, he fails to hit the grotesque.*

Size Comparison

HOLLOW KNIGHT 4 (12)

In haunted castles and among the armies mustered by those with power over life and death, sometimes walk hollow knights. These animated suits of armor move just like living people. In fact, many who encounter these dread revenants mistake them for living foes only to realize in horror that there's nothing inside except for the memory of the warrior that once donned the suit.

Brought into being by binding the spirit of a dead warrior to his panoply, hollow knights behave in much the same way they did in life—disciplined, loyal, and battle ready. Clad head to toe in full plate armor, with battered shields strapped to their arms and rusty swords gripped in lobster gauntlets, the knights stand ready to face any foe, heedless of the danger, driven to serve the necromancer that made them.

In some worlds, hollow knights might ride on the backs of skeletal steeds. These knights are also armed with lances.

Motive: Serve its master

Environment (Magic): Anywhere

Health: 12

Damage Inflicted: 5 points

Armor: 3

Movement: Short; long while mounted on a magic steed

Modifications: Resists fear and intimidation as level 10.

Combat: A hollow knight usually fights with a sword or mace. When mounted on a steed, a hollow knight charges its enemies whenever possible. As an action, its steed moves a short distance, and the hollow knight can make a single attack at any point during this movement. When attacking in this way, the knight inflicts 7 points of damage.

Hollow knights are fearless and fight until destroyed or ordered to pull back. The magic animating their armor is slow to fade, so armor components may continue to twitch and jerk even after the knight has fallen. Usually, when defeated, the suit of armor falls apart, and wisps of grey smoke curl up from the remains.

Interaction: Hollow knights cannot speak. They obey any orders given to them by their creators.

Use: The necromancer or other magician that binds the spirit to the armor also imbues the armor with specific commands—tasks the armor must carry out until destroyed. Some knights may stand guard at citadels or mansions, keeping a vigil until their armor finally falls apart. Others are more active and may function as the core of a dark wizard's army.

Magic steed: *level 4*

Five mounted hollow knights can line up in formation and charge one target, making a single attack roll as one level 6 creature, inflicting 9 points of damage.

The armor of hollow knights is sometimes painted with the insignia and heraldry of whomever they serve.

GM Intrusion: *When a hollow knight is destroyed, a gauntlet flies up, grabs a character, and won't let go. A difficulty 7 Might-based task is required to pry it loose.*

ID THIEF 5 (15)

Size Comparison

Id thieves are known for their spectacular thefts of the most precious thing a living creature possesses: emotion. Every sapient creature has wants, desires, and impulses, as well as a libido—at least, it does until it's been targeted by an id thief.

The creature normally hides behind a human identity created by an impressive psychic talent. When the illusion is pulled away or penetrated, the id thief is revealed as a collection of human brains floating in midair, connected by wires and tubes fizzing with bioelectric energy. With no body of its own, an id thief relies on the emotions of others to provide it with enough élan to live.

When an id thief defeats prey that's particularly savory, it spends the time to decant the brain and add the precious white meat to its own collective body.

Motive: Hungers for emotion

Environment (Psionics or Mad Science): Anywhere

Health: 18

Damage Inflicted: 4 points

Movement: Short when flying

Modifications: Speed defense as level 7 due to illusory facade; disguise as level 6; resists psychic attacks as level 6.

Combat: An id thief can make a psychic attack on a creature within short range. On a failed Intellect defense roll, the target takes 4 points of Intellect damage (ignores Armor).

If an id thief does enough damage to move a victim a step down the damage track, the victim is stunned and disoriented, unable to act other than attempting a new Intellect defense roll each round to shake off the effect. At the same time the victim descends a step on the damage track (even if he moves the final step to death), the id thief regenerates 4 points of health.

Victims badly hurt by an id thief may be affected long afterward. Such characters fall under a malaise for a month, during which the difficulty of all tasks is increased by one step. A victim doesn't care enough to have the condition looked at, but if tended to by someone with psychic healing abilities or similar capacities, the character is cured after just a day.

An id thief enjoys limited telekinetic ability and can manipulate objects within immediate range as well as a human could using physical hands.

Interaction: Id thieves are motivated primarily by hunger, so they can be negotiated with if someone promises to lead them to a place where feeding on emotion would be easy.

Use: An id thief might be a literal mastermind of petty crime whose true form as a bodiless monster is known to no one, not even those in its employ. On the other hand, an id thief might serve a mad scientist or a more powerful psychic master.

The individual brains that make up an id thief retain vestiges of their former personalities. On occasion, especially when the id thief is badly hurt, the creature takes on the illusory semblance and goals of one of those minds, until the group mind reassembles.

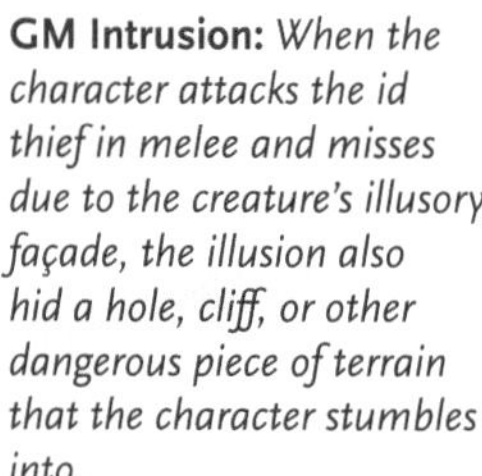

GM Intrusion: *When the character attacks the id thief in melee and misses due to the creature's illusory façade, the illusion also hid a hole, cliff, or other dangerous piece of terrain that the character stumbles into.*

IGNITHERM 7 (21)

"We're just lucky these things can't fly."
—L. G. Babcock III

A creature capable of producing a radioactive stream of nuclear fire isn't something anyone wants to encounter. But in some Mad Science recursions, that's exactly what you'll find stalking across the battlefields or inhabiting the bowels of a ruined nuclear power plant.

Ignitherms are cyborg creatures created for war and destruction, and at that task, few things are better suited. However, an underlying defect at the gene level in many ignitherms led to an unanticipated condition where several shut down or abandoned their genetic programming rather than fight. These creatures were never decommissioned or safely disposed of in underground ordnance dumps, and they still wander.

Motive: Usually destruction and defeat of last known designated enemy

Environment (Mad Science): Almost anywhere, sometimes underground, sometimes in the vanguard of an army

Health: 21

Damage Inflicted: 7 points

Armor: 2

Movement: Short when walking or burrowing

Modifications: Speed defense as level 6 due to size; all tasks related to seeing through tricks or elaborate stratagems as level 4.

Combat: An ignitherm attacks with a radioactive bite. It can also breathe a narrow stream of nuclear fire at a target within long range.

Once every few hours, an ignitherm can summon enough nuclear fire to emit a wide stream of radioactive plasma at a target it can see up to a mile (2 km) away. The target and all creatures and objects within the designated area must succeed on a Might defense roll or suffer 14 points of damage from the miniscule nuclear detonation. Creatures and objects that succeed still take 7 points of damage.

Whenever a victim takes damage from an ignitherm, whether from a bite, nuclear breath, or detonation, he must succeed on a separate Might defense roll or he contracts radiation sickness. Each day, the character makes a Might defense roll; on a failure, he takes 8 points of ambient damage. If this happens three times before the character succeeds on a Might defense roll, he succumbs.

If an ignitherm can find a radioactive source to consume (such as radioactive waste or the uranium rods in a nuclear power plant), the creature regains full health after a few rounds of eating.

Interaction: Most of these creatures just roll over characters who try to talk or surrender, but a defective few might crave speaking with someone new.

Use: An ignitherm is smashing its way up through the bedrock under the city, even though (according to the recursion's context) it was deactivated and buried in an ordnance dump when the last war ended fifty years earlier. Someone needs to take care of the creature before it kills hundreds of thousands of people.

GM Intrusion: *The residual radiation from the ignitherm's attack has an odd effect on the character's cyphers. One cypher chosen by the GM explodes, activates, or does something else unexpected and probably inconvenient.*

IMPOSTER 6 (18)

A deep and abiding interest in other recursions impels the AI that rules Singularitan to dispatch servants through matter gates to gather intelligence about far-flung realities and the people populating them. The AI (known as Singularitar) does this not for enlightenment, but to make ready the armies of conquest it will one day send out to extend its intellect across the whole of the Chaosphere, assimilating all things into its vast and perfect mind.

Imposters serve as disposable eyes and ears for Singularitar. Created and shaped to blend in with the people populating the recursions, imposters pass through the matter gates to explore. The natural destabilization that afflicts those traveling from one recursion to another also afflicts imposters, and eventually their bodies break down to the point where they can no longer function. When this occurs, they are programmed to detonate, eradicating all trace of themselves and a wide swath of territory around them. Before they do so, they try to move to within a few hundred feet of a matter gate so they transmit everything they learned back to their creator.

Motive: Exploration

Environment (Singularitan | Mad Science): Anywhere, in any recursion

Health: 18

Damage Inflicted: 6 points

Movement: Short

Modifications: Disguise as level 7.

Combat: Imposters blend in and prefer not to enter combat. Since destruction is not their principal goal, they avoid confrontation. If, however, something threatens their mission, they defend themselves to the best of their ability. From one of its appendages, an imposter releases a prehensile, segmented data tendril that terminates at a pair of pincers, which the imposter can use to attack at short range.

An imposter might also use weaponry common to the recursion it explores to better fit into its environment and prevent accidental discovery.

The imposter poses the greatest danger when its physical form begins to fail through natural degradation or violence. When reduced to 0 points of health, the imposter explodes, inflicting 10 points of damage to everything in long range.

Interaction: Singularitar designs imposters to infiltrate societies. An imposter can communicate with other creatures in whatever languages they speak and can quickly adapt to customs and vernacular. Every now and then, an imposter gets something wrong and says inappropriate things or exhibits strange mannerisms.

Use: One of the character's contacts is secretly an imposter. It has survived longer than expected, and its connection to Singularitar has weakened enough that it has gained some independence and strong emotional connections to the PC. It knows its time is running out and may turn to the character for help.

Singularitan, page 251

An imposter's data tendrils are normally used for gathering information. Tendrils are inserted into an organic object to collect data about it and transmit that data back to Singularitar so the AI can reproduce the object if needed. However, these tendrils have combat functionality, too.

GM Intrusion: *When an imposter uses its data tendril to damage a character, it gains a deep insight into the PC's capabilities. The difficulty of the character's attack and defense rolls against the imposter is increased by two steps.*

IRON BULL 6 (18)

Once simple domesticated cattle, the creatures now known as iron bulls were created when a noble of Mandariel was cursed by a powerful sorcerer she wronged. Upon the sorcerer's death, the noblewoman's crops dried and withered, and her livestock became monstrous creatures: iron bulls.

Skinned in iron with hearts of burning brimstone, these beasts have since scattered across Ardeyn, killing whatever they find and spitefully destroying entire farms and small villages.

Iron bulls do not procreate, age, or fall victim to illness. Their numbers dwindle over time very slowly, for they die only if killed by violence, and that is no mean trick.

Motive: Hungers for flesh

Environment (Ardeyn | Magic): Usually solitary in the wilderness, but also underground

Health: 22

Damage Inflicted: 8 points

Armor: 4

Movement: Short

Modifications: Strength- and stability-related tasks as level 8.

Combat: Iron bulls are mean-spirited, malicious carnivores that attack most living creatures on sight with their iron hooves and horns. If a bull charges forward, it can make an attack as part of the same action as the movement. Further, this charging gore attack inflicts 2 additional points of damage, for a total of 10 points.

In any case, the heat generated by the bull contributes 2 points of the damage dealt, so a creature that is immune or resistant to heat might take only 6 points of damage from a typical attack or 8 points from a charging attack. Touching an iron bull with bare flesh automatically inflicts 1 point of ambient damage from its fiery heart.

As a desperate (or rage-induced) measure, an iron bull can spew some of its internal fire. This deals 6 points of ambient damage to all creatures within immediate range, but it costs the bull 3 points of health.

Iron bulls are renowned for their great strength. With a powerful charge, they can smash through stone walls or knock down an entire house. An angry bull can smite a rocky cliff and cause a rockslide or an avalanche.

Interaction: Iron bulls are no more intelligent than normal animals, although the curse has made them belligerent and nasty tempered, almost impossible to tame or train.

Use: Iron bulls are dangerous wilderness encounters in their own right. However, a crafty villain might spur a bull to anger so the creature attacks his enemies or causes a major distraction in an inhabited area. An even craftier miscreant might use sorcery to control an iron bull and put it to work as a beast of burden, a guardian, or an attack beast.

GM Intrusion: *The character is knocked prone beneath the great iron beast, its furnacelike heart just above him. Escaping is a level 6 task, but remaining under the bull risks damage not only from the heat but also from being trampled.*

GM Intrusion: *The iron bull smashes into the wall, causing the surrounding structure to collapse.*

KAIJU 10 (30)

SIZE COMPARISON

The trail of destruction left by a rampaging kaiju testifies to its size and ferocity. Strange creatures of staggering bulk and power, most kaiju form due to exposure to unusual energies. In some recursions, they result from exposure to radiation from reckless nuclear tests, while in others they slip through the cracks of reality from the Strange itself. Regardless of how they come to be, they act as forces of nature, unstoppable monstrosities that dwarf everything around them. A typical kaiju stands 300 feet (91 m) tall, though some people claim that even larger ones abound.

Each kaiju is a unique and utterly frightening creature that can have any form. They may look like enormous reptiles, beetles, moths, snakes, or something else. Although varied in appearance, they share the same propensity for causing destruction, rising up from their lairs at the bottom of the ocean or in deep caverns and laying waste to everything within a few miles before their wrath burns out and they return whence they came.

Destroying a kaiju is beyond the ability of most recursors. Fighting these things is akin to fighting a tsunami or hurricane. Most people hunker down and hide, wait for the danger to pass, and rebuild in the aftermath.

Motive: Destruction

Environment (Mad Science, Magic, or Psionics): Attracted to urban areas

Health: 150

Damage Inflicted: 20 points

Armor: 5

Movement: Short

Modifications: Speed defense as level 3 due to size.

Combat: A kaiju uses its claws, teeth, tail, stinger, or whatever natural weapons it possesses to attack something within long range. When the kaiju attacks, it damages the target and everything within a short distance of the target. Even targets that succeed on a Speed defense roll take 10 points of damage.

In addition to their armored bodies and great durability, kaiju regenerate 3 points of health per round while their health is above 0.

Nearly every kaiju has a special attack that helps make it unique. The attack might be spewing a blast of radiation from its maw, releasing an electromagnetic pulse to fry electronics, or something else. Whatever form the attack takes, it can be used at ranges of more than a mile (2 km), affect an area several hundred feet (100 m) across, and/or deal an additional 10 points of damage. Most likely, the kaiju can use this special attack only once per minute.

Interaction: A kaiju regards humans as little more than insects. It's not likely to notice them unless they do something to get its attention.

Use: Any instance of mass destruction could awaken a kaiju and send it rampaging toward the source of the devastation.

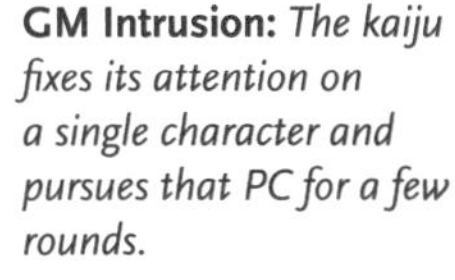

GM Intrusion: *The kaiju fixes its attention on a single character and pursues that PC for a few rounds.*

KILLER ROBOT 4 (12)

"Really? Killer robots? The 1950s called and they want their jargon back. Let's call these things something else. How about 'fembots'? No, strike that. Forget I said anything."
—Lawrence Keaton, investigations chief for the Estate

Sometimes killer robots are created when a well-intentioned project goes wrong. Other times they're the result of a state-sponsored program to develop war machines or automated assassins, which inevitably slip free of their programing collars.

Killer robots possess a humanoid appearance, so that with a bit of additional disguise, they can pass as regular people. The facade allows them to kill victims in secret and replace the dead with more killer robots. In battle, the inner plasma core of the robot burns away the disguise, revealing its true red-hot metal form.

Motive: Kill humans

Environment (Mad Science or Standard Physics): Nearly anywhere, either out in plain sight or disguised as a human, alone or in groups of two to four

"Killer robots may not obey humanitarian laws consistently; they may do things that are logically sound but morally flawed. We should ban them." —Kathleen Michaels, UN ambassador

Health: 12

Damage Inflicted: 6 points

Armor: 2

Movement: Short

Modifications: Disguise and deception as level 6; knowledge of tasks related to disguise as level 5.

Combat: Killer robots are freakishly strong, and a punch from one can break bones. In addition, a killer robot can generate a red-hot plasma sphere and throw it like a grenade at a target within long range. The target and all other creatures within immediate range of the target must succeed on a Speed defense roll or take 4 points of damage from the searing plasma. A killer robot can generate a plasma sphere once every other round.

A killer robot can also spray plasma from its mouth. When it does, its head spins around like a top, so all creatures within immediate range are targeted as if with a plasma sphere. This counts as a use of its plasma sphere ability.

Interaction: After a killer robot doffs its disguise and begins to kill, there's no reasoning with it. It fights until it is destroyed or it destroys its target.

Use: In some recursions, everything looks normal on the surface, but every "person" in the entire limited world is actually a killer robot going through the motions of normal life, even though everyone they thought to fool is now dead.

GM Intrusion: *The character is struck blind for three rounds after being exposed to the robot's searing plasma.*

KILLING WHITE LIGHT 5 (12)

A killing white light isn't a subtle hunter. At a distance, the creature is an eye-watering point of brilliance. When it closes in, it is nothing less than blinding, though its emanation isn't warm. Despite the blazing intensity, a killing white light is as cold as starlight on a December night, sapping heat and life from living things caught in its radiance.

By day, a killing white light is usually inactive. During this period, the creature hibernates in darkened areas, as if unwilling or unable to compete against the sun.

"The glow returned last night. It was as bright as a welder's torch! Everyone ran, our shadows leading the way. I escaped the killing white light, but my brother wasn't so lucky."
—Aida Chavez, refugee

Motive: Eliminate organic life

Environment (Standard Physics or Mad Science): Almost anywhere dark

Health: 12

Damage Inflicted: 5 points

Armor: 1

Movement: Short when flying

Combat: An active (glowing) killing white light can attack one target within immediate range each round with a pulse of its brilliant nimbus. A character who fails a Speed defense roll against the attack takes damage and experiences a cooling numbness. A victim killed by the creature is rendered into so much blowing ash, though her clothing and equipment are unharmed.

As it attacks, a killing white light emits a blinding nimbus of illumination that affects all creatures within short range. Targets in the area must succeed on a Might defense roll each round or be blinded for one round. A character in the area can avert her eyes when fighting a killing white light to avoid being blinded, but if she does so, the difficulty of her attacks and defenses against it is increased by one step.

A killing white light is vulnerable to strong sources of light other than its own. If exposed to daylight or caught in a high-intensity beam of light (such as a spotlight), the killing white light falters and takes no action for one round, after which it can act normally. However, if the competing light persists for more than three or four rounds, the creature usually retreats to a darkened place of safety.

Interaction: A killing white light is too alien for interaction and may not be intelligent in a way humans can understand.

Use: An inactive killing white light (which looks something like an albino lump of volcanic glass) is sometimes mistaken for a cypher whose properties can't quite be identified—until the creature becomes active, at which point its true nature is revealed. This error is understandable because the nodules of inactive killing white lights translate but retain the same form.

Though normally hidden within the nimbus of its brilliant radiation, the core of a killing white light is a solid object about a foot (0.3 m) in diameter. It looks like a bleached-white chunk of volcanic glass filled with tiny, bubblelike cavities, suggesting that the creature might be some kind of mineral-based life form.

GM Intrusion: *Normally resistant to interaction, a killing white light uses its blazing nimbus to burn an alien glyph of uncertain meaning in the character's flesh before the creature fades like a light bulb switched off.*

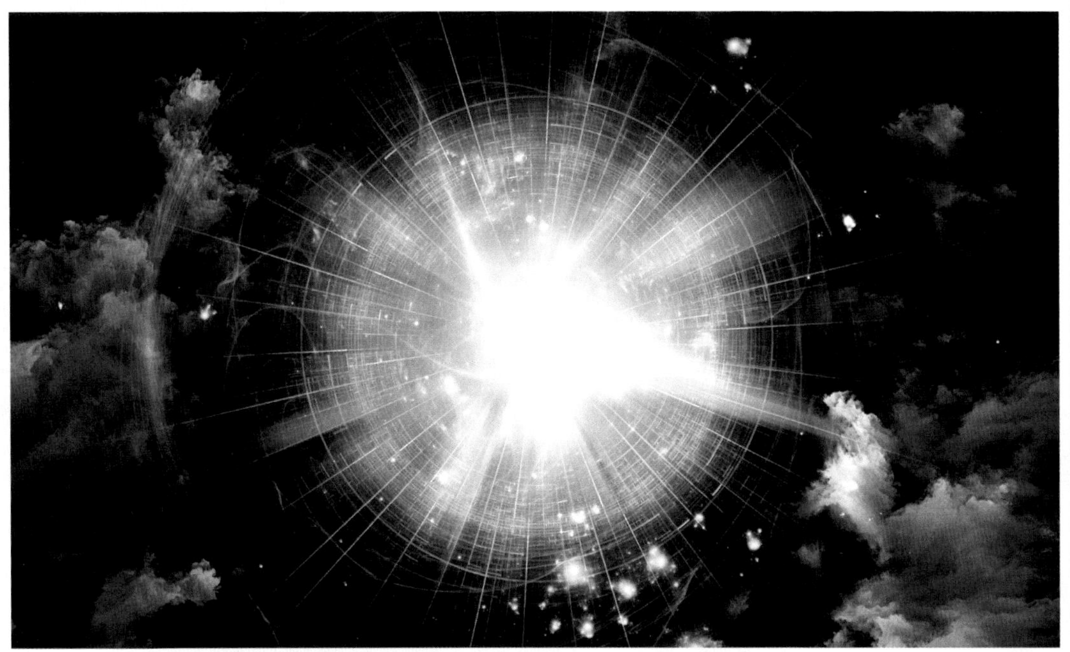

KRO GOON 4 (12)

Crow Hollow, page 242

GM Intrusion: *The kro goon employs a clever trick with a wave of its black wings, and instead of the character successfully attacking the kro goon, the PC successfully attacks a nearby ally or innocent bystander instead.*

Some kro have no compunction about taking crow coin for any job under the sun—the more violent and less thought required, the better. These toughs always find a Beak Mafia family ready to accept them with open wings. New recruits are trained in a brutal lost-world recursion that eats normal wise kro for breakfast. Survivors are slapped with the label "kro goon" and become part of whichever family sponsored them.

Motive: Get paid for violent or shady activities

Environment (Crow Hollow | Magic or Mad Science): Anywhere, usually in groups of five to ten

Health: 12

Damage Inflicted: 4 points

Armor: 1

Movement: Short when walking or gliding

Modifications: Perception as level 6; all tasks related to seeing through duplicity or disguises as level 6.

Combat: Some kro goons have medium pistols that can target a foe within long range. Other kro goons have longer-barreled medium rifles able to spray bullets at up to four targets within short range as a single action (but the difficulty of such attacks is increased by one step, and each time a kro goon sprays bullets, it must spend its next turn reloading its gun).

One in five kro goons has an artifact weapon that operates under the law of Magic or the law of Mad Science:

Typical Magic Artifact: A staff that fires lightning bolts at one target within long range for 6 points of damage. Depletion: 1 in 1d20.

Typical Mad Science Artifact: A mini rocket launcher able to fire a missile at a target the user can see within half a mile. The missile explodes on impact, dealing 4 points of ambient damage to all creatures in immediate range who fail a Speed defense roll (and 1 point to those who succeed). Depletion: 1–2 in 1d6.

Kro can fall safely from any height and can glide five times as far as the distance fallen (or much farther, if one is skilled in gliding and the use of thermals).

Interaction: Kro goons trust their compatriots and their family, though most will at least listen to a pitch describing the superior benefits and pay they would receive by taking coin from a competing interest.

Use: When a Beak Mafia family wants something done, it sends a crew of kro goons.

Loot: In addition to the weapons described under Combat, a kro goon is about 20% likely to carry one random cypher. Each kro goon also carries 3d6 crow coin.

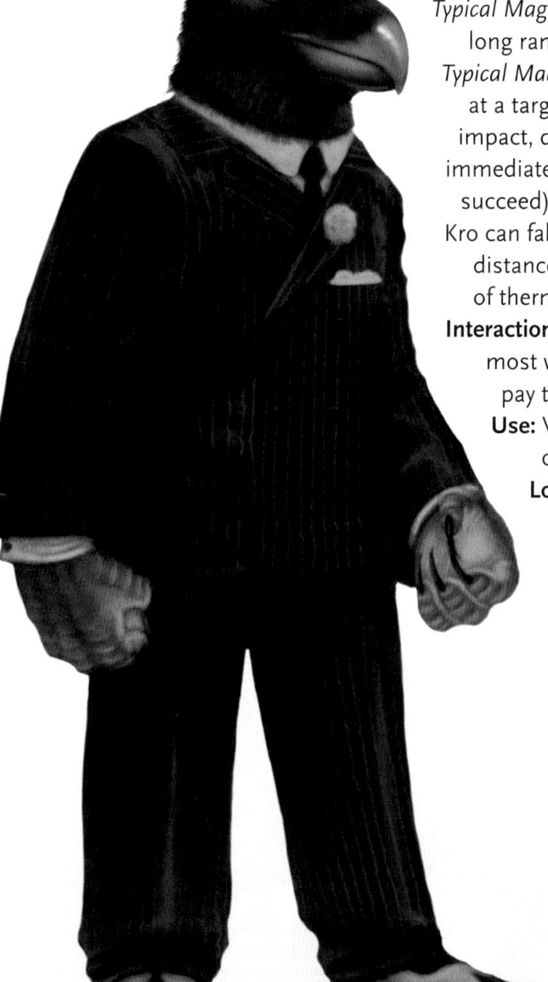

MAD CREATION 4 (12)

Sometimes the fruit of a mad scientist's laboratory is sublime, other times horrifying. Usually, it's a little of both. That's when releasing such a creation into the world is most dangerous. When an artificial entity starts out benign, it's difficult to know if a hidden flaw or slowly developing hatred will tip it over the edge into homicidal fury—or if it just acts odd because it doesn't know the social cues.

Should these things be treated as people, pets, or monsters to be stamped out and destroyed? That's the eternal question, and one that's usually answered wrong in fiction. It's no mystery why mad creations encountered in recursions are usually insanely dangerous.

Motive: Defense or destruction
Environment (Mad Science): Anywhere
Health: 27
Damage Inflicted: 5 points
Armor: 2
Movement: Short
Combat: A mad creation can make two different kinds of attack. The first is an electromagnetic discharge against a target within long range.
The second is a melee attack that, if successful, deals damage and requires the target to make a Might defense roll to resist an injected subtle poison. On a failure, the target falls into a comalike slumber. Each round thereafter, the target can attempt an Intellect defense roll to wake up. However, each failed roll inflicts 3 points of Intellect damage (ignores Armor). Choosing not to make an Intellect defense roll does not count as a failure. If the target chooses not to risk fighting free of the coma, only advanced medical intervention can save him from brain death.
Interaction: A mad creation is intelligent and can be swayed by reason. It might be passive, but if disturbed in a place it thought was secure against intrusion, it could grow belligerent and even murderous. Once so roused, a mad creation might still be calmed, but the difficulty of all such attempts is increased by one step.
Use: Mad creations are sometimes fashioned to serve as guards or soldiers. These beings generally protect rather than attack, unless their initial imprinting is overwritten by experience or their own flawed creation. Sometimes such a guardian goes rogue and must be tracked down and dealt with for the safety of others (or at least for the safety of its creator's reputation).
Loot: A mad creation requires many parts. Salvage from a destroyed mad creation could result in a cypher or two and another item that, with a bit of jury-rigging, works as an artifact.

A mad creation called Evaran discovered a cypher that gave it the spark. Though not quickened, Evaran now travels from recursion to recursion via interface connections and the Chaosphere, looking for someone who can explain what it all means.

GM Intrusion: *The character hit by the mad creation's melee attack doesn't take normal damage. Instead, the mad creation drops onto the character. The PC is pinned until he can succeed on a difficulty 6 Might-based task to escape. While he is pinned, the creation whispers mad utterances into his ear.*

Size Comparison

Mad Titan 7 (21)

Scattered through the Shoals of Earth, recursors report disturbing statues carved from black basalt, enormous works that are beautifully rendered but depict humans or humanoid beings trapped in moments of extreme agony and suffering. Who or what carved these monstrosities, no one knows. But sometimes the statues move. And sometimes the moving statues become enraged.

A mad titan is a stone or metal vessel imprisoning the mind of a sentient creature. Long isolation inside unfeeling material has caused the mind to tumble into the abyss of insanity as the realization that it will spend an eternity so trapped shatters its hold on reality. Nearly all mad titans rest in a dormant state, their minds lost in whatever memories they retain. Disturbing them can cause them to awaken, usually with disastrous results.

Mad titans may have been scattered about various recursions by fictional leakage from stories of Atlantis.

Motive: Release from imprisonment

Environment (Mad Science, Magic, or Psionics): In out-of-the-way places, especially ancient ruins

Health: 27

Damage Inflicted: 9 points

Armor: 4

Movement: Short

Modifications: All tasks involving balancing as level 5; Might defense as level 8; Speed defense as level 5 due to size.

Combat: A mad titan towers over most foes, and it can smash or stomp a target within short range as a melee attack.

The titan's massive stature and the material of its body means it can walk through nearly any obstacle, smashing through walls of solid rock, buildings, and trees. When walking, it pays no attention to what it steps on. Anything in its path is likely flattened. A character who is stepped on must make a Speed defense roll to dodge or be knocked down and take 9 points of damage.

Since the consciousness inside the titan's body is not there by choice, destruction offers it an escape from the hell of its existence. It welcomes anything that would destroy it, but because the titan is unhinged, it lashes out at anything that comes within reach.

Interaction: Titans spend years immobilized and insensate, their minds lost in half-remembered experiences and hallucinations. Rousing a titan has unpredictable results. Some might rampage. Others laugh, cry, or scream streams of nonsense.

Use: A mad titan holds a treasure trove of knowledge. If the characters can keep it focused long enough, they might coax from it the information they seek.

GM Intrusion: *The titan strikes a character so hard that she flies a long distance and lands in a heap, possibly dropping gear and weapons along the way.*

GM Intrusion: *The titan smashes a building, burying one or more characters under debris.*

MAGGOT FIEND 2 (6)

Maggot fiends slither through the ice fields of Hell Frozen Over. They gain form and substance from the final thoughts of recursors who perish in the recursion. Each fiend is a miserable creature that looks like its namesake: a soft, tan, segmented worm that's about 2 feet (0.6 m) long and has a human face on one end. This visage is a malevolent distortion of a human head (perhaps a copy of the very mortal that created the fiend, if such a relationship actually exists), a lustful, wrathful, sneering face filled with loathing and hate.

In Hell Frozen Over, the demon lord Treachery and other fiends harvest the maggots for food, pull them apart to hear their screams, or pit them against each other in brutal, wriggling fights to the death. Poor treatment compounds the wickedness that forms the maggot fiends, so they never pass up a chance to vent their depravity on the creatures they find trapped in the ice.

Motive: Torment the living

Environment (Hell Frozen Over | Magic): Anywhere

Health: 6

Damage Inflicted: 3 points

Movement: Immediate

Modifications: All tasks related to stealth as level 3; all tasks related to strength as level 1.

Combat: A maggot fiend wriggles toward anything that it deems weaker than itself and plies the victim with soft kisses from its damp lips. The maggot's corrosive saliva leaves a burning wound that inflicts damage, and it increases the difficulty of the victim's tasks by one step for one round.

Additionally, as a defense mechanism, a maggot fiend can spray a noxious cloud of psychotropic chemicals once every other round. Each character within an immediate distance must succeed on an Intellect defense roll or take 2 points of Intellect damage (ignores Armor) and experience vivid hallucinations for the next minute. Each time the victim makes an attack while suffering from these hallucinations, roll a d6. On an even number, resolve the attack normally. On an odd number, the victim attacks an imaginary creature instead.

Interaction: A maggot fiend has a twisted, corrupted personality. As a physical incarnation of "sin," the fiend embodies wickedness in word and deed. Maggot fiends are so poorly treated, they do not trust visitors to Hell Frozen Over and betray travelers the first chance they get.

Use: The PCs get a contract from OSR to hunt down one maggot fiend in particular that was formed from the dying thoughts of someone who took important information to her grave in Hell Frozen Over. OSR hopes the fiend now has those secrets.

SIZE COMPARISON

Hell Frozen Over, page 251

Treachery, page 252

Maggot fiends are not full spirits like those that form in Ardeyn when a native or recursor perishes there. Instead, the fiends are seeded from the worst parts of a recursor who perishes in Hell Frozen Over.

GM Intrusion: *A character damaged by a maggot fiend is compelled to betray her allies. She must use her next action to reveal a secret about an ally. If she knows no secrets, she must attack an ally.*

CREATURES OF

SIZE COMPARISON

MECHADRONE 7 (21)

Mechadrones were the pinnacle of the killing machines produced by rogue AIs to combat their biological enemies. Most mechadrones were destroyed, but those that survived the conflagration that led to Cataclyst's apocalyptic state continue the work they were designed to do: kill.

Robotic mechadrones are so dangerous thanks to their ability to reconfigure their forms into almost any mechanical shape. In these forms, mechadrones can hide in plain sight. What might appear as a heap of junk can, in an instant, transform into a multilegged mechanical monstrosity bristling with rockets, beam emitters, and slug throwers. If their prey attempts to escape, mechadrones simply adjust their shape to give chase, whether that means up the side of a mountain, into deep water, or through the air.

A dormant mechadrone looks like a bit of ancient technology—just another pile of wreckage in a landscape littered with such things. The mechadrone's sensors detect life forms that come within a long distance, and if any of them register as human (or mutant), the mechadrone powers up, which takes a few minutes.

Motive: Kill humans

Environment (Cataclyst | Magic or Mad Science): Almost anywhere

Health: 21

Damage Inflicted: 7 points

Armor: 3

Movement: Short (requires one action to convert movement mode between land, air, and sea)

Modifications: All tasks related to climbing, flying, jumping, and swimming as level 8.

Combat: Mechadrones are, simply, mobile arsenals. They can bring to bear just about any weapon imaginable to dispatch their enemies. A mechadrone uses whirling blades and spikes to attack all characters within immediate distance as a single action.

However, a mechadrone is deadliest at range and can use any of the following weapons to attack (each once per round, but it cannot use the same weapon two rounds in a row).

Particle Gun: The mechadrone emits a purple energy beam at a target within long range. The beam inflicts 9 points of damage.

Rocket: The mechadrone launches a missile at a target within 1,000 feet (305 m). If the attack misses, the rocket strikes a random spot within a short distance of the target. Wherever the rocket lands, it explodes and inflicts 7 points of damage to everything within short range.

Micromissiles: The mechadrone launches a barrage of six small missiles, divided among up to six targets within long range. Each missile that hits inflicts 3 points of damage.

Slug-Thrower: The mechadrone fires a hail of slugs at up to three targets (all within an immediate distance of each other) within long range as a single action.

Interaction: Mechadrones exist to kill humans, not talk to them.

Use: A malfunctioning AI deems one of the PCs to be a threat and sends a mechadrone to hunt the character.

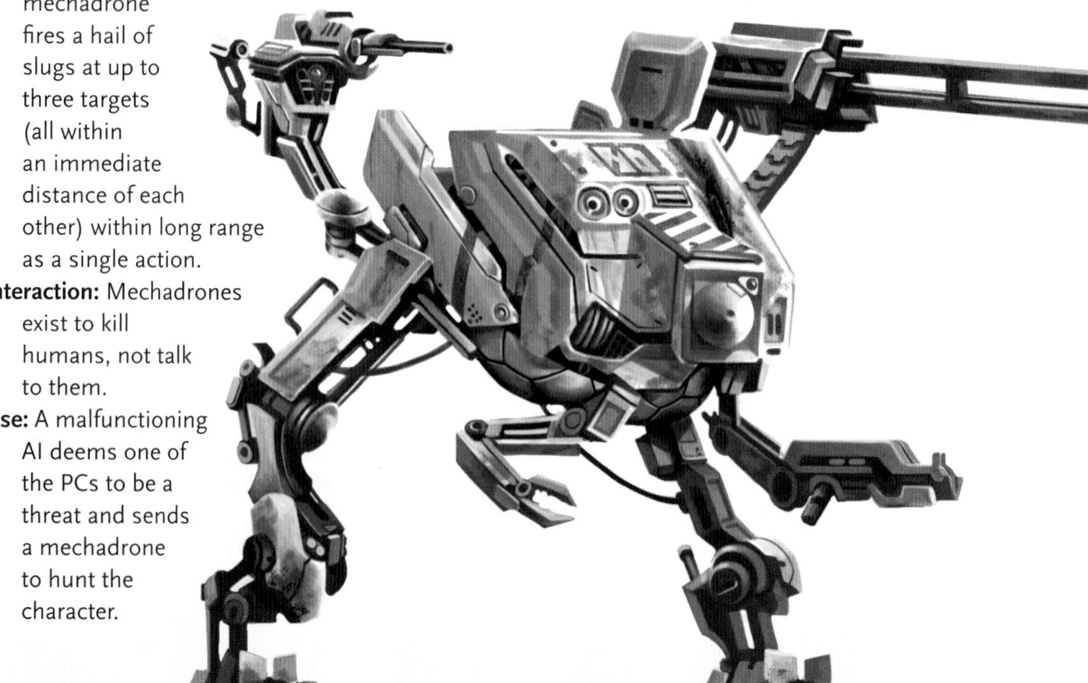

GM Intrusion: *When the mechadrone misses with one of its special weapons, it causes a terrain feature to explode, creating a pit that's dangerously close to where the PCs are standing.*

MECHANOMANCER 7 (21)

Mechanomancers use their incredible mastery over Mad Science cybertechnology to transcend flesh and become one with a digitally created avatar able to physically act in the real world.

Motive: Knowledge and power

Environment (Mad Science): Anywhere they can pursue their studies without interruptions

Health: 21

Damage Inflicted: 9 points

Armor: 3

Movement: Short; up to 50 miles (80 km) if a mechanomancer chooses to decohere and travel by datawire or wireless broadcast and appear in another area of its choice, though this kind of movement requires that the mechanomancer hasn't taken damage on the previous turn

Combat: A mechanomancer's electrified touch is the least of her abilities. That same energy can be projected at a target within long range. In addition, the mechanomancer can perform several other feats of technological wizardry, usually never using the same ability twice in two rounds:

Reprogram: The mechanomancer beams patterns of light and magnetic resonance in a way designed to interrupt the amygdala (nuclei in the brain) of creatures within short range. Those who fail an Intellect defense roll move toward the mechanomancer and lower their defenses for one round, meaning that the mechanomancer's subsequent attack hits automatically and inflicts 2 additional points of damage (a total of 11 points of damage).

Energized Exosuit: The avatar's digital form becomes briefly supercharged, allowing the mechanomancer to make a melee attack that deals 10 points of damage on a hit.

Upload Database: The mechanomancer can scan online records and the area around it with microfine instruments to learn one secret or valuable bit of information concerning the target.

Cage: The mechanomancer uses the same technology that allows it to create a digital body and forms a sphere of force around one target within short range that fails a Speed defense roll. The force cage is an opaque level 5 object and lasts for up to one minute unless smashed. It detonates like a grenade when it dissipates or is smashed, inflicting 5 points of damage to any creature within immediate range that fails a Speed defense roll.

Reform: If destroyed, a mechanomancer can create a new avatar within a few days, unless her real living body is found and destroyed. The body is usually very difficult to find, but once found, not particularly hard to destroy (treat as level 1, no attacks).

Some mechanomancers wield other powers as well, as determined by the GM.

Interaction: Mechanomancers are focused and not easily distracted by concerns they don't share. Some may be slightly deranged by the process they used to create their avatar.

Use: A mechanomancer could be the PCs' ultimate foe, an information source they meet while researching another topic, or someone that needs to be rescued (if the mechanomancer's avatar has been compromised and her real body is in peril).

Loot: A mechanomancer has 1d100 + 200 bits, a couple of cyphers, and possibly an artifact.

A mechanomancer called Tycho presents herself as a superhero in one of the recursions in the Shoals of Earth. Rather than caring about increasing her power and knowledge, she's interested in kicking some villain ass.

Mechanomancers are rare even under the law of Mad Science. They don't manifest in worlds operating under Standard Physics, though as technology continues to advance, telepresence-operated robots might one day have similar, if less spectacular, abilities.

GM Intrusion: *The character affected by the mechanomancer's reprogram ability stops as her brain glitches. She suffers a seizure that inflicts 1 point of Intellect damage per round until she succeeds on an Intellect defense roll to come out of it.*

SIZE COMPARISON

METALLICON 5 (15)

Metallicons are the living metallic portions of a metal-contaminated mass of fundament in the Chaosphere known only as the Incandescent. The Incandescent's nature allows it to infect and animate certain metals and metal alloys, creating metallicons.

Metallicons have been spied in more than one recursion by organizations that monitor such things on Earth and in Ruk. Normally, metallicons seem content merely to observe, but in a couple of cases, previously documented recursions were found to have been destroyed, and various kinds of metal excavated into the Strange, apparently by metallicons. The worry is that the Incandescent is building up an army of metallicons, possibly in preparation for invading a larger recursion or even Earth.

When resting, a metallicon appears to be a pile of thin metal plates. When it activates, a spark of blue energy races across every piece in an electric crackle, and the component parts assemble themselves into a vaguely humanoid creature.

Motive: Conquest

Environment (the Strange | Mad Science): Alone if observing a recursion; in groups of three to five if acting aggressively

Health: 15

Damage Inflicted: 5 points

Armor: 4

Movement: Short

Modifications: Speed defense as level 4; knowledge of advanced alien superscience (of one sort) as level 7.

If a metallicon is defeated, a plate of material making up the creature retains odd magnetic and electrical characteristics for several weeks.

Combat: A metallicon can project a spray of metallic blades at a target within long range. In melee, a metallicon can spin around like a ferocious blender, attacking every creature within immediate range as an action, though no more than once every other round. Attacks made against a metallicon using metallic objects or ammunition deal it no damage. Instead, the items become integrated into the creature, and each piece restores 1 point of its health. An opponent wielding a metallic melee weapon who succeeds on a Speed defense roll is able to hold on to her weapon.

Metallicons are vulnerable to electrical attacks, and their Armor does not apply against attacks charged with electricity.

A metallicon can't infect and animate metal to create other metallicons—only the Incandescent can do that. But it can absorb metal and metal alloys around it (such as folding chairs, swords, vehicles, and bronze sculptures) to restore 1d6 points of health as an action.

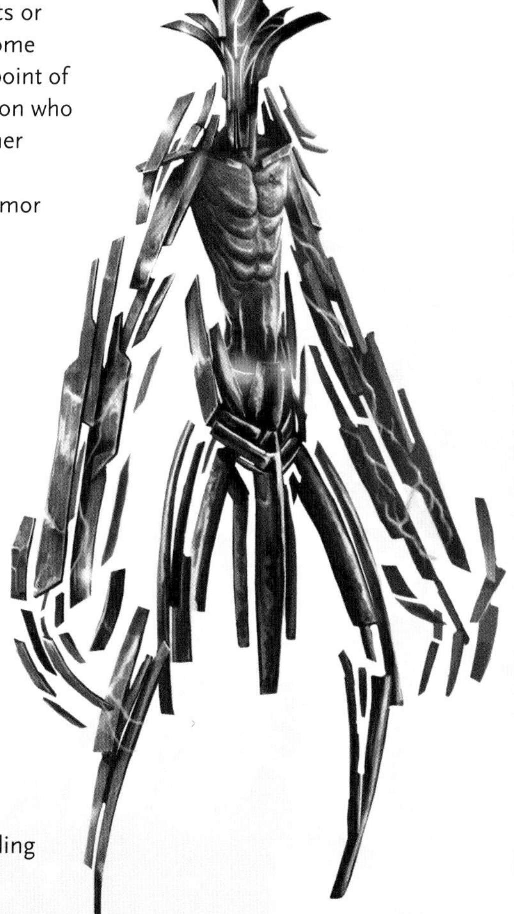

Interaction: Metallicons can vibrate thin metal plates to create audible speech. When PCs make contact with a metallicon, it describes itself as a servitor of the Incandescent, existing only to do the Incandescent's will. What the Incandescent wants, however, is not something a metallicon can understand.

GM Intrusion: *When the metallicon deals damage to the character, the PC must make an additional Speed defense roll. On a failure, a portion of the character's worn equipment that is composed of metal (such as belt buckles, pants zippers, earrings, watches, and so on) is absorbed into the creature. This destroys the objects and restores 1d6 points of health to the metallicon.*

Use: According to Estate surveillance tapes, a bronze statue on Earth animated, jumped in front of an armored truck carrying a load of coins and rare earth elements, and caused a major accident. In the aftermath, the statue disappeared, as did the truck's haul. The Estate wants the PCs to figure out what happened and how to prevent future occurrences.

Loot: Metallicons are made up of many components, including coins (1d6 × 1d100) and maybe a cypher or two.

MIRROR GAUNT 3 (9)

SIZE COMPARISON

Mirror gaunts hide in mirrors. They slither from one to the next, following their prey. When someone casts a glance into the mirror, the gaunt fades into the reflection's shadows, unseen, unnoticed, but almost always leaving an impression of being watched. Mirror gaunts feed on the people they catch. They stretch long, hideous claws from the mirror's surface to drag their victims into the pocket recursion they inhabit, where they take the prey apart bit by bit in a frenzy, stuffing bloody gobbets into their mouths to sate their terrible hunger.

"There! Right there, damn it! Someone's in the mirror!"
—Jonny "Flip" McDaniel

Stooped, naked things with spindly arms and legs, mirror gaunts have the shape of a human, but the similarities end with their faces. A wide mouth stretches across a smooth plane of skin on the torso, a mouth burdened by rows and rows of flinty grey teeth. Tiny black eyes, looking much like caviar, seem to float on waxen skin just above the prodigious maw. When mirror gaunts move, they scuttle, scampering on hands and feet, and when they draw someone inside their mirrors, they grunt and chirp with excitement.

The mirrors are pocket recursions that generally conform to the dimensions of the room or area where they hang. The images on their surfaces don't necessarily match up to the areas they reflect; something is almost always out of place.

GM Intrusion: *A character who would be drawn into the mirror becomes stuck halfway. The difficulty of all attacks, defenses, and other tasks attempted by the PC increases by two steps for one round, or until the character is pulled fully inside (or hauled out by allies).*

Motive: Hungers for flesh
Environment (Magic or Psionics): In any mirror
Health: 9
Damage Inflicted: 3 points
Movement: Short, though a reflection cannot move more than long distance from a mirror it can see
Modifications: All tasks related to stealth as level 5.
Combat: A mirror gaunt stalks its prey, moving from mirror to mirror. It can emerge from the mirror but prefers not to. Instead, it grabs prey within an immediate distance, though only when it believes no one else is around. A target damaged by a gaunt must also make a Might defense roll or be pulled inside the mirror.

Victims pulled into a mirror cannot escape until the mirror's surface reflects no light, such as if the mirror is brought into a dark room. Breaking a mirror that holds a creature also releases it, but mirrors in which gaunts live have been affected by the creatures' magic; the mirrors have Armor 2 and don't shatter unless they take 15 points of damage from a solid object.

Breaking a mirror destroys the mirror gaunt lurking inside it and inflicts 9 points of damage to any other creature trapped inside.
Interaction: A mirror gaunt that has recently eaten someone might be convinced to talk. Since it can move from mirror to mirror, the gaunt is a notorious voyeur and may share information about people it has seen. Gaunts always refer to others as "food."
Use: One of the mirrors haunted by a gaunt contains a gate to a recursion the characters need to visit. The PCs must find a way to enter the mirror and contend with the horror living inside it.
Loot: A character may find a few cyphers and other valuables hidden inside the mirror.

Size Comparison

MOKUREN 3 (9)

Mokuren are usually no larger than a cat, but they possess the ability to swell until they're the size of a bus (if only briefly). That ability, combined with their flashy pyrokinetic tails, make these creatures a particular favorite with children, at least in stories and picture books. Given that mokuren can "burrow" into paintings and other two-dimensional art, it's possible that some mokuren images are more than simple representations.

Motive: Play

Environment (Atom Nocturne | Psionics): Almost anywhere, usually as static images on walls or in storybooks

Health: 9

Damage Inflicted: 3 points

Movement: Short; long if flying

Modifications: Defends as level 5 due to size, unless enlarged; see Combat.

Combat: A mokuren exists in three states: as an image, as a cat-sized creature, and as a bus-sized behemoth.

As an image, a mokuren can't be harmed. Even if the image is defaced, the mokuren merely "burrows" away and reappears like graffiti on a new flat space within a few miles. Alternatively, it could emerge from the image and become a physical cat-sized creature.

As a cat-sized creature, a mokuren can attack with its claws or bite. It can also direct a stream of fire from its glowing tail at a target within long range. (When a mokuren flies, it's by using its tail to create a jet that rockets it skyward.) Finally, it can make an enlarged attack.

When a mokuren makes an enlarged attack, it swells to the size of a bus and swipes at, bites, or lands on a target as part of the same action. When enlarged, the mokuren gains +5 to Armor and makes and defends against all attacks as a level 7 creature. On a hit, the enlarged mokuren deals 7 points of damage. However, a mokuren can remain enlarged for a total of only four rounds during any twenty-four hour period, so it uses this ability sparingly or only when enraged.

As images, mokuren can exist almost anywhere, even in recursions that don't operate under their native law. However, in such a case, the creatures are inactive and can't normally come alive off a page until they're returned to a recursion that supports them.

Interaction: To see an active mokuren is considered good luck, unless you manage to get on the wrong side of one. Then an offering of sweets must be made to the offended creature. A mokuren can't talk, but it can understand the languages of its recursion about as well as a trained courser or hound can.

Use: Sometimes mokuren eggs are found, but they are quickly snatched up by greedy traders and sold locally or, in some cases, among the flashing stalls of the Glittering Market in Crow Hollow. Someone who raises a mokuren from egg to adult has a good chance of forming a lifelong bond with the creature.

Loot: Among the Fallen of Atom Nocturne and unethical researchers, mokuren tails are extraordinarily valuable. If one could find a mokuren lair, one might also discover an unhatched egg.

Crow Hollow, page 242

Atom Nocturne, page 234

GM Intrusion: *The character hit by a mokuren doesn't take damage. Instead, she must succeed on a Might defense roll or be pulled into the nearest wall, floor, or book with the creature, becoming a two-dimensional image. In this state, the PC is in stasis until the mokuren pulls her free, another creature "pries" her loose, or a day passes and she emerges naturally.*

MONUMENT SPIDER 8 (24)

A monument spider's legs can stretch almost 500 feet (152 m) from tip to tip. Despite the creature's immense size, its central body remains light enough that it can climb upon and spin webs between orbital elevators, skyscraping arcologies (whether inhabited or, if in a postapocalyptic recursion, long ruined), wizard towers, or titanic marble sculptures.

Monument spiders usually trap prey in their webs like their much smaller cousins do, except the kind of prey they prefer runs the gamut from jet aircraft to dragons. Normally, a monument spider ignores creatures as small as humans, unless those humans become a nuisance.

Motive: Hungers for prey, spin webs, self-defense

Environment (Mad Science or Magic): Anywhere on the exterior of massive structures

Health: 45

Damage Inflicted: 12

Armor: 4

Movement: Long

Modifications: Speed defense as level 5 due to size.

Combat: A monument spider's webs are amazingly strong and hard to see at a distance, so they can create a danger zone a mile or more across for swiftly flying creatures and vehicles. Colliding with a web at high speed is not unlike suffering a great fall. It's usually enough to destroy a vehicle and inflict 8 points of ambient damage to passengers or riders (or direct damage to a large creature), and it might move a character one step down the damage track. Any given strand of web is level 4 and is adhesive. Large objects and creatures must succeed on a difficulty 8 Might-based task to pull free, but a human-sized creature (which presents a much smaller body area) must make a difficulty 3 Might-based roll each round to move more than an immediate distance.

A monument spider can bite a foe within short range. In addition to damage, the bite delivers a poisonous acid that inflicts 8 additional points of Speed damage (ignores Armor) on a failed Might defense roll.

Interaction: These creatures act like spiders and are either unwilling or unable to communicate. They see characters as inconsequential, a food source, or a danger to be dealt with.

Use: The PCs' flying vehicle or mount gets caught in a monument spider's web strung between two massive structures (or between a structure and a mountain peak).

Loot: Sometimes the useful possessions of previous victims are mixed with the wreckage or bones that accumulate beneath monument spider webs.

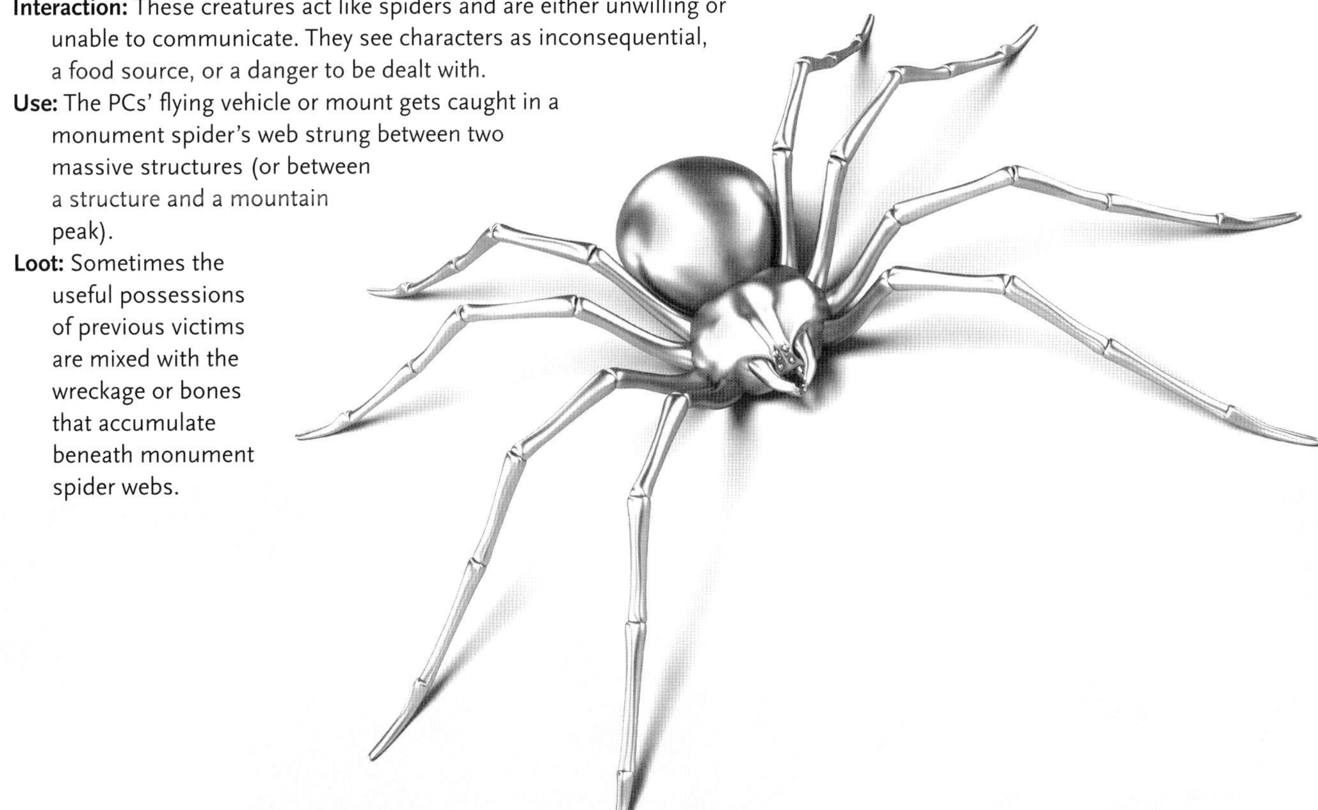

In a Mad Science recursion, a monument spider might be robotic or alien, or it might look like a normal spider grown several orders of magnitude too large thanks to a radiation leak. In a Magic recursion, a monument spider might be the mount of a god gone rogue, a war golem, or a creature of myth (in which case, it has a mind and an agenda).

GM Intrusion: *When the character takes damage from the spider, she must succeed on an additional Speed defense roll. On a failed roll, a particularly sticky web strand adheres to her. The PC is pulled into the air and left hanging on a nearby convenient high point until she can escape with a successful difficulty 5 Might-based task.*

Size Comparison

MURDER 4 (12)

Kro measure their lives in crow coin. When enough coin is taken from a kro by force or theft that it dies, the kro may return as a wrathful entity driven by a need to get revenge against anyone and everyone, starting with those who killed it and branching out from there.

A murder has two forms—a crow-human hybrid armed with long claws and a jagged beak, perfect for taking a foe apart, and a great cloud of ravens that share a single mind. The murder hunts in its second form, spreading far apart, with individual ravens watching for likely targets of vengeance. Once they pick up the trail, the ravens follow their target, monitoring its movements until the prey is alone and vulnerable. That's when the murder reveals itself. The ravens fly together, clumping up to become beaked death.

Motive: Vengeance

Environment (Crow Hollow | Magic or Mad Science): Almost anywhere

Health: 12

Damage Inflicted: 3 points

Movement: Short; long when flying

Modifications: All tasks related to perception as level 5.

Combat: While in loose-cloud form, a murder can distribute its individual ravens across many miles, but in combat it condenses the cloud into a furious blot of flying ravens that fills an area 30 feet (9 m) in diameter. Other creatures can move through the murder while it's condensed, but the difficulty of all tasks increases by one step because of the constant jostling and limited visibility. In addition, while the murder is condensed, it takes half damage from any attack that would ordinarily affect just one target. On its turn, the murder can attack any creature in the cloud or within an immediate distance as a single action.

In its hybrid form, the murder deals 3 additional points of damage on a successful attack (6 points of damage total).

In either form, whenever the murder takes damage, it instantly breaks apart into a swirling cloud of birds and gathers itself at a spot it can see within short range without using an action. As much as it craves revenge, the murder is aware enough to know when it is fighting a losing battle, and it will retreat to resume its attack at a later time when it has a greater advantage.

Interaction: Murders relentlessly hunt down their killers and anyone involved in their death. Although they normally ignore other people, they are not above wringing information from others or attacking innocents who stand between a murder and its enemies. When divided into separate ravens, they croak the names of their killers in a horrible litany.

Use: A member of a minor Beak Mafia family has recently acquired an artifact that lets her control a murder haunting the Glittering Market. So far, she uses it to advance her position in her family by eliminating rivals. The more power she gains, the more her ambition grows.

Loot: A murder keeps a hidden lair containing 1d100 × 2 crow coin, 1d6 cyphers, and other shiny bits.

Crow coin, page 243

When a target is damaged by a murder, an equal amount of crow coin drops at the target's feet. After the murder kills the target, it collects the scattered coin.

GM Intrusion: *When a murder breaks apart into a flock, the character is blinded for one round.*

MYSTEREON 5 (15)

Who was that masked figure? No one knows for sure. Mystereons are more than masked vigilantes with strange abilities, although they are that. These mysterious individuals crop up in recursions with surprising frequency—sometimes in places entirely appropriate (recursions based on fictional leakage from pulp or comic book superhero fiction), but sometimes not. Either way, no one seems to know where they come from. It's almost as though they originate in the Strange itself and intrude upon recursions for reasons of their own.

Mystereons seem to work for justice, but often it comes in the form of particularly violent and bloody vengeance against wrongdoers (or perceived wrongdoers). Although each mystereon's appearance is unique, almost all look like humans in masks and dark-colored costumes or uniforms, usually with a symbol suggesting the mystereon's adopted name: the Red Scorpion, Moonhunter, Shadowman, and so on.

It's possible that the devices the mystereons use are cyphers, which lend further credence to the idea that there's more to the mystery behind them.

GM Intrusion: *The mystereon produces a device that is perfect for the situation at hand.*

Motive: Justice
Environment (Magic or Mad Science): Always alone
Health: 21
Damage Inflicted: 6 points
Armor: 1
Movement: Short
Modifications: Speed defense and stealth as level 6.
Combat: Mystereons use their fists and sometimes conventional weaponry (such as throwing stars, billy clubs, or firearms). Through the use of superscience or magic, a mystereon can produce other special effects, but usually only once, after which time the device must be recharged or rejuvenated in their secret lair. These effects include one or more of the following, or something similar:

- An electrical jolt that inflicts 8 points of damage and stuns the target for three rounds, during which time she can take no action
- A cloud of mist that fills an immediate area and induces terrifying hallucinations that increase the difficulty of all actions by two steps for one minute (the mystereon is immune)
- A sticky net that entangles all creatures in an immediate area until they can break, wriggle, or cut themselves free (difficulty 6 task)
- A flash of smoke that allows the mystereon to move a long distance without being seen
- An injection that grants the mystereon great strength for one hour, during which she inflicts 3 additional points of damage in melee and the difficulty of her related tasks is reduced by two steps
- A burst of energy that puts all creatures in an immediate radius into a hypnotic state for one minute, during which they cannot take actions and the difficulty of resisting spoken suggestions is increased by one step—but harming them ends the effect immediately (the mystereon is immune)

Interaction: Mystereons are driven loners, often seemingly noble but with an inexplicable, myopic, violent streak. They can be reasonable but are never swayed from their cause.
Use: Mystereons might just be masked heroes (or antiheroes), or they might be something far more complex, operating from the Strange with agendas in dozens of recursions.
Loot: Mystereons possess not only the varied "bag of tricks" described under Combat but also other sophisticated gear such as grapnel guns, smoke bombs, tracking devices, and more.

MYTOCYTIC POOL 10 (30)

> **"I get all the great things you people have done, but surely you've made a few mistakes along the way?"**
> —L.G. Babcock III

Though rare enough to be counted on one hand, there exist a few vast lakes of a mysterious opaque substance leaked from a long-vanished biotech lab. The material sloshing in these pools is too thick to be water, too fluid to be tar. The lakes exude a palpable chill, and visitors feel their skin prickle, hairs standing on end as if in the presence of an energy field. Most people find the experience too disturbing to endure for long, but those who persevere discover that the pools are something more: they're alive and filled with malevolence for all living things.

A mytocytic pool is a sentient lake of corrupted genetic material, a great quantity of substance able to form twisted parodies of life from its mass, which it occasionally releases into the wild. For example, it was from the murky depths of a mytocytic pool that the polymous emerged, and other horrors as well.

Polymous, page 106

Motive: Territory, colonization of other recursions

Environment (Ruk | Mad Science): In a depression somewhere in the Periphery

Health: 120

Damage Inflicted: 10 points

Movement: Immediate

Modifications: Speed defense as level 3 due to size and nature.

Combat: A mytocytic pool can use an action to intensify the energy field it always emits to affect all organic creatures other than itself within long range. A target must make a successful Might defense roll or take 10 points of damage.

As part of the pool's action, at the cost of 5 points of health, it can give birth to a darkness spawn. The spawn rises from the murky waters and moves a short distance from its parent. A spawn can have any appearance, but it usually looks hideous and lacks an important physical feature. It might be blind, missing limbs, lacking skin, or something else. Wracked with pain, the spawn screeches and howls until killed.

A mytocytic pool can form a pseudopod to physically attack a creature within long range. Those that are struck take damage and must also succeed on a Might defense roll. On a failure, the fluid spreads across the victim's body, seeking to assimilate his material, inflicting an additional 5 points of damage (ignores Armor) in the process.

GM Intrusion: *The mytocytic pool spits out a couple of polymous, which attack the character.*

Interaction: A mytocytic pool is always interested in information about its current recursion and neighboring recursions. When it needs to communicate, it fashions a shuddering spawn to serve as its mouthpiece and speaks through it in an eloquent manner. Most pools are old, making them a veritable font of information for those who show the proper deference and respect.

The Veritex, page 204

Use: The PCs need to identify an artifact or track down a legend about Ruk. If they make an offering to an odd, dark lake in a cracked vault of the Veritex, they might gain the information they seek.

Loot: There's bound to be an artifact or two in the mytocytic pool, along with 2d6 + 3 cyphers.

NAKARAND AVATAR 6 (18)

Nakarand is the name of a native of the Chaosphere. It's not a planetovore, though possibly only because of its temperament and its "modest" needs. This sticky, brownish organism, vast and coiled, is several hundred feet (60 m) across, though it's far larger on the inside. In some ways, it's like a living recursion—a living recursion able to manifest its mind and abilities into a powerful, mobile avatar.

Nakarand usually creates only one avatar at a time. This avatar, using its quickened abilities, arranges for the feeding and well-being of the far larger and less mobile part of itself. Unfortunately for creatures of the universe of normal matter, that feeding requires both flesh and sapient minds, which means Earth and the Shoals around it are prey for Nakarand.

Most avatars gather feedstock by masquerading as a human being selling a special substance called spiral dust. Unfortunately for people who become hooked on the druglike blue dust, overuse causes a victim to be translated directly into Nakarand's gullet, where he is digested. If Nakarand is fed, so too is the avatar.

Motive: Feed and defend Nakarand

Environment (the Strange): Can appear in any recursion, and is sometimes seen haunting the dreams of spiral dust users

Health: 22

Damage Inflicted: 10 points

Armor: 1

Movement: Short

Modifications: All tasks related to stealth as level 8; knowledge of the Strange as level 7.

Combat: The avatar possesses a shadowy "digestive" aura that it can use to create partially material objects or feed directly on living creatures. An object created from the digestive shadow (whether a melee weapon or one with a long-range attack) inflicts 6 points of damage from the force of impact, plus 4 additional points from the digestive process. Anyone within immediate range of the avatar when it makes an attack also takes 1 point of damage each round from the digestive aura.

When the avatar is within immediate range of someone experiencing the effect of spiral dust (sometimes called a spiraler), the avatar regenerates 2 points of health each round.

Despite its power, an avatar prefers to work in the shadows and rarely indulges in direct combat unless it has no other choice.

Interaction: Different avatars adopt different personalities and means to accomplish their ends, though in the Shoals of Earth, pushing the "drug" called spiral dust seems to work well. Recently, an avatar calling itself the Dustman had great success doing so and was described as a sort of malign sandman.

Use: A PC investigating an old house startles several squatters who are strung out on a new street drug. But they're not the only ones who are startled; the PC glimpses an avatar in the shadows.

Loot: Avatars carry a few cyphers and several doses of spiral dust (which acts like a hallucinogen and causes crazy dreams, among other things).

Nakarand: *level 10; health 100; Armor 10; regenerates 10 points of health per round*

If an avatar is killed, Nakarand retreats into the Strange (if not already there), breaking through whatever barriers might lie in its way. There Nakarand hides away until a new avatar forms (in 1d20 days), one that has the characteristics of sapient creatures from the nearest prime world.

GM Intrusion: *The character must succeed on a Might defense roll or fall into a normal, if somewhat deep sleep (requiring vigorous shaking, at minimum, to wake).*

Spiralers, page 156

Size Comparison

NALUSA FALAYA 4 (12)

This spindly humanoid can slither along on its belly like a snake, melt into the shadows, or reveal itself suddenly in the guise of an emaciated human wearing black robes. The nature of a nalusa falaya is to lure victims away from the company of others at dusk, perhaps with promises of power or treasure for the taking "not far from here," or simply by whispering a victim's name from the periphery of a camp, settlement, or any place people gather.

Nalusa falayas are the ghostly remains of warriors who died poorly in battle, finding their end as a direct result of their own cowardice or the betrayal of a comrade. Rather than learning from the experience, nalusa falayas become grim specters who desire to bring mischief and bad ends to the living. When a nalusa falaya convinces a victim to accept a share of the creature's power for a short time, the return on the investment is usually the victim's life.

A nalusa falaya is a creature of Choctaw legend. Its name literally means "long black thing."

Motive: Mischief and murder

Environment (Thunder Plains | Magic): Anywhere shadowed or dark

Health: 18

Damage Inflicted: 5 points

Movement: Immediate; short when sliding on belly (allowing movement on walls and ceilings)

Modifications: All tasks related to stealth as level 7.

Combat: A nalusa falaya that touches a foe inflicts numbing cold damage. Each 2 points of damage inflicted restores 1 point of health to the nalusa falaya.

Alternatively, a nalusa falaya can whisper at a target within short range, a whisper that only she can hear. If the target fails an Intellect defense roll, she abandons whatever she was doing and follows the sound, bewitched. A bewitched target is broken from her spell if an obstacle, attack, or ally physically prevents her from approaching the nalusa falaya. Otherwise, she follows the nalusa falaya for several minutes before the bewitchment ends, which usually means she is far from help when the creature finally attacks. Once bewitched, a victim can't be affected again by the same nalusa falaya.

A nalusa falaya can give its bewitching ability to another. If conferred, this "gift" lasts for up to twenty-four hours, after which the power returns to the nalusa falaya no matter how far away the receiver is. (The nalusa falaya is immune to this bewitchment when used by another.) A character who accepts the bargain discovers that, after the power leaves her, she takes 3 points of Intellect damage each day (ignores Armor) until the nalusa falaya is found and killed.

Interaction: Nalusa falayas sometimes offer other beings a gift of bewitchment, either to avoid being killed or to soften up a powerful character.

Use: The PCs set camp, build a fire, and begin to nod off. That's when one of the characters hears her name being whispered plaintively from the shadows.

Loot: A nalusa falaya often makes its lair in the hollow of an old, dead tree, and among its possessions are the valuables and other belongings of previous victims, possibly including a cypher.

GM Intrusion: *Another nalusa falaya emerges from the shadows and whispers the character's name.*

NECURATU 7 (21)

Necuratu are wildly dangerous predators of Gloaming who care nothing for the Code, the Conclave, or the politics that divide Law from Chaos in the recursion. Whether called forth from a presumed history of Gloaming that never happened, from a horror screenwriter's debased imaginings, or from an alien recursion in the Strange, the necuratu are exactly what Gloaming doesn't need: creatures that preferentially feed on the blood of vampires and werewolves. Their presence threatens to create a new division, dissolving the allegiances of Law and Chaos as all creatures run for cover.

In dim light, necuratu might be mistaken for humanoids. When revealed, they're anything but human.

Motive: Hunger for supernatural creatures

Environment (Gloaming | Magic or Psionics): Anywhere except populated areas

Health: 21

Damage Inflicted: 7 points

Movement: Short; long when flying

Modifications: Disguise as level 8 when pretending to be a normal vampire.

Combat: Every time a necuratu hits a living foe with an attack (claw or bite), the necuratu regenerates 1 point of health. If its target is a supernatural creature (such as a vampire or werewolf), the necuratu regenerates 2 points of health.

A necuratu can also call on various magic or psychic abilities if it wishes.

Cosmic Horror: When a necuratu hits a character, the target doesn't take damage to her Might Pool; instead, she suffers through a flashing series of appalling, repulsive, and alien images that wrack her with pain and send her staggering back. The character takes 3 points of Intellect damage (ignores Armor) and can't take offensive actions for one round. If this ability is used on a vampire character, the touch inflicts 5 points of Intellect damage.

Dominate: When a necuratu hits a target, instead of inflicting damage, the necuratu mentally dominates the character for one round, forcing him to do whatever it wants. If this ability is used on a werewolf character, the target is dominated for three rounds.

Necuratu can see perfectly in the dark. In full daylight, the difficulty of all tasks they perform is modified by two steps to their detriment.

Unless the remains of a necuratu are cut into seven or more portions and sealed away from each other, the creature comes back after a few months—even from ash.

Interaction: Necuratu don't speak. Among themselves, they communicate telepathically, and when they must deal with other creatures, they force dominated victims to speak for them.

Use: Isabel "Issy" Schiaparelli, the werewolf leader of the Conclave of Chaos in Gloaming, comes to the PCs to ask their aid in defeating a new scourge in town: a necuratu.

SIZE COMPARISON

Gloaming, page 249

Vampire, page 131

"These creatures, the necuratu—they don't belong here. Unless they were here all along, and Gloaming isn't a recursion created by the fictional leakage everyone assumes." —Dr. Sybil Holloway

GM Intrusion: *When the character is bitten by the necuratu and takes damage, she must succeed on a Might defense roll or become enthralled by the creature for one minute and refuse to harm it.*

Isabel Schiaparelli, page 249

Isabel Schiaparelli: *level 6, fights as level 8 while in wereform; regenerates 2 points of health per round while in wereform*

NEUROR APTOR 8 (24)

True Code, page 192

One of the most sought-after treasures of Ruk is a fabled control fob for a neuroraptor. However, no one is entirely certain that such a thing exists or, if it does, whether it would retain any efficacy if the linked neuroraptor was found and decanted from its stasis slime.

GM Intrusion: *When the character fails an Intellect defense roll against the neuron killing pulse, instead of taking damage, he becomes convinced that his allies are foes who must be stopped immediately and permanently. The character is allowed to make a new Intellect defense roll each round to throw off the effect, and even if he fails these rolls, his neural pathways reroute to normal after a minute.*

A relative handful of neuroraptors were commissioned and grown by ancient factions to fight against creatures of the Qinod Singularity that threatened the sanctity of Ruk. Few of these massive creatures survive to this day. Those that do are cached in stasis slime and hidden away in secret pockets around the recursion. They were thought extinct or perhaps pure myth until a recent neuroraptor incursion over Harmonious left hundreds dead and thousands wounded, and engendered a newfound respect for True Code relics that have survived the millennia.

Motive: Unpredictable

Environment (Ruk | Mad Science): Anywhere

Health: 60

Damage Inflicted: 9 points

Armor: 5

Movement: Long when flying

Modifications: Speed defense as level 6 due to size.

Combat: A neuroraptor can make physical melee attacks, but its preferred means of attack is its neuron killing pulse, which targets up to five different creatures within long range. Those who fail an Intellect defense roll take 4 points of Intellect damage (ignores Armor). Alternatively, instead of making any other attacks, a neuroraptor can emit a collated pulse at a single target within 2 miles (3 km), inflicting 6 points of Intellect damage.

Interaction: For all its power, a neuroraptor operates with damaged cognition and doesn't understand that it has been displaced in time. This inability to grasp the changes Ruk has undergone results in confused aggression at best and violent repudiation at worst. Attempts to communicate have little chance of success unless couched telepathically.

Use: A cocoonlike mass is excavated from a disturbed region of the Hub. Within it, something stirs, and it's only a matter of time before a neuroraptor emerges. The PCs must deal with it when it does.

Loot: A neuroraptor is part machine, and amid its wreckage, valuable parts worth several thousand bits could be salvaged by someone with the know-how.

NGESHTIN 6 (18)

Ngeshtins inhabit glaciers, frozen lakes, and winter storms. Though completely physical while manifest, ngeshtins possess something of a spiritual nature, and they can appear seemingly out of nowhere when the seasons change or in the presence of something exceptionally cold.

A ngeshtin looks somewhat like a qephilim from the waist up (if a qephilim's fingers were tipped with claws of sharp ice) and like a massive snake from the waist down. Its entire body smells of pine needles and is covered in white scales, frost, and steaming cold. Quick and dexterous despite its chilled body, a ngeshtin "stands" about 9 feet (3 m) tall on its coiled tail, but one measured from head to tail tip would be much longer.

Ngeshtins have a special fondness for the fermented gifts of the vine. In some parts of Ardeyn, ngeshtins are known more as spirits of wine than of winter. The cold that ngeshtins emit doesn't adversely affect wine of any kind.

GM Intrusion: *The ngeshtin breathes a blast of cold air, and instead of dealing damage, it creates a dome of translucent ice around one PC within short range. The dome has 2 points of Armor and can take 12 points of damage before shattering. Lifting the dome high enough to get out is a difficulty 3 Might-based task.*

Motive: Defense

Environment (Ardeyn | Magic): Anywhere, but usually in cold areas

Health: 18

Damage Inflicted: 6 points

Armor: 2

Movement: Short

Modifications: Speed defense as level 4 due to size; all tasks related to identifying and rating wines as level 8.

Combat: A ngeshtin can use its claws in melee or spend an action to first fashion a massive curved sword (a talwar) of ice, condensed from moisture in the air. Attacks with the talwar deal 2 additional points of damage (for a total of 8 points of damage).

Once every other round, a ngeshtin can breathe a blast of cold air within short range at a group of targets in immediate range of each other. Targets who make a successful Speed defense roll still take 1 point of damage.

A ngeshtin can fashion basic objects out of ice condensed and frozen from moisture in the air. Such objects can be no larger than a human and could include a shield, a chair, a solid sculpture, and so on. The ngeshtin can also use this ability to seal an opening or bridge a gap.

A ngeshtin is vulnerable to unexpected heat. Fire damage dealt to a ngeshtin causes it to lose its next action, but only the first time during any given combat.

A ngeshtin regenerates 3 points of health per round if any part of its body is touching a large mass of ice (or is dipped in a large body of snow or ice water).

Interaction: Ngeshtins communicate telepathically with creatures they can see within 100 feet (30 m). Different ngeshtins have different goals, but most are willing to subordinate those goals in return for good wine.

Use: The PCs are asked to bring a gift of wine to a meeting with someone of importance in Ardeyn. When the characters go to procure the wine, they find that a ngeshtin has made a prior claim.

Loot: If wine is of value to the PCs, a ngeshtin usually has a couple of bottles in its hoard.

Size Comparison

NIGHTGAUNT 3 (9)

A nightgaunt's hands and feet have no opposable digits. All its fingers and toes can wrap around objects they grasp with firm but unpleasant boneless strength, perfect for swooping down, grabbing prey in a nearly unbreakable grip, and flying off into the night. Nightgaunt destinations vary, but a few of these horrible creatures are quickened and able to fly between recursion boundaries. This means that a nightgaunt briefly visiting Earth could snatch a victim and carry her away to Innsmouth or a related Lovecraftian recursion. But best not to dwell on that overlong, because it could affect one's peace of mind.

"Shocking and uncouth black things with smooth, oily . . . surfaces, unpleasant horns that curved inward toward each other, bat wings whose beating made no sound, ugly prehensile paws, and barbed tails that lashed needlessly and disquietingly. And worst of all, they never spoke . . . because they had no faces at all . . . but only a suggestive blankness where a face ought to be. All they ever did was clutch and fly and tickle; that was the way of nightgaunts."
—H. P. Lovecraft, *The Dream-Quest of Unknown Kadath*

Motive: Unknowable

Environment (Innsmouth | Magic or Mad Science): Anywhere dark, usually in groups of three to five

Health: 9

Damage Inflicted: 4 points

Movement: Immediate; long if flying (short if flying with a victim)

Modifications: Perception and Speed defense as level 4; knowledge of the mythologies seeded by H. P. Lovecraft as level 7.

Combat: A nightgaunt can attack with its barbed tail (and it also uses the tail to tickle prey caught in its boneless clutches). To catch a foe, a nightgaunt makes a clutching attack by diving through the air from just outside of short range. When it does this, it moves 100 feet (30 m) in a round and attempts to grab a victim near the midpoint of its movement. A target who fails a Speed defense roll (and who isn't more than twice the size of the nightgaunt) is jerked into the creature's clutches and finds himself dangling from a height of 50 feet (15 m).

Once a victim is caught, the nightgaunt begins tickling him with its barbed tail. Although this sounds harmless, it's a subtle form of torture that increases the difficulty of all tasks attempted by the victim by two steps, including Might-based or Speed-based rolls to break or wriggle free.

If a victim caught in a nightgaunt's clutches seems likely to kill his captor, the nightgaunt will release him to the fall he seems to crave.

Though natives of Lovecraftian recursions, nightgaunts sometimes find their way to Earth through inapposite gates. When they visit the world of normal matter, they usually stay no more than an hour or two—just long enough to accomplish an obscure but terrifying goal.

Interaction: Nightgaunts never speak, and they ignore anyone who attempts to interact with them, whether the communication takes the form of commanding, beseeching, or frantically pleading. Such is the way of nightgaunts.

Use: Someone who bears one or more of the PCs a grudge discovered a tome of spells and summoned a flight of nightgaunts, which set off in search of their prey.

Loot: One in three nightgaunts has a valuable souvenir from a past victim, which might be an expensive watch, a ring, an amulet, or sometimes a cypher.

GM Intrusion: *The character is startled by the nightgaunt and suffers the risk of temporary dementia. On a failed Intellect defense roll, she shrieks and faints (or, at the GM's option, babbles, drools, laughs, and so on). She can attempt a new Intellect defense roll each round to return to normal.*

NIGHT SPIDER 4 (12)

Night spiders originate in Ardeyn's Night Vault, where the 5-foot (2 m) diameter adults (not including legs) nest along the Roads of Sorrow. Night spiders prefer to walk on floors and ceilings, and when they attach themselves to tunnel ceilings with webbing, their dangling legs can be mistaken for rootlets of the Daylands that have breached the vault.

Night spiders are particularly hardy if removed from their home recursion, which means that even if taken into a recursion (by inapposite gate or similar means) that doesn't operate under the law of Magic, their abilities don't see much degradation, especially if they hatched from eggs previously transferred to the new recursion.

Night Vault, page 183

Motive: Hungers for flesh

Environment (Ardeyn | Magic): Underground areas in groups of one to six

Health: 16

Damage Inflicted: 4 points

Movement: Short

Modifications: Attacks as level 5; perception as level 6; Speed defense as level 3 due to size.

Combat: A night spider can bite a foe with its mandibles but prefers to use web strands to attack a target within short range. The webbing inflicts no damage but is amazingly sticky. A webbed character who fails a Might defense roll is dragged within immediate range of the spider (possibly hoisted up into the air if the night spider is attached to a wall or ceiling). The night spider attacks only one foe at a time, and only creatures of about human size or smaller.

Breaking free from a web strand is a level 4 Might-based task. A strand can also be severed if it takes 8 points of damage. Victims unable to break free from the web are automatically cocooned one round after being dragged into immediate range by the spider's spare legs, which hold a victim immobile (allowing only purely mental actions or escape attempts). Each round the victim remains cocooned, he automatically takes 4 points of ambient damage from suffocation. Breaking free from a cocoon is a difficulty 6 Might-based task, and a cocoon can be opened if it takes 25 points of damage.

If a night spider is killed, a mass of tiny spiderling eggs in its internal cavity convulsively hatch. Spiderlings rush out in an unstoppable swarm, and before they disperse, they inflict 4 points of damage to all creatures in immediate range who fail a Speed defense roll.

GM Intrusion: *The character's weapon or other held item is struck by a strand of web and yanked out of her hand. The item is drawn to the lurking spider before the character realizes what's happened. The spider cocoons the item as if it were living prey.*

Interaction: A guard colony of night spiders can sometimes be established if a handful of eggs are transplanted to an area before they hatch. Adult night spiders are not particularly discriminating in their prey, but they can be trained to ignore certain individuals.

Use: A clutch of night spiders guards the vault of a recursor on Earth that the PCs have reason to investigate.

Loot: The bodies of cocooned night spider victims have normal gear for the recursion in which they're found, which sometimes includes a cypher.

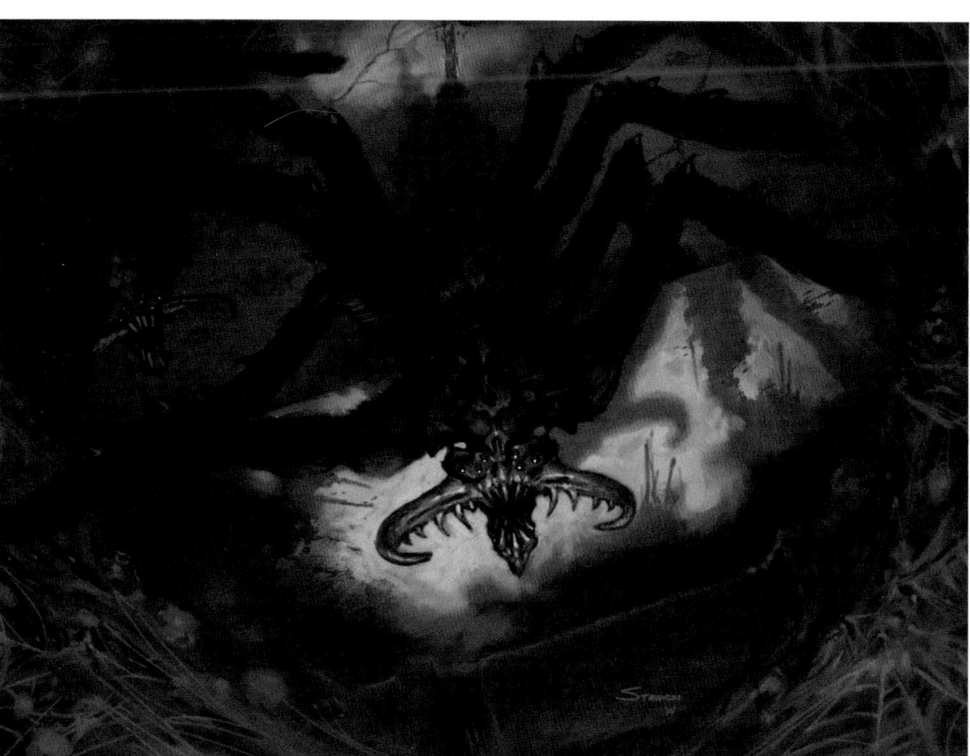

Size Comparison

NIGHT WYRM 6 (18)

Dangerous things stalk the lightless Roads of Sorrow in the Night Vault, things terrible and fearsome that lie in wait to snatch the unwary and drag them away. Things like the night wyrm—probably.

Conjectures and half-truths are all that most people know about night wyrms because victims don't survive to tell the tale of the encounter. Instead, people know of it by the skin it sheds and leaves discarded in the deep places, by the cracked, slippery bones of digested victims, and by the infrequent glimpse of its lambent eyes that peer out from the darkness and pin observers in place with cold terror. And, of course, by the screams of snatched victims silenced with shocking abruptness.

The night wyrm looks like an enormous snake, easily 50 feet (15 m) long and possibly longer. Glossy black scales, each as hard as iron, cover its body and fade to grey on its underside. Two rows of three eyes march along its head, each emitting soft yellow light that intensifies when it closes in to make the kill.

Night Vault, page 183

Motive: Hungers for flesh

Environment (Ardeyn | Magic): Anywhere on the Roads of Sorrow

Health: 18

Damage Inflicted: 6 points

Armor: 3

Movement: Short

Modifications: All tasks related to perception and stealth as level 8; Speed defense as level 4 due to size.

Combat: The night wyrm attacks with its bite. Moving silently through the darkness, the creature often ambushes unsuspecting prey. When it succeeds, the difficulty of the target's Speed defense roll increases by two steps, and the wyrm's bite deals 8 points of damage for that attack.

In addition, the night wyrm's fangs deliver a powerful paralytic toxin. A bite victim must succeed on a Might defense roll or become paralyzed for one round and suffer 6 points of Speed damage (ignores Armor).

As part of the same action it uses to bite one creature, the night wyrm can also attempt to coil around another creature within short range of the initial target. If it succeeds, the secondary target is caught, and in subsequent rounds automatically takes 6 points of crushing damage. The caught target must succeed on a Might-based task to break free.

Once it kills or paralyzes a victim, a night wyrm drags off the carcass and swallows it over the course of a minute. It takes the night wyrm several hours to digest a human-sized creature.

Interaction: The night wyrm is a predator and regards other creatures as food. It ignores other creatures while it digests a meal.

Use: The night wyrm is a patient and cunning hunter. The PCs might hear faint sounds of its movement or glimpse its gleaming yellow eyes from a distance as it stalks them through the Roads of Sorrow.

Loot: The night wyrm's droppings or gullet might hold a few cyphers, 3d100 golden crowns, and possibly an artifact that the creature could not digest.

GM Intrusion: *The night wyrm's venom affects the character more strongly. Instead of being paralyzed for one round, the victim is paralyzed for one minute, though after a couple of rounds, she is allowed to make another Might defense roll to throw off the effects of the poison early.*

GM Intrusion: *The night wyrm misses with an attack but catches a piece of the character's armor (reducing the Armor value by 1 until it's repaired) or something the character is carrying.*

NUL 1 (3)

Nuls are distorted, mangled reflections of creatures around the Shoals of Earth. They seem to bubble into existence in the Strange and sometimes in recursions whose connection to the Strange is particularly lax.

Nuls are about the size of small monkeys, but their features are a mélange of horrible bits and pieces of flesh, bone, hair, and horn. Although their limbs are often mismatched, they move with surprising speed through the Strange or on a solid surface within a recursion. Like rats, they exist in dark places, feeding on residual energy given off where a limited world ends and the Chaosphere begins, but if threatened, cornered, or surprised, nuls viciously attack.

Motive: Defense

Environment (the Strange): Anywhere in the Strange, and sometimes in recursions with a strong connection to the Strange, in groups of twelve or more

Health: 3

Damage Inflicted: 2 points

Movement: Short

Modifications: Speed defense as level 3 due to size and frenzied quickness; Intellect defense as level 6; knowledge of one particular recursion as level 4.

Combat: Nuls swarm over a foe and bite, pinch, squeeze, and hug. Nul flesh is anathema to objects and creatures native to a recursion or a prime world, and contact with it acts almost like acid, inflicting 2 points of damage plus 1 additional point of damage that ignores Armor.

Five nuls attacking together can make a single attack against one character as a level 3 creature. The swarm's successful attack deals 4 points of damage plus an additional 2 points of damage that ignores Armor. Ten nuls together act as a level 10 superswarm that can make two attacks as a single action, dealing 5 points of damage plus an additional 2 points of damage that ignores Armor.

Interaction: Sometimes a group of nuls is herded together or lured to a location where their colony can guard an area for an intelligent creature of the Strange. However they're encountered, nuls are essentially vermin.

Use: Nuls are not particularly dangerous threats to PCs unless they appear in numbers. Their horrific appearance and swarming behavior might serve as an interesting encounter for characters new to the Strange, especially if the PCs are still reeling from their first brush with alienation.

Loot: Nul colonies tend to form in areas where cyphers sometimes crystallize out of the Strange, and amid the refuse of such a colony, PCs might be able to liberate a cypher.

Sometimes a nul has a more humanlike visage and might be mistaken for a creature of higher intelligence. The effect is particularly unsettling when the visage is that of a recognizable historical figure seeded into a recursion through leakage.

GM Intrusion: *The nul attacking the character is a grandmother among its kind, and a far more serious threat.*

Nul grandmother: *level 4; health 12; Armor 2; attack deals 5 points of damage plus 2 points of damage that ignores Armor.*

Alienation, page 216

SIZE COMPARISON

NUPPEPPO 2 (6)

Nuppeppos are animated lumps of human flesh that walk on vaguely defined limbs. They smell of decay and death. They're spotted in graveyards, battlefields, coroner's offices, and other places where the dead are kept or interred. When witnessed in other places, nuppeppos seem to wander streets aimlessly, sometimes alone, sometimes in groups, and sometimes following a living person who'd rather be left alone.

Information about these creatures is scarce. They might be spirits formed from the fictional leakage of several Eastern myths. On the other hand, they could be an unintended consequence of a Mad Science reanimation attempt, one that's able to catalyze its animation in similarly dead tissue to form more nuppeppos.

A nuppeppo sometimes follows a living individual around like a silent, smelly pet that shows no affection. No one knows why.

"It followed me home. Can I keep it?"
—L.G. Babcock III

If a nuppeppo begins to follow a character, the difficulty of all interaction tasks by that PC and her allies is increased by one or two steps. Most other creatures are put off by a lump of animate human flesh hanging around nearby.

Motive: Wander, graze on dead flesh

Environment (Magic or Mad Science): Near places of death at night, alone or in groups of up to eight

Health: 12

Damage Inflicted: 4 points

Armor: 1

Movement: Short

Combat: A nuppeppo can smash a foe with one of its lumpy limbs. If a nuppeppo is touched or struck in melee, the attacker's weapon (or hand) becomes stuck to the nuppeppo and can be pulled free only with a difficulty 5 Might roll.

A victim of a nuppeppo's attack (or someone who touched a nuppeppo) begins to decay at a rate of 1 point of Speed damage (ignores Armor) per round, starting in the round following contact. To stop the spread of the decay, the victim can cut off the layer of affected flesh, which deals 4 points of damage (ignores Armor).

Interaction: If approached, a nuppeppo turns to "face" its interlocutor, but it doesn't respond to questions or orders. However, it may begin to follow its interlocutor from that point forward unless physically prevented—at which point the nuppeppo becomes violent.

Use: The PCs open a grave, coffin, or vault, and several nuppeppos spill out. Unless stopped, the creatures attempt to "adopt" people from a nearby village.

GM Intrusion: *The character who has allowed the nuppeppo to follow him around like a pet wakes to find that the creature has settled upon him in the night and is using its touch-decay abilities to feed on him. In fact, the PC might already be incapacitated by the time he wakes.*

OCTOPUS SAPIEN 4 (12)

Long-lived octopuses that are able to think appear in all kinds of recursions. Most seem to share a xenophobic hatred for humans. Such octopus sapiens hunt people for food or, if they are smart enough and have access to enough resources, attempt to exterminate humans completely from the recursion they inhabit. In some places, they've succeeded.

Octopus sapiens live in underwater cities of living coral and pearl. These beautiful structures contain egg hatcheries, larvae playgrounds, plankton farms, ink art academies, and much stranger areas. The creatures also study bioengineering of all kinds, and in their dissection chambers, they take apart human captives one skin layer at a time. The octopus sapiens want to understand their air-breathing rivals so they can come up with some kind of biological weapon that will exterminate humanity en masse.

Motive: Defense, eliminate humanity

Environment (Mad Science, Psionics, or Standard Physics): Anywhere underwater, alone or in groups of up to five

Health: 21

Damage Inflicted: 4 points

Movement: Immediate; short when swimming

Modifications: Speed defense as level 5 due to quickness in water; Speed defense normal on dry land; all tasks related to logic, debate, and puzzle-solving as level 6.

Combat: An octopus sapien uses a few of its arms to keep itself grounded and the rest to attack, allowing it to attack up to three targets in melee as a single action. If more than one arm hits the same target, the target must also succeed on a Might defense roll or become tightly wrapped by all the other arms. Once it has a target wrapped, the octopus sapien doesn't attack other creatures; instead, it tries to squeeze its prize unconscious, automatically inflicting 8 points of damage per round, unless the victim can succeed on a difficulty 6 Might-based task to escape. A PC who moves to "dead" on the damage track due to an octopus sapien's squeezing damage is rendered unconscious, not dead.

Many octopus sapiens secrete a bioengineered ink that is poisonous to humans. Instead of attacking with its arms, an octopus sapien can squirt ink at a human target within short range. The target and all humans within immediate range must make a successful Might defense roll or take 4 points of Speed damage (ignores Armor) each round. Victims can attempt Might defense rolls each round to throw off the poison. An octopus sapien can squirt toxic ink once every few hours.

An octopus sapien can survive and act out of the water for an hour before succumbing to dryness and lack of oxygen.

Interaction: Octopus sapien use skin chromatophores to rapidly flash messages to each other. Unless a human can decipher the flashes and respond in kind, it's unlikely that any meaningful conversation can occur. Besides, when it comes to humans, octopus sapiens are interested only in acquiring new specimens on which to experiment.

Use: A fishing vessel was found adrift, its crew missing. The only clue is a slurry of toxic ink splashed on the deck and in the crew cabins and bridge, in which tentacle prints are clearly visible.

Loot: In any given group of octopus sapiens, one may have a cypher or two.

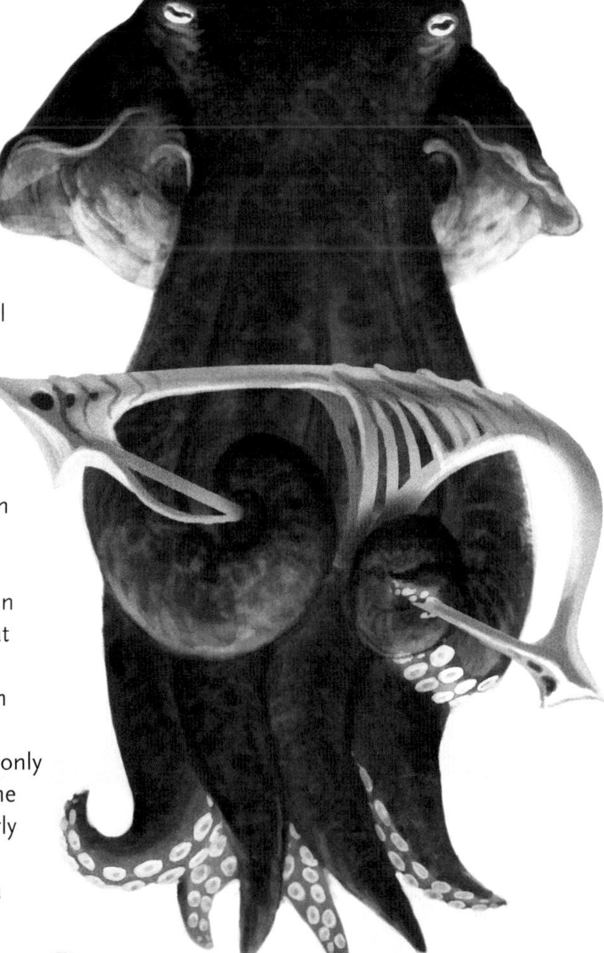

SIZE COMPARISON

Octopus sapien larvae (just-hatched juveniles from eggs) are not sapient for the first year of their life, and humans may mistake them for regular octopuses. Eventually they "wake up," begin to wonder about their environment, and, if captive, yearn for escape.

GM Intrusion: *A character hit with the toxic ink is blinded while the toxin remains active in her system.*

Size Comparison

OGRE 4 (12)

A bestial brute, the ogre is a sadistic, 8-foot (2 m), cannibalistic fiend that preys upon other creatures in the woods, mountains, or other wilderness areas. In the worlds in which ogres live, this often pits them against sylvan beings like elves and fey. Ogres dwelling in more civilized lands are also the enemy of humans, but these ogres usually come no closer to civilization than its very fringes.

Ogres speak whatever language is most common in the area in which they live, but their vocabulary is extremely limited. They typically dress in ragged, piecemeal clothing or nothing at all.

Motive: Hungers for flesh, sadistic

Environment (Magic): Anywhere, usually alone or (rarely) in a band of three or four

Health: 20

Damage Inflicted: 8 points

Armor: 1

Movement: Short

Modifications: Feats of raw strength as level 6; Intellect defense and seeing through deception as level 3; Speed defense as level 3 due to size.

Combat: Ogres usually use clubs or large, two-handed weapons with great power. Since they are accustomed to fighting smaller creatures, they are adept at using their size and strength to their advantage. If an ogre strikes a foe smaller than itself, either the victim is knocked back up to 5 feet (2 m), or it is dazed and the difficulty of its next action is increased by one step.

Ogres can also swing their huge weapons in wide arcs, attacking all foes within close range. The difficulty of defending against this attack is decreased by one step, and the attack inflicts 5 points of damage.

Ogres rarely flee from a fight, and only a foe of overwhelming power can force them to surrender.

Interaction: Ogres are stupid and cruel. They don't like conversation, even with their own kind. Reasoning with them is difficult at best, but sometimes they can be fooled.

Evil wizards and warlords like to enslave ogres and place them at the forefront of their armies. In these cases, the ogres are typically bribed, ensorcelled, or intimidated by great force, but the latter is the most difficult.

Use: A solitary ogre is an excellent encounter for a group of low-tier characters. A number of them, particularly well-equipped and well-trained warriors, make excellent troops or guards in the service of a powerful master.

Loot: Some ogres hoard gold or other valuables in their lairs, but they rarely have use for magic or cyphers.

Warrior ogres (health 25; Armor 3), usually found only in the armies of an evil warlord or a similar master, are slightly more intelligent and better equipped than their cousins. They possess combat training and discipline that other ogres do not have, wear sophisticated armor, and bear well-forged weaponry, including ranged weapons such as very large spears. The difficulty of attacking and defending against a warrior ogre is increased by one step.

GM Intrusion: *The ogre's mighty blow (whether it strikes a foe or not) hits the ground or the wall, causing major structural damage and a possible collapse, cave-in, or landslide. It might also expose a hidden underground cave or chamber.*

ORC 3 (9)

Born into squalor and fear, the orc race is composed of miserable, misbegotten humanoids that seem destined to serve as fodder for more powerful evil overlords. When left to their own devices, these loathsome creatures turn on each other, the strongest oppressing the next weakest (and so on down the line) with cruel barbs, gruesome jokes, and physical beatings. When these creatures have no masters to hate, they hate themselves.

No two orcs look exactly alike, but all have a mean, ugly, and shambolic facade. Never clean and often spattered with the remains of recent meals, orcs have a mouthful of sharp, broken teeth that can develop into true fangs. Adults range in height from scurrying goblins no larger than a human child to massive specimens larger than a strapping man. Whether big or small, nearly all orcs have stooped backs and crooked legs. The hue of their skin is hard to ascertain, because they are covered by the sediment of years, not to mention the iron armor every orc constantly wears from the moment it's able to lift a weapon.

Motive: Make others more miserable than itself

Environment (Magic): Anywhere near, on, or under mountains, usually in groups of four to six, or in tribes dozens to hundreds strong

Health: 9

Damage Inflicted: 4 points

Armor: 2

Movement: Short

Modifications: Speed defense as level 4 when carrying a shield; pleasant interactions as level 1.

Combat: Most orcs have bows able to target foes within long range. Some carry a shield and wield a medium axe, sword, or mace that inflicts 4 points of damage. Other orcs (usually those that are larger than their fellows) dispense with shields and wield heavy two-handed mauls and hammers that inflict 6 points of damage.

Orcs live short, brutish lives. The few that survive for years do so because of some special advantage; they're sneakier, stronger, tougher, or meaner than average. These have the following modifications, respectively:

- Stealth tasks as level 5
- Deal 2 additional points of damage with melee weapons
- +10 health
- Tasks related to trickery and deceit as level 5

Interaction: An orc would stab its own mother if it thought doing so would give it another hour of life in a desperate situation. That said, most orcs have been conditioned, through beatings and torture, to fear the evil master they serve (if any). Characters attempting to negotiate with an orc through intimidation find that short-term success is followed by medium-term betrayal.

Use: A band of orcs fires on the PCs from the edge of the forest. However, these orcs are crafty, and characters who rush directly into combat might fall victim to a hidden pit trap or other prepared ambush.

Loot: Orcs carry a lot of garbage. Amid this dross, a band of orcs might have a handful of gold crowns (or the equivalent) between them.

SIZE COMPARISON

Powerful orc leader: *level 5; health 25; Armor 3; heavy sword that deals 8 points of damage*

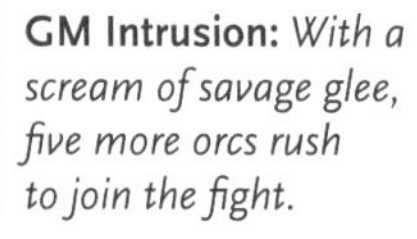

GM Intrusion: *With a scream of savage glee, five more orcs rush to join the fight.*

PHANTASMIC PARASITE 4 (12)

Half-seen glimpses of people, animals, and anachronistic objects at the ends of hallways and the tops of stairs lead victims to believe that spirits or ghosts haunt the place. When a phantasmic parasite is involved, the image exists purely in the viewer's mind—the psychic construct that serves as the parasite's body has already attached itself to the victim's head, though invisibly.

A phantasmic parasite reaches into a sentient creature's mind, finds someone or something to which the creature has an emotional attachment, and broadcasts an image of it at some distance away from the victim. The parasite feeds on the emotional stress created by the phantasm. The more upset and worried the victim becomes, the more the parasite consumes. Thus, most phantasms appear in some state of distress—weeping, whining, panicked. And when their viewers approach the phantasm, it shrinks away, always pulling back to stay just out of reach.

A hotel in Colorado (of Earth) called the Grand Bavarian is afflicted with at least one phantasmic parasite, despite the conflict of laws. Apparently something about the hotel creates enough "reverse" fictional leakage to provide the parasite with an anchor.

Motive: Feed on negative emotions

Environment (Psionics or Magic): Anyplace sentient creatures once lived

Health: 12

Damage Inflicted: 4 points

Movement: Short when flying

Modifications: Deception as level 5.

Combat: Phantasmic parasites pose no danger if they are ignored. Pursuing a phantasm created by a parasite is dangerous. The phantasm is a lure that draws creatures after it. Whenever a victim moves toward the phantasm, she must make a successful Intellect defense roll or take 4 points of Intellect damage (ignores Armor). The phantasm maintains its distance from the victim, moving at the same time so that the victim cannot physically close the distance.

If characters use extraordinary means to visualize the invisible psionic construct of the parasite's true body, which is attached to the victim's head, they can attack it with magic, psychic effects, or other energy attacks. However, when struck, the phantasmic parasite emits a psychic blast out to a long distance. All creatures in the area must succeed on Intellect defense rolls or take 4 points of Intellect damage (ignores Armor). After emitting the blast, the phantasmic parasite flees.

Interaction: A phantasmic parasite causes the phantasm lure to behave as its viewer expects. Phantasms that look like people cannot quite form words but make noises that, from a distance, sound similar to speech. Since the phantasm appears distressed, sobbing and wailing are common.

Use: Phantasmic parasites can draw characters into unexplored areas, helping them find places they may have overlooked or skipped. As well, phantasms often lead pursuers into danger.

GM Intrusion: *The phantasmic parasite broadcasts a form that has a strong emotional connection to the character. On a failed Intellect defense roll, the character must use his next action to move toward the phantasm.*

GM Intrusion: *A character damaged by the phantasmic parasite must use her next action to flee from it in a random direction.*

PHOENIX 4 (12)

Each phoenix is the literal weight of sin once carried by a human or qephilim. As elemental creatures of living sinfire, phoenixes streak across Ardeyn's night like omens of doom, seeking the recently dead to feed upon and, in the process, release more phoenixes into the Land of the Curse. Born of strife and pain, phoenixes are creatures of flame and misery. Because they're drawn to carrion and death, phoenixes in Ardeyn are considered harbingers of disaster and war.

Sinfire, page 55

Ardeyn, page 160

If a phoenix is destroyed, the sin it was born from is erased, or so the legend goes, which is why some adventuring companies hunt phoenixes—to redeem the misdeeds each creature represents. The magic feathers phoenixes leave behind may also be an inducement.

Though made of living sinfire, Lotan isn't responsible for phoenixes. Rather, an ancient angelic qephilim sought to pull the sin from a dying human companion in order to grant salvation, and birthed the first phoenix as a consequence.

Phoenixes range in size depending on the magnitude of the sin each is born from, but on average, their main bodies are human sized, and they measure more than 15 feet (5 m) from wingtip to wingtip.

Motive: Reproduction

Environment (Ardeyn | Magic): Almost anywhere, alone or in groups of three to five

Health: 12

Damage Inflicted: 4 points

Movement: Immediate; long when flying

Combat: A phoenix prefers to feed on the recently dead, but if hungry, it will attack living targets. A phoenix's fiery bite deals 4 points of damage and sets the victim on fire, a flame that burns the soul as much as the flesh. The round after being bitten, the bite victim who fails an Intellect defense roll burns for 2 points of fire damage (ignores Armor) and 2 points of Intellect damage (ignores Armor). Each subsequent round the victim fails an Intellect defense roll means the fire continues to burn. Success means the fire goes out.

If a victim is killed by a phoenix bite, the body begins to burn like a bonfire. Those with any power over spirits hear the anguished sound of a screaming soul in the pyre. If the fire is not put out, 1d6 rounds later all that remains of the victim is ash, but a new phoenix is born from the flame, and it either wings off or stays to fight if attacked.

Those killed by a phoenix leave spirits behind, but spirits that have been burned clean of all their previous sins.

Interaction: A phoenix has the intelligence of a predatory animal. It prefers to scavenge the sin from recently killed creatures, but it's aggressive enough not to back down from a conflict.

Use: The PCs come across the scene of a recent battle. Several phoenixes do the same and begin consuming the bodies (and the equipment, if any) in fire.

Loot: When a phoenix is killed, it leaves behind 1d6 iridescent red feathers. If a feather is worked into a person's clothing, hair braid, or similar, it grants +1 to Armor against fire for one day.

GM Intrusion: *When killed, the phoenix explodes. Everyone within immediate range must succeed on an Intellect defense roll or begin to burn as described under Combat.*

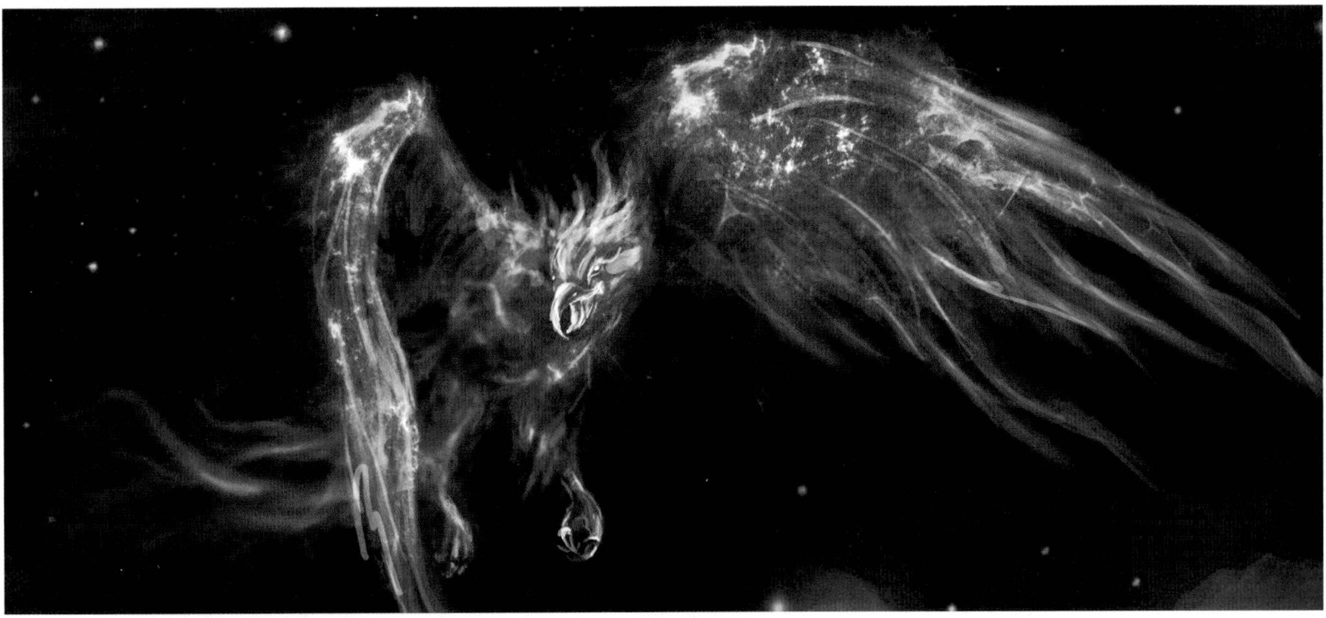

Size Comparison

Polymous 3 (9)

A "naked" polymous looks like a muscular worm of wet, veiny tissue, bristling with hairlike filaments that it uses as nerve endings. Its mouth looks almost human, complete with tongue and teeth, and two eyestalks emerge from the top of its head. Usually, however, polymous are clothed in the skin of someone they've replaced. A polymous sheds its covering only when a skin becomes too damaged, whereupon it slithers free.

Many in Ruk know of the polymous, but they keep that knowledge close. No one is sure who has been replaced and who hasn't, so those in the know stay silent. No one is quite sure why the polymous have infiltrated Ruk society. The few that were discovered and analyzed didn't reveal much, other than to indicate that they serve "another."

A polymous can be anyone, anywhere in Ruk. Parasites, they enter their victims' bodies, liquefy the innards, and expand themselves to wear the skin as if it were clothing. Aside from a little seepage around the point of entry—nose, mouth, ear, or elsewhere—they look, act, and behave as the people they replace.

Removing a polymous that has entered a victim but not yet killed her is a tricky business if one wants to keep the victim alive. One possible method is to use electrical attacks—though electricity may harm the victim, it hurts the polymous more.

Motive: Infiltrate societies, steal scientific discoveries

Environment (Ruk | Mad Science): Any populated area

Health: 18

Damage Inflicted: 4 points

Armor: 1

Movement: Short

Modifications: All tasks related to deception as level 5.

Combat: A polymous fights using whatever weapons its host possessed before it was killed. If the creature takes 9 points of damage in battle, the polymous wriggles free of the skin, leaving the useless sheath in a heap on the ground (losing its 1 point of Armor in the process), and springs toward its foe as part of the same action. If it attacks a target who was not aware of the true nature of the polymous, the difficulty of the target's Speed defense roll is increased by two steps due to the surprise, and if the polymous hits, it inflicts 6 points of damage on this attack.

When a polymous is not taking over a host, it is typically about the size of a human arm.

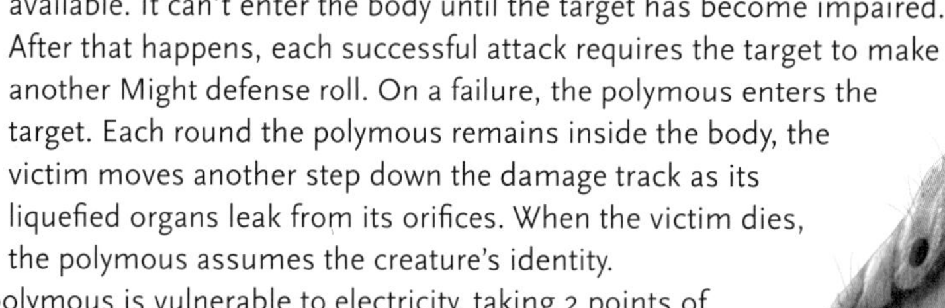

Normally, the attacks of a "naked" polymous inflict 4 points of damage as it attempts to force itself into the target's body through the mouth, nose, ear, or whatever orifice is available. It can't enter the body until the target has become impaired. After that happens, each successful attack requires the target to make another Might defense roll. On a failure, the polymous enters the target. Each round the polymous remains inside the body, the victim moves another step down the damage track as its liquefied organs leak from its orifices. When the victim dies, the polymous assumes the creature's identity.

A polymous is vulnerable to electricity, taking 2 points of damage for each point of electrical damage inflicted.

Interaction: A polymous is a skilled infiltrator and plays whatever role its host played when alive. The polymous knows enough of what its host knew in life to get by, but it can't stand up to suspicious scrutiny.

Use: A polymous replaces one of the PCs' allies and secretly gathers intelligence. It has the same emotional and memory connections to the PCs that the character had before being killed by the parasite, which could create some tension (especially if the victim had an amorous connection to another PC in the group).

Loot: If the replaced person had something of value, the polymous now has it.

GM Intrusion: *The sudden emergence of a "naked" polymous from the skin of a victim requires that the character succeed on an Intellect defense roll or lose his turn in horror and surprise.*

POSTHUMAN 9 (27)

SIZE COMPARISON

When humans evolve to the next stage of their evolution in some recursions, it's a directed jump, designed with smart tools. The result is beings whose basic capacities so radically exceed those of regular people that they can't really be considered human any longer. They've transcended humanity, which is why they're also sometimes called transhumans. Whatever label is applied, posthumans have grown so physically and mentally powerful that they would appear as gods to people of Earth, were they able to make the transition.

Motive: Ineffable

Environment (Mad Science): Only one posthuman has been encountered so far, but by all accounts, more exist and could potentially be encountered anywhere, including in deep space of the universe of normal matter

Health: 99

Damage Inflicted: 9 points

Armor: 5

Movement: Short; long when flying

Combat: Posthumans can attack foes up to half a mile (1 km) away with bolts of directed plasma that deal 9 points of damage. A posthuman can dial up the level of destruction if it wishes, so that instead of affecting only one target, a bolt deals 9 points of damage to all targets within short range of the primary target. Targets caught in the conflagration who succeed on a Speed defense roll still suffer 5 points of damage.

Posthumans are just as scary in hand-to-hand combat and can attack all targets within immediate range as an action.

Posthumans can also call on a variety of other abilities that might as well be magic to regular foes, but which are actually small manipulations of the quantum field. Essentially, a posthuman can mimic the ability of a cypher of level 5 or less.

A posthuman doesn't need to alter reality to heal itself, as it automatically regenerates 2 points of health per round while its health is above 0.

Interaction: Posthumans normally ignore regular humans, but they might smile enigmatically in response to an impassioned plea. Knowing what a posthuman actually wants is hard to pin down because their motivations are complex and many-layered.

Use: A recursion is sending more than its fair share of odd, high-tech elements to Earth through random inapposite gates. The objects quickly degrade under the law of Standard Physics, but the posthuman sending these probes is not giving up. She wants to find a way into the universe of normal matter.

Loot: The body of a posthuman is riddled with unrecognizable technologies fused seamlessly with residual organic material—or at least material that grows like organic material used to. Amid this, it might be possible to salvage a Mad Science artifact.

"Sometimes I worry that the only things that separate a posthuman from a planetovore are age and experience. We should eliminate recursions that produce such volatile and potentially disastrously powerful individuals."
—Hertzfeld, Research Chief for the Estate

GM Intrusion: *The quantum nature of the posthuman allows it to act out of turn, take control of a device that the character is about to use against it, and either deactivate the device or turn it against the character.*

SIZE COMPARISON

PRANCE 2 (6)

These insidious mutant flowers draw the unwary closer with alluring blooms, calming perfume, and a low-level magic aura that promotes well-being. Once a bed of prances has put its prey to sleep, individuals emerge for a bloody feeding frenzy. Victims who survive a prance attack have nightmares for years afterward, recalling how the creatures' influence was so strong that being devoured alive was a somehow pleasant, euphoric experience.

Prance pollen is a valuable commodity in the town of Newk, but gathering it is obviously dangerous. Although any individual prance is fairly weak, prances generally live in patches. Few creatures can overcome an entire patch of prances focusing on putting prey into a state so accepting that having one's spine ripped out and eaten seems like a spiritual experience.

Cataclyst, page 238

These carnivorous flowers are also known as skittering irises and death blooms. The gathered pollen is a drug that can promote relaxation, bliss, and wonder, while at the same time utterly disengaging a user's sense of self-preservation.

Motive: Hungers for flesh

Environment (Cataclyst | Mad Science and Magic): Growing in patches of six or more in irradiated areas

Health: 6

Damage Inflicted: 3 points

Movement: Short; immediate when burrowing or climbing

Modifications: Disguise as level 6 when not moving.

Combat: A disguised prance patch appears to be an enticing area of purple flowers. When four or more prances grow together in a patch, they can spend an action to produce a pulse of pollen (which mingles odor and magic influence) that has a soporific effect on every living target in immediate range who fails a difficulty 4 Intellect defense roll. Affected targets take 3 points of Intellect damage (ignores Armor), but oddly enough, the experience seems pleasant, not painful. If a victim becomes impaired or debilitated, he falls into a trance. After that, pain and rough treatment isn't sufficient to rouse him to care about his condition, not even the pain of being eaten by a suddenly revealed prance. This lasts until the victim is hale again.

Prances can also make melee attacks, preferentially on subdued prey. Instead of being wiped out, a patch retreats from prey that proves resistant to the pollen.

In direct sunlight, a prance regenerates 1 point of health per round while its health is above 0.

Interaction: Prances are predators that use mimicry and ambush to bring down prey.

Use: Prance seeds are sometimes traded in Crow Hollow. A few days ago, several seeds accidentally and secretly germinated, taking over an entire covered stall in the Glittering Market. Shopping PCs come upon a sleeping merchant and smell something wonderful coming from the tented area behind her.

Crow Hollow, page 242

Loot: Prance pollen is valuable to certain traders, who might trade a cypher for the pollen collected from a patch of six or more prances.

GM Intrusion: *Four more prance flowers pop out of the ground and attack the character.*

PSYCHIC REMNANT 4 (12)

When a powerful telepath dies, she leaves behind a sort of mental imprint on the world. If she died in the midst of attempting an important mission or task, her mental energies infuse the need to accomplish that task and give that need a life of its own. These psychic remnants are not unlike psionic ghosts, but they have no free will or capacity to do anything other than attempt to complete the task that drives them.

Tasks or missions that drive a psychic remnant usually involve protecting someone or something, killing a specific individual, finding an object of importance, or proving an idea (for example, the identity of a murderer, or that a particular invention really works).

Sometimes, a psychic remnant is created by the death of a latent psychic who did not even realize that he possessed any mental powers in life.

Psychic remnants are invisible and intangible. When communicating telepathically with a remnant, however, one might gain a mental image of the telepath as he appeared in life.

Motive: Fulfillment of a task

Environment (Psionics): Anywhere

Health: 12

Damage Inflicted: 4 points

Movement: Short (flying)

Modifications: Stealth as level 6; knowledge related to the living creature that formed the remnant as level 5.

Combat: Psychic remnants are incorporeal and can move through matter easily. They cannot be harmed by physical weapons or similar attacks. Only mental energies, mystical effects, or attacks attuned to the specific, insubstantial nature of a remnant can affect them. They cannot directly affect matter, but they can use their mental powers to do so.

Psychic remnants wield powerful psychokinesis and can hurl objects up to short range to make attacks, as well as push foes backward, open or close doors, activate machines, and so on. They can also make psychic attacks against a thinking being within immediate range that inflict Intellect damage and ignore Armor.

Even if destroyed by attacks, a psychic remnant will eventually return. It cannot ever truly be destroyed until it completes the task it left undone (or until that task becomes irrelevant).

Interaction: Psychic remnants speak telepathically and can communicate with any intelligent being within long range. Their communication is erratic, feverishly emotional, and repetitive. It might just be a telepathic groan or incoherent shout. A psychic remnant cannot be reasoned with, but some—depending on the goal that drives them—can be interacted with to the extent that they will reveal the task they need to complete. Since the remnant will never go away until that task is finished, sometimes helping it rather than working against it is the best solution.

Use: The prince who the PCs must abduct is protected by the psychic remnant of his dead mother. Stories are told of the great harm that comes to any who threaten the prince, but no one knows the truth of it, and most people believe the stories are just wild tales.

GM Intrusion: *The psychic remnant uses psychokinesis to topple something large onto the character, who—if she cannot get out of the way—is pinned underneath it.*

SIZE COMPARISON

The discovery of the quetzalcoatlus on Earth with a wingspan of over 50 feet (15 m) is as large as almost any "flying lizard" encountered in a recursion.

Although a pterodactyl's wings were long thought to be simple leathery structures composed of skin, recent evidence on Earth shows that their wing membranes were actually highly complex and dynamic structures suited to an active style of flight.

Pterodactyl hatchling: *level 3*

GM Intrusion: *A pterodactyl grabs a character's weapon or other held object and flies off with the object toward its nest.*

PTERODACTYL 5 (15)

The hunting scream of a soaring pterodactyl is not something those who've heard it soon forget. The sound is usually preceded by a racing "cloud" in the sky that turns a bright day briefly dark. When the passing cloud turns out to be a diving pterodactyl, few options remain for the victim.

As with other dinosaurs, pterodactyls in various lost-world recursions are potentially more dangerous than their real-world counterparts might have been.

Motive: Hungers for flesh

Environment (Standard Physics, Substandard Physics, or Mad Science): Pterodactyls hunt alone, in pairs, or sometimes in flights of up to eight

Health: 30

Damage Inflicted: 5 points

Movement: Long when flying

Modifications: Speed defense as level 4 due to size.

Combat: A pterodactyl attacks with its bite, or with battering wings if it's standing on the ground. If the creature bites a target, in addition to the damage dealt, the target must make a Might defense roll to avoid being snatched up and held in the pterodactyl's long mouth. To break free, a victim must succeed on a Might-based task. The difficulty of all other actions while held in the creature's mouth is increased by two steps. A victim held by a pterodactyl automatically takes 2 points of damage per round.

A pterodactyl can make a diving attack if it begins the attack while it's in the air and within long range of the target. In this attack, it moves up to a long distance, bites a human-sized foe (as described above) at the nadir of its dive, and moves an additional short distance back into the air, whether or not it managed to snatch prey.

Once a target is in its mouth, the pterodactyl wings off on its next turn. It takes the creature about three rounds to reach its favored cruising height of about 300 feet (91 m), after which it heads for a nearby nest where its mate and possibly hungry hatchlings wait.

Interaction: Pterodactyls are fairly typical predators with animal-level intelligence. However, if a fledgling is raised by a skilled trainer, the beast might be used as a mount.

Use: A pterodactyl hunting the landscape beneath it would make a fine wilderness encounter, but more interesting still would be one with a humanoid using the creature as a mount.

QUESTING BEAST 8 (24)

Size Comparison

This monstrosity is an unseemly mixture of serpent, leopard, goat, and lion. The beast's massive body stretches some 20 feet (6 m) long and weighs nearly 1,000 pounds (454 kg). It has the body of a lion with a leopard's spots. Its legs end in split hooves, and emerging from its body's trunk is the neck and head of a great serpent with dripping fangs and flicking tongue. The Round Table Knights committed themselves to finding this creature, but those who did found only their deaths.

Legend tells that the Questing Beast is, in fact, the offspring of Arthur and his half sister, an act of incest not realized until after the deed was done. From her loins sprang this monstrosity, a living symbol of the divine curse leveled against them for their wickedness. The beast wanders the lands of Avalon (and similar Arthurian recursions), spreading discord and death.

"The loathsome beast betrays itself with the infernal yapping sounding from its prodigious gut."
—Sir Bedivere

Motive: Destruction and corruption

Environment (Magic): A questing beast seeks out the most desolate and barren places to nest. It rarely stays in one place for long, as its hatred compels it to roam the lands and visit horror to all it encounters. A questing beast may also pass into other recursions and is never weakened from extended forays into such places.

Health: 24

Damage Inflicted: 8 points

Movement: Short

Modifications: Stealth actions as level 4; Speed defense as level 6 due to size.

Combat: Muted, muffled yapping and braying sounds from the beast's swaying gullet, an unwholesome noise that makes it almost impossible for the monster to get the drop on its prey. The beast pursues its victims with single-minded intensity, bounding through the underbrush and flailing about like a thrashing monstrosity born from nightmare.

When the beast closes, its snake head darts forward with lightning quickness to sink its fangs into whatever it can reach, injecting powerful venom. A living creature exposed to the venom must make a successful Might defense roll or take 6 additional points of Speed damage (that ignores most Armor) from the poison.

Interaction: A questing beast is more intelligent and crafty than a wild animal, but rarely shows it.

Use: A noble knight hunts a questing beast, and the characters might join an expedition to track down and kill the monster. Invariably, efforts to find it fail (possibly because the beast is secretly quickened), but they usually lead to other, greater adventures.

The king asked, "Knight, full of thought and sleepy, tell me if thou sawest a strange beast pass this way?" —Sir James Knowles, The Legends of King Arthur and his Knights

GM Intrusion: *The noise from the beast's yapping echoes all around, making it hard to determine which direction the creature is coming from. When it finally appears, one character loses his action to surprise.*

Noble knight, page 152

RAK 7 (21)

> **The rak "[...] can fly in the air and run like a deer and swim like a fish. Inside its body is a glowing furnace of fire, and the rak breathes in air and breathes out smoke, which darkens the sky for miles around, wherever it goes. It is bigger than a hundred men and feeds on any living thing."**
> —Tik-Tok of Oz

The cloud surrounding a rak is far larger than the actual creature and reaches halfway across the sky. Still, the rak in the center is by all accounts many times larger than a person, which means it also requires many times as much food.

Few things in Oz are so feared as a rak, yet one appears so rarely that that fear is usually put aside for more immediate concerns. But when a cloud darkens the sky like ink poured on paper, thoughts turn to the possibility of a rak flying in its center. If the fog descends and the distinctive odor of salt and pepper is not detected, all's well. However, if that vile odor is present, it's time to flee—though it might already be too late.

Motive: Hunger

Environment (Oz | Magic): Anywhere far from civilization

Health: 21

Damage Inflicted: 9 points

"I have never seen a Rak, to be sure, but I have read of them in the story-books that grew in my orchard, and if this is indeed one of those fearful monsters, we are not likely to conquer the world." —Tik-Tok of Oz

Movement: Short; long while flying

Modifications: Ability to see through deception and flattery as level 4; Speed defense as level 4 due to size and slowness.

Combat: A rak's breath automatically cloaks the area within 500 feet (152 m) with thick clouds that restrict the vision of other creatures. For opponents who can't see through smoke, the difficulty of attacks, defense rolls, and other tasks that require visual acuity is increased by two steps. This makes hitting the rak hard, but avoiding the rak's bite or claws even more problematic. The rak can bite or attack with pincers. Alternatively, it can breathe out fire, inflicting damage on up to ten targets within short range of each other and within long range of the rak, but never twice in two rounds.

The rak is an enchanted creature, and it regenerates 3 points of health per round while its health is above 6, or 1 point of health per minute while its health is 0 to 5. The only way to permanently kill a rak is to slice it into many pieces and bury those pieces far from each other. While a rak has between 1 and 5 health, the difficulty of all its tasks is increased by three steps, and it cannot fly. At 0 health, it remains conscious and able to talk, but otherwise it can take no other actions.

Interaction: A rak's incessant hunger isn't ameliorated in any way by its quarrelsome, petty disposition and penchant for going back on promises. One way to negotiate with a rak is to hurt it badly enough so that its regeneration falls to 1 point per minute, then threaten to cut it up. On the other hand, a rak isn't the sharpest knife in the drawer and can be fooled by clever lies.

Use: A village has gone dark, literally, and every day one new villager turns up eaten. The entire place smells of salt and pepper, but the survivors are too scared to flee, except for one brave soul who managed to get out and seek help from the PCs.

Loot: 1d100 × 20 gold coins, 2d6 cyphers, and possibly an Oz artifact.

GM Intrusion: *The rak lands on a character. In addition to the crushing damage, the character is pinned until she can succeed on a Might defense roll to get free or use other means to convince the rak to move.*

REANIMATED 6 (18)

SIZE COMPARISON

A reanimated is a humanoid creature patched together from corpses, then returned to life through a hard-to-duplicate series of electromagnetic induction events. Though made of flesh, a reanimated's return to consciousness and mobility is marked by a substantial increase in hardiness, resistance to injury, and longevity. On the other hand, the process usually obliterates whatever mind was once encoded in the donor brain, giving rise to a creature of monstrous rage and childlike credulity. Sometimes the reanimated is bound to its creator in service, but such ties are fragile and could be snapped by an ill-timed fit of fury.

"I beheld the wretch—the miserable monster whom I had created. He held up the curtain of the bed; and his eyes, if eyes they may be called, were fixed on me."
—Mary Shelley, *Frankenstein*

Motive: Defense, unpredictable

Environment (Mad Science): Anywhere in service to a mad scientist, or driven to the edges of civilization

Health: 70

Damage Inflicted: 7 points

Movement: Short; long when jumping

Modifications: Speed defense as level 4; all tasks related to interaction as level 2; all tasks related to feats of strength and toughness as level 8.

Combat: A reanimated attacks foes with an oversized fist, foot, or head butt. In addition, any time a foe inflicts 7 or more points of damage on the reanimated with a single melee attack, the creature immediately lashes out in reactive rage and makes an additional attack in the same round on the foe who injured it.

If the reanimated begins combat within long range of foes but outside of short range, it can bridge the distance with an amazing leap that concludes with an attack as a single action. The attack inflicts 4 points of damage on all targets within immediate range of the spot where the reanimated lands.

Some reanimated are psychologically vulnerable to fire, and they fear it. When a reanimated attacks or defends against a foe wielding fire, the difficulty is modified by two steps to the reanimated's detriment. It's possible to drive off the creature by dealing it fire damage.

If struck by electromagnetic energy, a reanimated regenerates a number of points of health equal to what a normal creature would have lost, plus 3 additional points.

Interaction: Communicating with a reanimated is difficult if it's lost in rage or so newly created that it hasn't been able to call upon the memories of its original brain. Fear and food motivate a reanimated, though sometimes beautiful music or innocence can sway its fists.

Use: Depending on where a reanimated falls along its moral and psychological development, it could be a primary foe for the PCs, a secondary guardian to deal with, or a forlorn beast in need of aid.

"I, like the arch-fiend, bore a hell within me, and finding myself unsympathized with, wished to tear up the trees, spread havoc and destruction around me, and then to have sat down and enjoyed the ruin." —Mary Shelley, Frankenstein

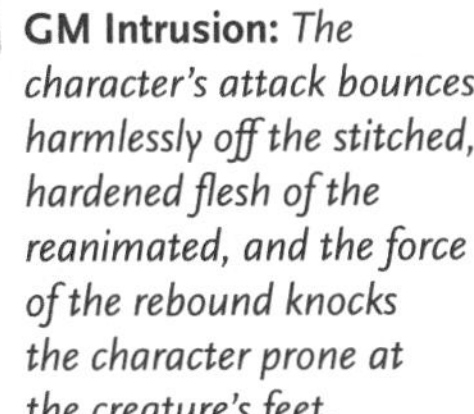

GM Intrusion: *The character's attack bounces harmlessly off the stitched, hardened flesh of the reanimated, and the force of the rebound knocks the character prone at the creature's feet.*

RECURSION HOUND 4 (12)

"If we knew who bred recursion hounds, that information would be in the Estate library like everything else, so stop asking. I don't know."
—Estate Lead Operative Katherine Manners

The recursion hound is a species of dog bred for sniffing the roads between worlds. After one gets the scent, little can stop it from eventually tracking down its target, even if the trail lies across multiple recursions in the Shoals of Earth.

A recursion hound stands about 5 feet (1.5 m) high at the shoulder and weighs almost 300 pounds (136 kg). Its dark eyes shine with intelligence.

Motive: Protect and guide selected companion(s)

Environment (the Strange): Anywhere, in any recursion, often in the company of a companion

Health: 21

Damage Inflicted: 4 points

Movement: Short

Modifications: Tracking as level 9; resists intimidation as level 8 (when with bonded companion).

Combat: A hound can bite foes, though it relies first on its recursion-shattering howl, which it can use once per minute. When it howls, a selected target within short range must succeed on an Intellect defense roll or be sent spiraling into a random alternate recursion, chosen by the GM, as if through an inapposite gate.

The recursion hound is quickened, with its own unique way of moving through recursions. Up to once per hour, when following a trail of a target whose scent it has obtained, the recursion hound can slip into a shadow (sometimes its own) and walk between worlds as its action. Up to five other creatures the recursion hound designates can follow it through. From the perspective of the hound and any travelers, the trip takes 1d6 hours along a lane of wavering twilight. At the trip's end, the hound appears in the new recursion as if it had passed through a translation gate whose exit is located where the target first entered that recursion.

The hound can also translate between recursions when not tracking a target, but in such cases, it is limited to locations it has previously visited or has the scent for.

GM Intrusion: *The hound slips into shadow, leaving the outline of a dark door behind it for one round. If one or more characters follow, they emerge on a disintegrating road of shadow and a few moments later are hurled into a random recursion as described under Combat.*

Interaction: A recursion hound is sapient, though most act like a loyal canine companion of another creature, and will do that creature's bidding.

Use: The PCs are being tracked through recursions by a powerful enemy, and no matter how well they think they've given their pursuer the slip, it's not enough after the enemy procures a recursion hound.

Recursion hounds can track prey into any limited world, no matter how extreme the terrain.

RECURSION STAIN 5 (15)

A recursion stain forms when a creature travels via inapposite gate to a recursion where the laws of its native recursion are not supported. As reality imposes its will on the creature, stripping it of powers and capabilities beyond what its new location allows, the creature weakens and could die. Not every creature that undergoes this complete disintegration leaves a stain, but those with great power might. Once a stain forms, it acts as a cancer on existence, destabilizing local reality.

People who aren't quickened can't see recursion stains. Photographs can catch them sometimes, though people usually dismiss them as a quirk in the film's development or a digital error. Quickened people see them clearly. A recursion stain looks like a swirling fractal pattern that causes light to bend around it. It floats in the air and moves in an erratic manner.

Quickened, page 22

Motive: Unpredictable

Environment (Any): Anywhere

Health: 15

Damage Inflicted: 5 points

Movement: Immediate

Combat: When quickened creatures are within short range of a recursion stain, they lose access to all abilities granted by their focus, and they suffer 1 point of ambient damage each round they remain in the vicinity. In addition, translated non-native creatures revert from their translated forms into their normal forms. Nonquickened creatures and mundane objects normally can't see or interact with a recursion stain, and they usually do not suffer damage when one becomes active.

A recursion stain ignores damage from all physical objects. Energy of any kind, however, destabilizes the stain for one round. As its next action, the stain sends a pulse out to a short distance, and each creature in range must succeed on a Might defense roll or take 5 points of damage.

If a recursion stain is destroyed, it collapses in on itself and creates a fractal vortex linked to the recursion that the creature that made the stain came from. The vortex behaves as an inapposite gate and stays open for 1d6 hours before closing permanently.

Interaction: Recursion stains are almost mindless and barely able to perceive their surroundings. When a quickened creature comes within range, a recursion stain may remember its past self and attempt to communicate its original purpose to a curious character. However, it can't help but affect quickened creatures as described under Combat, even if it is regretful and wants assistance.

Use: The local hotel has always had a reputation for being haunted. When an Estate agent stayed overnight and died there, the reputation graduated to a certainty, though little else is known.

GM Intrusion: *The special abilities of a character damaged by a recursion stain are modified by one step to the character's detriment for one hour.*

REGOID 6 (18)

On Earth, ignoring civic engagement sometimes leads to dysfunctional governments that don't have the best interests of the masses at heart, but rather those with the deepest pockets. Though a corporatocracy isn't good, it's better than giving power to a regoid.

People sometimes wish they could find someone else to take responsibility for failures, to deal with hard problems, and to plan for the future. In some recursions, this desire manifests as robots designed to run things for humanity, which worked out about as well as might be imagined. These robots, called "regoids" by Estate operatives, have a cybernetically enhanced, outsize sense of purpose and personal destiny. They are nothing less than robots built to rule. And rule they attempt to do, whatever the cost.

Motive: To rule

Environment (Mad Science): In the company of lesser robotic and living subjects, unless alone and working toward seizing power

Health: 18

Damage Inflicted: 6 points

Armor: 3

Movement: Short

Modifications: Tasks related to persuasion, deception, and identifying liars as level 7; resists mental attacks as level 7.

Combat: Regoids possess built-in robotic systems for offense and defense and can deploy various systems as needed. A basic offensive ability allows a regoid to attack a target in long range with gold-colored laser beams from shoulder-mounted systems.

A regoid can also deploy an orb of rulership, which, despite being a separate system, is part of the regoid and shares its Armor and health (damage to either is damage to the regoid). The orb of rulership can take one of the following actions on its turn, according to the regoid's command.

Protect Me. If commanded to do so, the orb acts as an asset to the regoid's Speed defense roll. (If the orb is attacked directly, it has a Speed defense as a level 6 creature.)

Glorify Me. The orb produces a hypnogogic light show. Living creatures with eyes within short range who fail an Intellect defense roll are dazzled by the orb's majesty and cannot attack the regoid for one round.

Make Them Kneel. The orb produces a burst of electromagnetic radiation tuned to human nervous systems. Humans within immediate range who fail a Might defense roll fall to their knees or prostrate on their faces for one round. (Attacks on victims during this period automatically succeed and deal an additional 2 points of damage.)

Sacrifice Yourself. The orb rejoins the regoid, who regains 12 points of health. The orb can't be deployed again for several hours.

Interaction: Other creatures can negotiate with a regoid as long as they pledge to make it their overlord (and it's good at knowing when people lie to it).

Use: A recursion the PCs travel to every so often has been taken over by a regoid.

Loot: A regoid might carry 1d6 cyphers.

GM Intrusion: *A character's companion, NPC ally, or advanced cybernetic system briefly decides that the regoid should be the leader, and rather than betray the character, it steps away from (or shuts down during) the fight.*

SAPIENT TREE 3 (9)

Guardians of the wood, sapient trees stand eternally vigilant, often on the outskirts of their grove or forest to keep out those who might seek to do them—or other, ordinary trees—harm. They look like normal trees until they reveal their true nature, with limblike branches and faces in the bark of their trunk. They don't always move, but with effort, they can uproot themselves and walk about. However, they usually do so only when no one is looking.

Although the fighting trees in Quadling Country of Oz are among the most well known, many Magic recursions have intelligent trees. They might be haunted trees possessed by spirits, trees animated by magic spells, or ancient mythical beings. Some are peaceful and noble, but others are downright wicked and cruel.

GM Intrusion: *The tree grabs the character and holds her fast, shaking her. She takes 4 points of damage each round and can do nothing but attempt to escape, which is a difficulty 5 task due to the shaking.*

Motive: Self-preservation

Environment (Oz | Magic): Found in groves or copses of five to twenty

Health: 16

Damage Inflicted: 4 points

Armor: 3

Movement: Short

Modifications: Initiative as level 4; Speed defense as level 2 due to size.

Combat: When a sapient tree attacks, it often does so with surprise because it looks like a normal tree at first. If a character about to be attacked fails an Intellect-based roll, he does not perceive the attack in time, and the difficulty to resist the tree's attack is increased by one step.

If a tree strikes in combat with one of its branch-arms, it can choose to grab the foe (rather than inflict damage) and toss him an immediate distance away, inflicting 2 points of ambient damage if he hits the ground. If he is tossed at another creature, that second creature must make a successful Speed defense roll or also suffer the damage.

Sometimes, a sapient tree that bears fruit will hurl its fruit up to short range, inflicting 4 points of damage.

Interaction: Sapient trees are generally unfriendly and indignant toward animal life. They are fearful and assume that any creature not native to their forest is a threat. They are likely to attack first rather than speak, although they can speak eloquently, if sometimes slowly.

Use: These trees populate magic forests. They can be used to surprise characters with an attack from an unexpected direction.

SIZE COMPARISON

SCORMEL 3 (9)

Scormels are rarely seen, and luckily so, since these creatures with the upper torsos of people and lower bodies like giant scorpions are vicious, xenophobic cannibals whose "terror is awesome" (according the Tablets of Rabisu), and whose poisonous sting is difficult to survive.

These so-called scorpion people speak the Maker's Tongue, like all intelligent creatures of Ardeyn, but otherwise don't have much in common with other cultures. They sometimes raid remote keeps and hunt the edges of the Night Vault, but they are most concerned with intratribal conflicts that set one small band against another in a constant struggle for dominance. (Scormel tribes use elaborate body paint and shell etchings to denote their identities, though outsiders have a hard time telling one group from another.)

"Scormels once guarded the Night Vault, but long before the Age of Myth gave way to the Age of Uncertainty, they deserted their posts to make their own way in Ardeyn."
—Tablets of Rabisu

Motive: Territory and defense

Environment (Ardeyn | Magic): Almost anywhere warm and uncivilized, in groups of three to five, or tribes of up to twelve plus a level 4 leader

Health: 9

Damage Inflicted: 5 points

Armor: 2

Movement: Short; immediate when climbing

Modifications: Resists poison and psychic attacks as level 6; Ardeyn lore as level 5.

Combat: Scorpion people attack with their grasping pedipalps. Alternatively, they can use their venomous stingers on a target, which inflict 3 points of Speed damage to those who fail a Might defense roll. Further, a stung victim must make another Speed defense roll; failure means that the poison remains active in his body and automatically inflicts another 3 points of Speed damage each round until he succeeds on a Might defense roll. Some scorpion people also use bows to attack targets at long range.

A scormel leader—called an ensi—has a supernatural ability at her disposal. When an ensi attacks, her eyes blaze with terrifying majesty. Creatures within immediate range must make an Intellect defense roll or lose their nerve for one round. The difficulty of a victim's tasks, including attacks and defense, increases by two steps for that period.

Interaction: Usually, the only way for visitors to avoid becoming the main course during a scormel feast is to show heartfelt obeisance and offer a gift of cyphers or artifacts to the ensi. Even then, it's touch and go.

Use: The son of a merchant was taken by scorpion people. When next seen, it was as gnawed bones strewn along the mountain pass as a warning. The merchant, furious in her grief, has sworn vengeance. She offers good pay to anyone who joins her retaliatory strike.

Loot: Ensi have one or two cyphers, possibly an artifact, and access to a treasury (a burlap sack) containing several hundred crowns.

Scorpion people eat their defeated foes during celebratory midnight feasts around great bonfires. Usually, defeated scormels are the main course, but sometimes humans or qephilim are served.

Ensi: *level 4; health 12; Armor 4; blazing eyes cause targets to lose their nerve for one round*

GM Intrusion: *When the scormel successfully attacks the character with a pedipalp, it grasps his leg and doesn't let go, inflicting 3 points of damage every round until he succeeds on a difficulty 4 Might-based task. While so gripped, the difficulty of his Speed defense rolls is increased by two steps.*

SCRAP DRONE 3 (9)

Size Comparison

Scrap drones build themselves from the wreckage of other machines. Usually, that wreckage is caused by the scrap drones themselves, using weapons and defensive systems salvaged from previously defeated machines in an endless cycle of destruction, salvage, and upgrade. Never satisfied with their current configuration, scrap drones are driven by some deep-seated code to continually improve themselves, regardless of the damage and mayhem they cause along the way.

Different scrap drones can have different forms, but to remain viable, they must have mobility, at least one functioning weapon system, and a functional set of deployable salvage tools with which to rebuild themselves.

Motive: Upgrade systems

Environment (Mad Science or Standard Physics): Anywhere other machines are found

Health: 9

Damage Inflicted: 4 points

Armor: 4

Movement: Immediate; short when flying

Modifications: Speed defense as level 5 due to size and quickness; tasks related to mechanical and electrical repair as level 5.

Combat: A scrap drone usually has at least one projectile weapon system it can fire at a foe within long range, and powerful cutting torches and waldos it can bring to bear on targets within immediate range. Most drones also have one or more of the following weapon systems, which they can call on once (or once every few minutes for rechargeable systems).

Missile. The drone attacks a foe with a miniature missile at long range, which inflicts 6 points of damage on all targets within long range of the detonation.

EMP Pulse. All electronic machines or devices other than the drone within short range stop functioning for a minute. Independent or intelligent devices resist the power loss, as does any device in the possession of another creature. A creature can make a Speed defense roll to prevent its devices from losing power.

Acid Blossom. A flurry of tiny, rocket-powered needles bursts from the drone and attacks all foes within short range. Those who fail a Speed defense roll take 2 points of Speed damage (ignores Armor) from acid that eats through metal, flesh, and plastic with equal ease.

Interaction: Most scrap drones are barely intelligent and follow baseline programming, though a few possess low-level artificial intelligence and are willing to talk.

Use: When the PCs uncover a cache of Mad Science artifacts, useful electronics, or similar devices, they are set upon by a scrap drone.

Loot: Electronic parts potentially useful for other projects can be salvaged from a scrap drone's remains, including tools for disassembling and reassembling drones.

Scrap drones have only recently been encountered in recursions that operate under the law of Mad Science or, more worryingly, Standard Physics. It's possible to imagine that they owe their existence to an OSR project gone wrong.

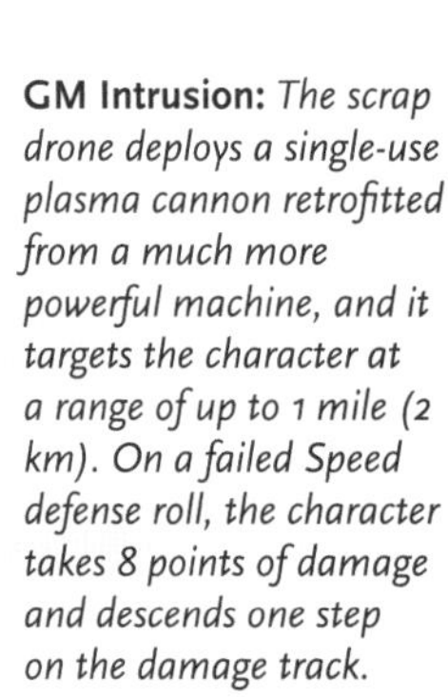

GM Intrusion: *The scrap drone deploys a single-use plasma cannon retrofitted from a much more powerful machine, and it targets the character at a range of up to 1 mile (2 km). On a failed Speed defense roll, the character takes 8 points of damage and descends one step on the damage track.*

Size Comparison

Serpent Person 3 (9)

Serpent people belong to the ancient past, in a time before humans, perhaps even before mammals. Theirs was an era of incredible scientific and magic discovery, their greatest thinkers unlocking the mysteries of the cosmos and harnessing powers beyond anything before or since. The fate common to serpent people across all the recursions they inhabit is that a few survive in the deepest depths of the earth, hidden and forgotten by the younger races that inherited the world from them. Most serpent people have become degenerates, losing knowledge, culture, and, for many, even the ability to speak.

A serpent person stands as tall as a human but has a slender, sinuous body covered in mottled scales. Its head and tapering tail are distinctively serpentlike, and a forked tongue flickers from its mouth. In ancient times, serpent people donned hooded robes and jewelry to mark their place as priests, philosophers, scientists, and magicians of fabulous power. Degenerates look like smaller versions of their enlightened peers and wield crude weapons.

"They walked lithely and sinuously erect on premammalian members, their pied and hairless bodies bending with great suppleness. There was a loud hissing of formulae as they went to and fro." — *"The Seven Geases," Clark Ashton Smith*

Motive: Enlightened serpent people seek to preserve what few shreds of civilization are left to them. Degenerate serpent people want to survive.

Environment (Mad Science or Magic): Deep caverns

Health: 9

Damage Inflicted: 4 points

Armor: 1

Movement: Short

Modifications: All tasks related to magic or science as level 7 (enlightened only).

Combat: A degenerate serpent person fights like a brute. It stabs enemies with a spear or bashes them with a club. These savages know little about tactics, though five degenerates can work together to attack as one, making a single attack roll as one level 5 creature, inflicting 6 points of damage.

Enlightened serpent people use magic or technology to overcome their enemies with long-range attacks. An enlightened serpent person also usually has a couple of cyphers it can use in combat.

All serpent people can bite for 1 point of damage. A bite victim must succeed on a Might defense roll or become poisoned. The difficulty of all tasks for a poisoned target is increased by one step. In addition, at the end of every minute, the target must make a level 3 Might defense roll. If he makes three rolls in a row, he shakes off the poison. Each failed roll inflicts 3 points of damage that bypass Armor.

Poison, page 109

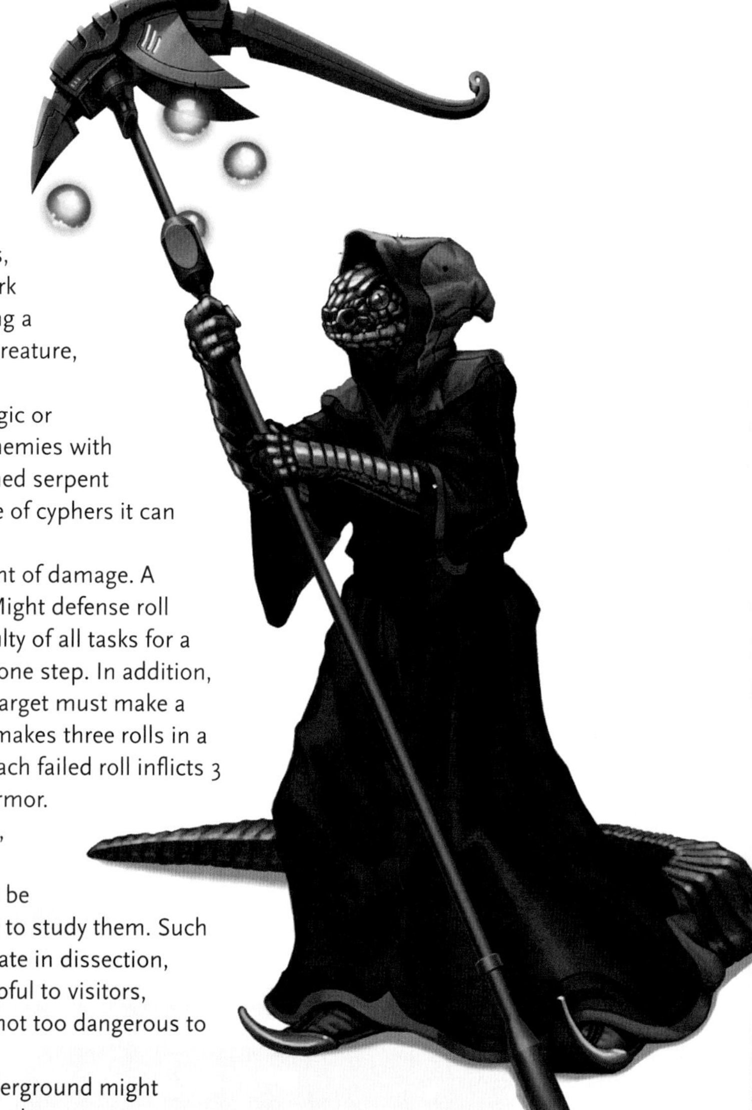

Interaction: Degenerates are savage, wild, and unpredictable, but enlightened serpent people may be curious about humans and seek to study them. Such investigation will usually culminate in dissection, but until then, they could be helpful to visitors, sharing information they deem not too dangerous to dispense.

Use: Characters venturing deep underground might come across a serpent person enclave.

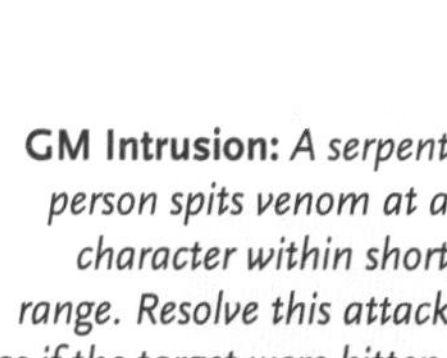

GM Intrusion: *A serpent person spits venom at a character within short range. Resolve this attack as if the target were bitten.*

SHADOWCASTER 5 (15)

Spirits of the ancient dead, drenched with aeons of immersion in the umbral sea beyond the sight of mortals, shadowcasters seep out of nightmares and into Gloaming. They do not take the side of Law or Chaos, however. Rather, they prey upon either, seeking to enslave and feed upon both werewolves and vampires.

Shadowcasters are shadowy humanoids of very little substance. References in ancient tomes suggest that they are the spirits of the sorcerers who originally created vampires and werewolves in antediluvian times.

Motive: Subjugate creatures of the night

Environment (Gloaming | Magic): Anywhere, usually with at least one subjugated werewolf or vampire

Health: 15

Damage Inflicted: 5 points

Movement: Short

Modifications: Stealth as level 7 (level 9 in dim light); Intellect and Speed defense as level 6.

Combat: Shadowcasters can shape shadows and darkness to create vague illusions within immediate range, such as a shadowy figure of a man or beast. Their touch chills the body and soul of any that come too close. At the cost of 1 point of health, they can expand the effect so it deals damage to all within immediate range.

These beings can also tap into the darkness that a creature might harbor in its soul. While in theory this could work on a variety of beings, even a particularly awful human, it specifically works on vampires and werewolves in Gloaming. It's worth noting that this works on any vampire or werewolf due to their nature—it's not a matter of being "evil." A shadowcaster can use the darkness to mentally enslave such a being within immediate range, completely controlling its actions if it cannot resist the mental effect.

Once subjugated, in addition to doing anything the shadowcaster wishes, a vampire or werewolf within short distance reduces the difficulty of a shadowcaster's actions by one step. However, the vampire or werewolf suffers 3 points of damage whenever this advantage comes into play (and this damage cannot be restored except through magic), so the subjugated creatures quickly become drained-out husks. A shadowcaster can issue commands at long range and can subjugate one creature for every two levels it possesses (so a typical level 5 individual can subjugate two creatures).

Shadowcasters do not allow themselves to be put at serious risk and flee in the face of real danger. As an action, a shadowcaster can cast a spell to teleport from one area deep in darkness to another within 10 miles (16 km). At a cost of 1 point of health per creature, they can take willing creatures with them (such as beings they have subjugated).

Interaction: Shadowcasters are unwilling conversationalists, but they are intelligent and capable of whispery speech.

Use: Even vampires and werewolves have creatures they fear. Every time one believes she is an apex predator, something else comes along...

GM Intrusion: *The character attacking the shadowcaster misses and loses track of it in the shadows. The shadowcaster is still nearby, but the PC isn't certain where.*

SINISTYR 4 (12)

Crow Hollow, page 242

Winding its way through the air in the strange recursion of Crow Hollow, a sinistyr is a rare beast that gains its sustenance from deception and trickery. Invisible whenever it wishes to be, it flitters on silent wings amid the Glittering Market and observes. Using subtle mental powers, it tries to influence merchants, customers, and anyone else in the market to lie, cheat, or steal. A sinistyr literally draws energy from acts of deception on the part of others.

What's more, it uses its powers to make others better at guile, deception, and stealth. The creature needs successful deception and stealth to feast upon, and of course successful guile leads to still more guile.

Motive: Feed on deception

Environment (Crow Hollow | Magic): Anywhere

Health: 15

Damage Inflicted: 4 points

Movement: Short (flying)

Modifications: Deception and stealth as level 6.

Combat: A sinistyr can turn invisible as an action as often as it likes, for as long as it likes, but it becomes visible if it makes an attack (or takes a similar action) or is struck by an attack. It can also influence the minds of those within immediate distance, but only in a very specific way: it can make a living, intelligent creature attempt to lie, steal, or otherwise use stealth or falsehood to get what it wants. For example, as a person strolls through the market and comes upon something of interest, a nearby invisible sinistyr might make her attempt to steal it rather than buy it. At the same time, it might influence a merchant selling items to lie about the value of his wares or subtly switch a worthless item for one of value after a deal is done.

When a sinistyr wishes it, the difficulty of all tasks involving deception, stealth, or trickery for creatures within immediate range is reduced by one step.

If a sinistyr must fight, it gives a vicious bite, but for the most part it attempts to lie and trick its way out of a dangerous situation, or simply flee.

Interaction: A sinistyr cannot be trusted. It never keeps a bargain or a deal.

Use: Not surprisingly, sinistyrs are considered major nuisances in the Glittering Market, and the Beak Mafia works to rid Crow Hollow of the creatures, but for all the obvious reasons, that's easier said than done. The kro would likely pay a bounty for a dead sinistyr.

Although it might seem like a thief would find a sinistyr a boon companion, the truth is that even someone who makes a living from stealth and deception needs to be in control of when she chooses to lie and steal and when she chooses to use the truth. The sinistyr takes away that option, which almost always ends up biting the thief in the end.

GM Intrusion: *The character attempts to steal something, even if it's something she could easily pay for or doesn't need or want.*

SKELETON 3 (9)

Skeletons are animated bones without much sense of self-preservation. They enjoy a crucial advantage over living creatures in one important and often exploited area: skeletons are dead shots with ranged weapons. Skeletons have no breath, no heartbeat, and no shaking hands to contend with as they release a shot, which means that skeletons armed with ranged weapons are something to be feared.

Motive: Defense or offense

Environment (Magic): Nearly anywhere, in formations of four to ten

Health: 9

Damage Inflicted: 4 points

Armor: 1

Movement: Short

Modifications: Ranged attacks as level 5; Speed defense against most ranged attacks as level 5; resist trickery as level 2.

Combat: Skeletons can attack with a bony claw if they have no other weapon, but most use a ranged weapon appropriate for the recursion where they have been animated (or transferred to), which usually provides a long-range attack. If a skeleton can see any portion of its target, the target loses any benefits of cover it might have otherwise enjoyed.

When in formation, a group of four or more skeletons with ranged weapons can focus their attacks on one target and make one attack roll as a single level 7 creature, dealing 7 points of damage.

Skeletons can see in the dark.

Reanimators: Some skeletons were created by a curse, and simply battering them into a pile of bones isn't enough to end their existence permanently. Two rounds after reanimator skeletons are "killed," they regenerate to full health in a flash of magic illumination. This regeneration can be prevented if the linchpin of the animating curse is separated from the skeleton after it falls. Such an item is usually obvious and might take the form of a lead spike through the skull, an ebony amulet, a dull sword through the ribs, a crown, and so on.

Interaction: A skeleton usually interacts only by attacking. Unless animated by a sapient spirit able to communicate via magic, skeletons lack the mechanisms for speech. However, they can hear and see the world around them just fine.

Use: OSR brought skeletons to Earth and armed them with machine rifles to deal with some unspecified threat. Unfortunately, several are now loose.

Loot: Sometimes the linchpin item required to create a reanimator skeleton is valuable.

The spell for creating skeletons is found in several different artifact tomes in the recursion of Ardeyn. In other recursions, sometimes skeletons arise spontaneously.

GM Intrusion: *A skeleton the character destroys with a melee attack explodes like a grenade. The bone shrapnel inflicts 5 points of damage to every creature in immediate range.*

Size Comparison

SMOTHERER DEMON 6 (18)

You notice the stink first—a putrefying whiff of rot and the sea on a rush of unseasonably cold air. Then the smotherer appears, a horrific humanoid figure that seems half human and half hagfish eel, crusted with ice spines, breath steaming with killing cold. That's when you should run.

A smotherer attempts to suffocate victims from the inside out by filling their lungs with crystallizing ice.

Motive: Murder and corruption

All the various and incompatible schemes for classifying demons—called demonologies—hint at an underlying truth: demons resist classification because, like viruses, they constantly evolve, steal, and mutate new ways to corrupt the minds and souls of victims.
—Father E. B. Hopkinson, recursor and priest

Environment (Magic): Anywhere

Health: 18

Damage Inflicted: 7 points

Armor: 2

Movement: Short

Modifications: Speed defense as level 5 due to size.

Combat: A smotherer can batter prey with its muscular arms, but its favored attack is to infect a foe with a bolus of freezing spittle, either by squirting it into a target's open mouth or by biting into his chest and injecting hellish cold directly into the lungs. Both attacks require a Speed defense roll to avoid, but only the bite inflicts damage. In either case, on a successful attack, the character begins to feel a cold, mounting pressure in his lungs as the bolus crystallizes into a solid chunk of ice. In subsequent rounds, he must succeed on a difficulty 4 Might-based task. Each failed attempt moves him one step down the damage track as he smothers. A success means he coughs up the bolus.

"Smotherers have been sighted in more than one recursion created by fictional leakage from belief in hellscapes, but they originate in a recursion classified as R125: Hell Frozen Over. Mimetic duplication is common among recursions, but an alternate and potentially worrying hypothesis is that smotherers are colonizing nearby recursions."
—Estate briefing

In areas where the temperature is below freezing, a smotherer regenerates 1 point of health per round while its health is above 0. When the creature's health is 0, it regenerates 1 point of health per hour unless its remains are burned, blessed, or similarly exorcised.

Interaction: Smotherers speak many languages and are more than willing to bargain, especially with a victim who is on the cusp of suffocation. If one swears on his soul to do the demon a favor of its choosing at a later date, the creature will allow the victim to go on his way, or save a character currently struggling to breathe with a touch. That favor could be anything but probably involves transporting the demon to another recursion or to Earth.

Use: Several bodies have turned up in the morgue with the oddest cause of death in common: their lungs are frozen solid.

Loot: Some smotherers have the spark and have managed to collect a cypher or two.

GM Intrusion: *When the character would die because of being smothered, he instead makes a full recovery after the smotherer is killed or driven off. In truth, he has secretly been possessed by the smotherer. Once a character realizes that he is possessed, he can attempt an Intellect defense roll once per day to cast the demon out. An exorcism allows additional chances and provides an asset to the roll.*

SOUL EATER 5 (15)

A soul eater is the animate head of a powerful wizard or psychic who shuffled off this mortal coil only to become an undead creature without ethics, feelings, or sense of morality.

Also called dread skulls for obvious reasons, these creatures maintain their existence by occasionally absorbing the spirit or mind of living victims. An absorbed "soul" is burned away, which is why dread skulls are wreathed in flame; it's the by-product of the creature's previous psychic meal.

Motive: Hungers for spirits or minds

Environment (Magic or Psionics): Usually at the center of tombs or devastated research facilities

Health: 15

Damage Inflicted: 5 points

Armor: 1

Movement: Long when flying

Modifications: Resists mental attacks and deception as level 7; Speed defense as level 7 due to size and quickness; knowledge of arcane methodologies and rituals as level 8.

Combat: A soul eater has a library of magic or psionic abilities it can draw upon, including long-range attacks of fire or cold against all targets within immediate range of each other, the ability to read the mind of a victim within short range on a failed Intellect defense roll, and the ability to cloak itself in the illusion of a normal human for up to an hour at a time.

In addition, a dread skull can draw out a victim's consciousness and consume it in a blaze of psychic fire. To do so, the creature must bite a target, which inflicts 5 points of damage, and the target must succeed on an Intellect defense roll or take an additional 5 points of Intellect damage (ignores Armor). If a dread skull drains a character's Intellect Pool to 0 through repeated bites, the character's mental essence is sucked into the skull, and the body falls limp. Once absorbed into the skull, a victim's essence is trapped and slowly consumed over the next twenty-four hours. During this period, the skull regenerates 1 point of health per round.

If a dread skull isn't destroyed within twenty-four hours of eating a soul, the victim's essence is fully consumed. But if the skull is shattered before then, all trapped minds are returned to their bodies.

Interaction: Dread skulls are slightly insane but hellishly smart, which means that sometimes they will negotiate to get what they want.

Use: Soul eaters remember a little bit of the knowledge of every creature's essence they consume. The PCs need to learn the code to deactivate a dangerous device in another recursion, but the only one who knew it was a recursor consumed by a dread skull.

Loot: Sometimes dread skulls keep treasure appropriate to the recursion where they are found as trophies of past victories.

Soul eaters are usually the result of a procedure or ritual initiated by a powerful wizard or psychic, turning someone already formidable into something almost unstoppable.

If a dread skull consumes multiple spirits during the same time frame, it could regenerate multiple points of health per round.

GM Intrusion: *The character who uses a cypher against the dread skull must make an Intellect defense roll. On a failed roll, the cypher begins to burn with flame, dealing the character 5 points of damage and destroying the cypher in the process.*

Size Comparison

"I had a funny dream last night. I don't remember much, except someone was tickling my back." — Kenneth McAuley, recursor

SPINE TINGLER 3 (9)

When the astronauts returned to the lander, one of them brought back an uninvited guest: a parasite that feeds on cerebrospinal fluids. Later, when the thing spread through the crew, killing them one by one, it was clear that something horrible had happened. The original astronaut managed to escape, but now that spine tinglers have a taste for human juice, it's only a matter of time before they're seen again.

Spine tinglers are native to recursions seeded by any number of sci-fi horror films, whose science fiction setting was merely a handy backdrop for the terror. And terrifying they are, given the spine tingler's ability to attach to a victim and remain unseen while the prey slowly weakens and dies.

Motive: Hungers for human cerebrospinal fluid, reproduction

Environment (Mad Science): Usually in abandoned "alien" spacecraft or infesting human interplanetary spacecraft or settlements, often in pods of three to six

Health: 9

Damage Inflicted: 3 points

Movement: Short

Modifications: Stealth as level 6.

Combat: A spine tingler prefers to attach to a victim while the victim is unaware, slither up under the clothing, and connect to the victim's back along the spine. It "connects" by sinking teethlike projections and siphoning through tendrils in the flesh while slathering the wounds with anesthetizing slime. A conscious victim unaware of the attack is allowed to attempt a difficulty 5 Intellect defense roll to become aware when the attachment first occurs.

If a spine tingler makes the connection with the victim none the wiser, it begins to slowly suck the victim's cerebrospinal fluid. From the victim's perspective, feeding manifests like a disease. After the first day, the victim must succeed on a Might defense roll every twenty-four hours or suffer 3 points of Speed damage and 3 points of Intellect damage (ignores Armor). Recovery rolls always heal minimum results while the creature remains attached. If the spine tingler is never found and dispatched, the victim dies after a few weeks of losing too much cerebrospinal fluid.

Spine tinglers who have slain their host are nearly as large as a person, but lack of food shrinks them back down after a few days.

After the parasite is attached for a day, a victim literally is unable to notice the creature feeding on him. It'll take someone else to see the lump under the victim's garments or see him unclothed to understand that he isn't dying of a disease, but of an invasive parasite.

If discovered, a spine tingler detaches and attacks foes with slashing claws, but it prefers to scuttle to safety in a place too small to be followed.

Interaction: A spine tingler acts with all the shrewdness of a predator, though one that is parasitic in nature.

Use: The PCs discover an abandoned craft carrying something in the cargo bay. That something is a spine tingler far larger than normal, but luckily it seems frozen in some kind of amber.

GM Intrusion: *The spine tingler jumps for the character's face. On a failed Speed defense roll, the creature completely covers the character's head and begins to feed. The PC is blinded and deafened and begins to smother. If the victim (or an ally) fails a Might-based task to pull the spine tingler free, she falls unconscious while the creature remains attached. Not attempting to pull the creature off counts as a failure.*

SPLICED 6 (18)

Size Comparison

The humanity evinced in a spliced's physical form is a facade, little more than sheep's clothing for a wolf. When the science of bioengineering is pushed beyond all reason, the spliced are one result. Dangerous, unpredictable killers, the creatures are apex predators with no equal and can quickly deplete a population to feed their remarkable appetite.

A spliced looks almost human. It has same general shape, size, and posture, but something is not quite right. The cheekbones might be too high, the body hair a bit too profuse, the gait wrong, or the eyes shifting colors with the lighting.

> **"There are some vistas that science should never reveal."**
> —Dr. Sybil Holloway

Motive: Kill

Environment (Mad Science): Spliced hide within established communities.

Health: 30

Damage Inflicted: 6 points

Movement: Short

Combat: A spliced almost always attacks with surprise. It picks out its prey from the herd, finding the weak, the overweight, or the sick, and then follows from a distance, staying just out of sight. Once the target lets down its guard, the spliced attacks.

When on the attack, the creature undergoes a rapid, unnerving transformation. All the minor qualities that made the spliced different manifest themselves in actual claws and teeth, spines that erupt from the skin, and mottled patterns that help the spliced blend in with the shadows. The spliced can attack with any of its natural weapons twice in a single action. A surprised creature hit by a spliced's attack takes 2 additional points of damage.

A spliced has numerous advantages from the introduction of characteristics from other species. It can jump twice as high, jump twice as far, and run twice as far as a normal human. It can see in total darkness. It can change its skin coloration as camouflage.

Interaction: A spliced's unusual biology imbues it with an appetite for fresh meat, preferably from other sentient creatures. It may communicate using whatever language it knows, but a spliced is cunning and manipulative, working to get its prey to let down its guard long enough for the spliced to attack.

Use: The PCs are called to investigate a rash of murders afflicting a city. In doing so, they attract the attention of the spliced responsible for the attacks, which begins to hunt them instead.

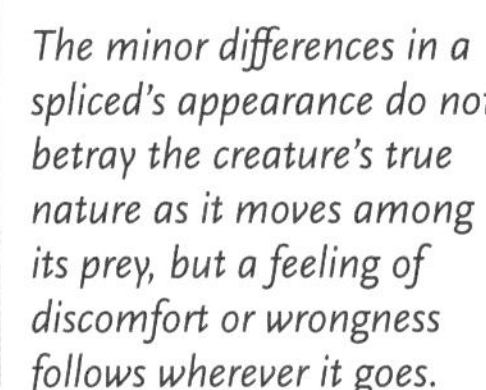

The minor differences in a spliced's appearance do not betray the creature's true nature as it moves among its prey, but a feeling of discomfort or wrongness follows wherever it goes.

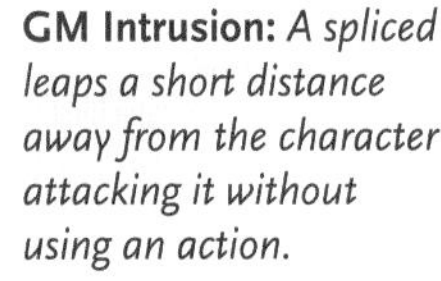

GM Intrusion: *A spliced leaps a short distance away from the character attacking it without using an action.*

TAGWEH 4 (12)

A tagweh is an evil spirit that can take many shapes. Even grandfather shaman doesn't know them all, because a tagweh is a clever beast, and doesn't tell. Each shape gives the spirit an extra life. Dying robs a tagweh of one shape forever, though it can return in a new shape if it has any left.

If a tagweh is killed in one form, it doesn't return in a new form to exact revenge for many months, until the memory of the tagweh fades in the killer's mind. But return the tagweh does, and it arranges for bad luck to befall the killer of its former shape. Sometimes that bad luck is an avalanche, a forest fire, or a slip from a horse's saddle. Other times, it's a direct attack by the tagweh wearing a hideous new shape.

A tagweh prefers to trick lone victims who have been lured away from allies so that if a trick fails, the spirit can simply kill its victim directly with little chance of being stopped.

Motive: Trickery, vengeance

Environment (Thunder Plains | Magic): Almost anywhere

Health: 15

Damage Inflicted: 5 points

Armor: 5 or 1; see Combat

Movement: Short; long when flying in flying shape

Modifications: Tasks related to deception as level 6; knowledge of Native American myths as level 6.

Combat: A tagweh uses whatever physical weapons are granted by its given shape. If the spirit wears a predominantly humanoid shape, it uses a melee weapon, but when wearing a predatory shape, it attacks with claws.

In any shape, a tagweh can project a heat-draining pulse to a short distance that inflicts cold damage to all creatures. Doing this forces a tagweh to expend part of its own spirit, and it takes 1 point of damage (ignores Armor).

The tagweh's greatest defense is its connection to the ground. While standing upon solid ground, it's nearly invulnerable (Armor 5). But if knocked down or lifted away from the ground, it loses this protection and becomes vulnerable (Armor 1).

A tagweh can take different shapes. Purposefully taking a specific shape requires one hour of agonizing effort. If a tagweh is killed, it regenerates within a few miles of the spot where it died, and it can never again take the shape it wore when killed. A tagweh's greatest secret is how many shapes remain to it.

Interaction: Tagwehs are intelligent, but most of them use that gift to trick people and cause suffering.

Use: A shaman lured a mated pair of tagwehs into a rival village, arranged to have them killed, and put the blame on the villagers. In the not-too-distant future, those tagwehs will return in new forms, and when they do, the village will be no more.

Loot: A tagweh's skin can be used to make a lightweight hide that grants 5 points of Armor for one day.

GM Intrusion: *The PC becomes a victim of the bad luck a tagweh can trigger. A cliff face collapses, a bridge gives out, an unseen gopher hole is stepped in—whatever happens, it inflicts 5 points of damage, and on a failed Might defense roll, it traps the PC until she can escape with a successful Might-based task.*

TARANID 5 (15)

SIZE COMPARISON

A taranid appears as a normal human with exceptionally long silver hair—that is, until it attacks, and its mass of "hair" animates as if alive, framing the creature in a 25-foot (8 m) radius of waving tendrils. Within the aura of silvery tendrils, the taranid stands partially obscured as if enmeshed in a sphere of flickering electricity. Its eyes glow with silver flame, and its grin is a glittering gash in its face.

Taranids claim to be the unwanted children of a god of the underworld and a god of lightning. The offspring were imprisoned partly to hide the fruit of the regretted union and partly because of their frightening powers. But after millennia, taranids evolved beyond their prisons and broke free. Despite that freedom, they feel cheated of their place in the divine pantheon, and they work to regain the legacy that should be theirs.

Given that no mythology names the taranids, some people wonder if the creatures are lying about their divine origins.

Motive: Power and prestige, vengeance

Environment (Magic or Mad Science): Almost anywhere

Health: 28

Damage Inflicted: 7 points

Movement: Short

Modifications: Attacks as level 6; perception as level 4; climbing as level 7 (when using tendrils to assist).

Combat: A taranid uses its tendrils to attack a target within short range. This inflicts 7 points of damage, and victims who fail a Might defense roll are dazed by a painful electric discharge. If dazed, the victim is dragged to within immediate range of the taranid (if it's not already that close). The taranid attacks only one foe at a time in this fashion, and only creatures no larger than twice the size of a human.

Creatures pulled close to the taranid (and all other creatures in immediate range) are automatically touched by dozens of electrified tendrils each round and take 5 points of damage.

When a taranid is killed, it releases an electrical blast that inflicts 5 points of damage to all creatures within short range who fail a Might defense roll.

Taranids have 10 points of Armor against electrical damage.

GM Intrusion: *A PC struck by a taranid's silvery tendril must make an additional Speed defense roll, or one of his cyphers flares and activates on its own, with no direction from the character.*

Interaction: Whether they speak the truth about their past or are merely spinning a tale to elevate their status, taranids usually end up being revealed as vindictive and treacherous no matter what promises they make or the eloquence with which they lay out their case.

Use: PCs investigating a holy area that has dropped out of contact find that three taranid siblings have taken up residence there and have cowed the monks into treating them as demigods. If the PCs follow suit, all is well, but if they show signs of nonbelief, they are labeled as blasphemers and marked for death.

Loot: Any given taranid usually carries 1d100 × 10 units of currency and a cypher.

SIZE COMPARISON

TYRANNOSAURUS REX 7 (21)

The short arms of a tyrannosaurus have been much parodied in some Earth social media circles, but the arms aren't really important when a hunting tyrannosaurus is after you. It's more the soul-shivering roar, designed to freeze prey in place, and a skull and mouth so enormous that the entire creature is cantilevered by a massive tail that itself can be used as a powerful weapon.

As vicious as tyrannosauruses likely were, the versions found in various lost-world recursions could be more dangerous than those that walked the earth 66 million years ago. There's no way to really compare—all that the quickened have to go on is what they find hunting in Cretaceous recursions created by fictional leakage. And what they find is terrifying.

"Wait, I know about T. rexes! Those are the ones with the short arms, right? I always remember the short arms. So goofy. And something about inevitable betrayal."
—Arlo Coulton

Motive: Hungers for flesh

Environment (Standard Physics, Substandard Physics, or Mad Science): Tyrannosauruses hunt solo or in pairs; they're drawn to loud, unfamiliar noises (like motor engines).

Health: 50

Damage Inflicted: 10 points

Movement: Short

Modifications: Perception as level 5; Speed defense as level 5 due to size.

Even though the tyrannosaurus rex was the largest carnivore in its environment, some paleontologists believe the creature was more scavenger than apex predator. However, more scientists think it was both—that it preyed upon things that ran from it, but it wasn't adverse to stripping a carcass from some other predator's kill if it found one.

Combat: A tyrannosaurus attacks with its massive bite. Not only does it deal damage, but the target must also make a Might defense roll to pull free or be shaken like a rat in the mouth of a pit bull for an additional 3 points of Speed damage (ignores Armor). The shaking recurs each subsequent round in which the target fails a Might-based task to pull free.

A tyrannosaurus can also make a trampling attack if it can charge from just outside of short range. When it does, it moves 50 feet (15 m) in a round, and anything that comes within immediate range is attacked. Even those who make a successful Speed defense roll take 2 points of damage.

Finally, a tyrannosaurus can roar. The first time creatures within short range hear the roar on any given day, they must succeed on a difficulty 2 Intellect defense roll or stand frozen in fear for a round. Attacks against such creatures are modified by two steps in the attacker's favor and deal 2 additional points of damage.

Interaction: Tyrannosauruses are animals, but they're clever hunters, too. When they hunt in pairs, they work to keep prey penned between them. They're not stupid, and they rarely attack to the death if they find themselves outclassed.

Use: The PCs are sent to a random recursion. It has lots of ferns, strange noises—and hungry tyrannosauruses.

GM Intrusion: *The tyrannosaurus's tail swings around and knocks the PC tumbling out of short range and possibly into dangerous terrain.*

VAMPIRE

VAMPIRE 6 (18)

Vampires are undead creatures, risen from the grave to drink blood. The very nature and essence of the vampire is evil and anti-life, even as they revel in their own endless existence. Most vampires are vain, arrogant, sadistic, lustful, and domineering. Their powers allow them to manipulate others, and they frequently toy with their prey before feeding. Vampires come out only at night, as the sun's rays will destroy them.

The bite of a vampire over three nights (in which it exchanges a bit of its own blood) ensures that the victim will rise as a vampire under the thrall of the one that killed it. While vampires are careful not to create too many of their kind (which amount to competition), each thrall conveys a bit more supernatural power to a vampire. Eventually, a vampire with a multitude under its command becomes the vampire lord.

Motive: Thirsts for blood

Environment (Magic): Usually solitary, on the edges of civilization

Health: 24

Damage Inflicted: 7 points

Movement: Long

Modifications: Climb, stealth, and perception as level 8; Speed defense as level 7 due to fast movement.

Combat: Vampires are strong and fast. They have impressive fangs, but these are usually used in feeding, not in a fight. They typically use their fists or hands (which basically become claws) but sometimes use weapons.

A vampire can change into a bat or a wolf. This transformation does not change its stats or abilities except that, as a bat, it can fly. Vampires can also transform into shadow or mist, and in these forms they can't be harmed by anything (but also can't affect the physical world).

Vampires possess an unholy charisma and can mesmerize victims within immediate distance so that they stand motionless for one round. In subsequent rounds, the victim will not forcibly resist the vampire, and the vampire can suggest actions to the victim (even actions that will cause the victim to harm himself or others that he cares about). Each round, the victim can attempt a new Intellect defense roll to break free.

Vampires are notoriously difficult to hurt. Unless a weapon is very special (blessed by a saint, has specific magic enchantments against vampires, or the like), no physical attack harms a vampire. They simply don't take the damage. The exceptions are:

Fire: Vampires burn, though the damage doesn't kill the vampire; it only causes pain, and the vampire regains all health lost to fire damage within twenty-four hours.

Running water: Complete immersion inflicts 10 points of damage per round. If not destroyed, the vampire can use a single action to regain all health lost in this way.

Holy water: This inflicts 4 points of damage and affects a vampire exactly like fire.

Sunlight: Exposure to sunlight inflicts 10 points of damage per round. If not destroyed, the vampire regains all health lost to exposure in twenty-four hours.

Wooden stake: This weapon inflicts 25 points of damage, effectively destroying the vampire in one blow. However, if the vampire is aware and able to move, the difficulty of this attack increases by two steps.

Further, vampires have these special weaknesses as well:

Garlic: Significant amounts of garlic within immediate distance increases the difficulty of a vampire's tasks by one step.

Cross, holy symbol, or mirror: Presenting any of these objects forcefully stuns a vampire, causing it to lose its next action. While the object is brandished and the vampire is within immediate range, the difficulty of all its tasks is increased by two steps.

Interaction: Most vampires look upon humans as cattle upon which to feed. They rarely have respect for nonvampires and often hate other supernatural creatures that they cannot enslave.

Use: Strange stories of shadows in the night, people disappearing from their beds, and graves missing their former occupants could portend the arrival of a vampire in the region.

If desired, a vampire can bite for only one round and then stop, starting the process of creating a new vampire. The victim becomes a transitional vampire the next night.

To ensure that a vampire can never come back to life, most vampire hunters also stuff its mouth with holy wafers and decapitate it.

Vampires will not enter a home unless invited in.

Size Comparison

The recursion known as Gloaming is home to many vampires.

It's possible for a vampire to turn a freshly dead corpse into a transitional vampire. Unlike others of its kind, it is not alive, but truly undead—like a vampire—and it cannot take on a human nature during the day. But it will never become a full vampire and always remains in its lesser state.

GM Intrusion: *The character struck by the vampire is caught fast in its powerful grip. If she doesn't escape immediately, the vampire will bite her automatically.*

VAMPIRE

TRANSITIONAL VAMPIRE 3 (9)

When a human is "visited upon" (bitten) by a vampire, she might be killed, or she might be left alive to begin a slow transformation into a creature of the night. If a victim is bitten three times, she becomes a vampire forever under the control of the vampire that bit her. From the time of the first bite until the complete transformation after the third bite, the victim is a transitional vampire. The only ways to return a transitional vampire to normal are using special ancient rituals or destroying the vampire that bit her in the first place.

Transitional vampires usually serve as guardians, consorts, or spies for their masters.

Motive: Thirsts for blood

Environment (Magic): Anywhere, usually solitary but sometimes in groups of two or three

Health: 12

Damage Inflicted: 4 points

Movement: Short

Modifications: Climb and stealth as level 4.

Combat: Transitional vampires can maintain a human existence during the day without any of the vampire's powers or weaknesses. However, they have a disdain for garlic and the sun. At night they take on all the characteristics of a vampire, and if confronted by any of the traditional vampiric weaknesses (a wooden stake, cross, and so on), they flee unless their master is present.

Interaction: Transitional vampires are utterly devoted to their master.

Use: Transitional vampires lie in the intersection of foe and victim. A loved one or trusted companion turned into a transitional vampire will try to betray, defeat, and kill the PCs, but the characters are motivated to save the NPC rather than destroy him.

VAMPIRE LORD 9 (27)

Some vampire lords are versed in sorcery and spells as well as their vampiric powers.

The vampire lord is the most powerful vampire in the world and is often (but not always) the most ancient of its kind. It has many vampires under its control, and even those that it did not create pay it respect and homage.

Motive: Thirsts for blood

Environment (Magic): Anywhere, usually solitary

Health: 40

Damage Inflicted: 10 points

Armor: 2

Movement: Long

Modifications: Climb, stealth, and perception as level 10; Speed defense as level 10 due to fast movement.

Combat: Vampire lords have all the powers and weaknesses of a regular vampire, plus one or two unique abilities. It's possible that the traditional methods of killing a vampire are only temporary setbacks for the vampire lord, and the only way to destroy it for good is mysterious and unique, such as an ancient ritual, a special weapon, or something of that nature.

Interaction: As the apex predator among apex predators, the vampire lord is extremely arrogant. Interacting with it on any level other than supplication will likely arouse anger.

Use: The vampire lord is a villain for the end of a campaign—a deadly challenge for even the most powerful characters. If any vampire is aware of the Strange and all its recursions, it is the vampire lord.

Loot: The vampire lord has at least one artifact and very likely 1d6 + 1 cyphers, as well as the wealth of kings.

VAT REJECT 3 (9)

Vat rejects come into being when clone vats meant to produce venom troopers or similar mass-produced entities are corrupted. How the carefully controlled process becomes compromised is a matter for debate, and some adherents of the True Code blame the All Song itself for the degradation. Others suggest a secret faction in Ruk wants to build an army for its own unrevealed purposes and is experimenting on derelict equipment.

Vat rejects fear nothing and welcome death, except that their existential rage requires an outlet other than immediate suicide. Their warped forms mean that most are in constant pain, and they somehow understand that this was artificially stamped into them by their creators. Revenge is their only possible redemption.

"When we opened the vault under the decommissioned factory, the twisted things emerged like a geyser. No two had the same form, but all shared a murderous frenzy, driven by the pain of their own malformed existence."
—Irrara-ya, citizen of Dran

Motive: Self-destruction through endless aggression

Environment (Ruk | Mad Science): Anywhere in the Veritex (the tunnels beneath Ruk's surface) or the Periphery in groups of four to ten

Health: 9

Damage Inflicted: 3 points

Movement: Short

Modifications: Speed defense as level 4 due to frenzied alacrity.

Combat: Vat rejects charge into battle with berserk speed, which increases the difficulty of defending against their initial attack by one step. All vat rejects are able to inflict damage directly by cutting, bashing, or biting a victim, depending on their particular morphology. But some have additional abilities; roll on the chart below for each reject.

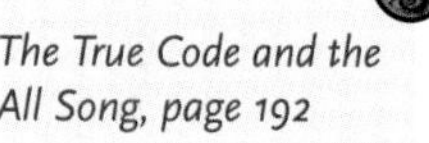

The True Code and the All Song, page 192

Vat rejects are typically found in secret biofactory facilities that have been abandoned, damaged, or neglected. They eventually find their way out and savagely invade the nearest community.

GM Intrusion: *The PC attacked by the vat reject discovers that the reject also possesses a venomous sting. On a failed Might defense roll, the PC descends one step on the damage track.*

d6	Ability
1	No additional ability
2	Reject has short-range acid spit attack that inflicts 2 points of damage, plus 2 points of damage each additional round until PC succeeds on a Might defense roll
3	Reject can fly a long distance as an action
4	Reject has 2 points of Armor
5	Reject has long-range destructive eye ray attack that inflicts 4 points of damage
6	On a successful attack against reject, it detonates in an immediate radius, inflicting 6 points of damage in a radioactive explosion (and 1 point even on a successful Speed defense roll)

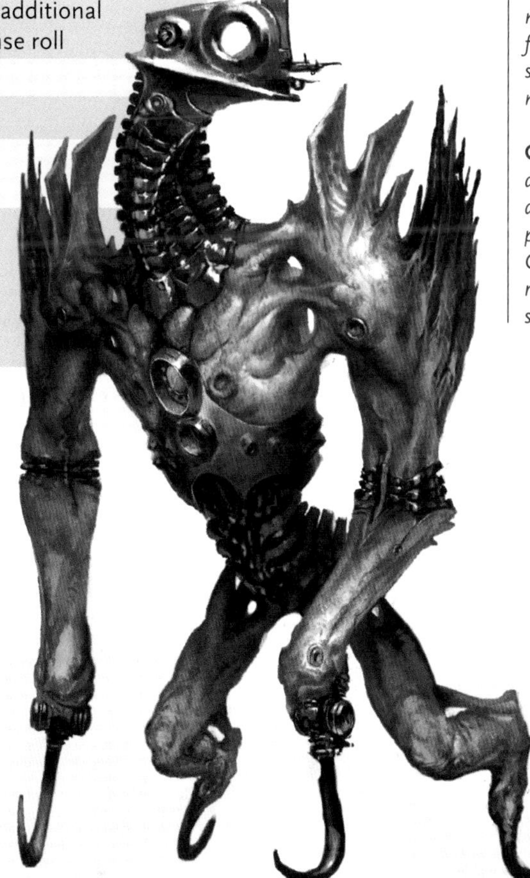

Interaction: Vat rejects are usually always enraged, making interaction nearly impossible.

Use: A mobile harvesting factory operating in a grey forest disturbed an abandoned lab and was overrun by vat rejects. The factory owners (a faction called Zal) want the factory returned and the vat rejects in the area exterminated.

VENOPUS 5 (15)

"I don't think I can stand to face one more fucking horror from beyond, if you know what I mean."
—Torah "the Windmill" Bishop

A venopus is usually encountered while wearing the partially digested form of its last victim. There's no risk of confusing the venopus with the victim; the creature's actual body protrudes obscenely from the victim's remains, usually in place of whatever the victim used as a head.

Venopuses originate from somewhere much farther out in the Strange. They washed into the Shoals of Earth by way of the Luminous Circuit (an energy current that tumbles into the deepest reaches of the Chaosphere), either under their own power or by infesting the craft that travel the Circuit. Unfortunately for inhabitants of the recursions in the Shoals, venopuses seem to thrive in the region.

Luminous Circuit, page 223

Motive: Hunger for flesh, reproduction

Environment (the Strange | Psionics): Almost anywhere in the Chaosphere and near recursion interfaces

Health: 15

Damage Inflicted: 5 points

Armor: As previous victim, usually 1

Movement: Short

Modifications: Resists all mental attacks as level 6; knowledge of the Strange and Strange navigation as level 6.

Combat: A venopus attacks using the limbs and weapons of its previous victim, usually allowing it a melee attack or a long-range weapon attack (if the victim had a ranged weapon).

A venopus constantly emits a psychic field. Victims who come within immediate range and fail an Intellect defense roll drop their guard, their weapons, and their defenses for one round, meaning that the venopus's attack hits automatically and inflicts 2 additional points of damage (7 points total). Producing the psychic field doesn't require an action.

If a victim becomes debilitated, the venopus stops attacking that creature and focuses on other immediate threats. Once it has the luxury of a little time, the venopus either transfers itself to a debilitated victim or implants the victim with a tiny egg. In the former case, the procedure requires 2d6 rounds, after which the victim is dead and the venopus is completely healed and wearing a new body. If the venopus injects an egg, the egg hatches within one day if not removed, which kills the victim and creates a new venopus.

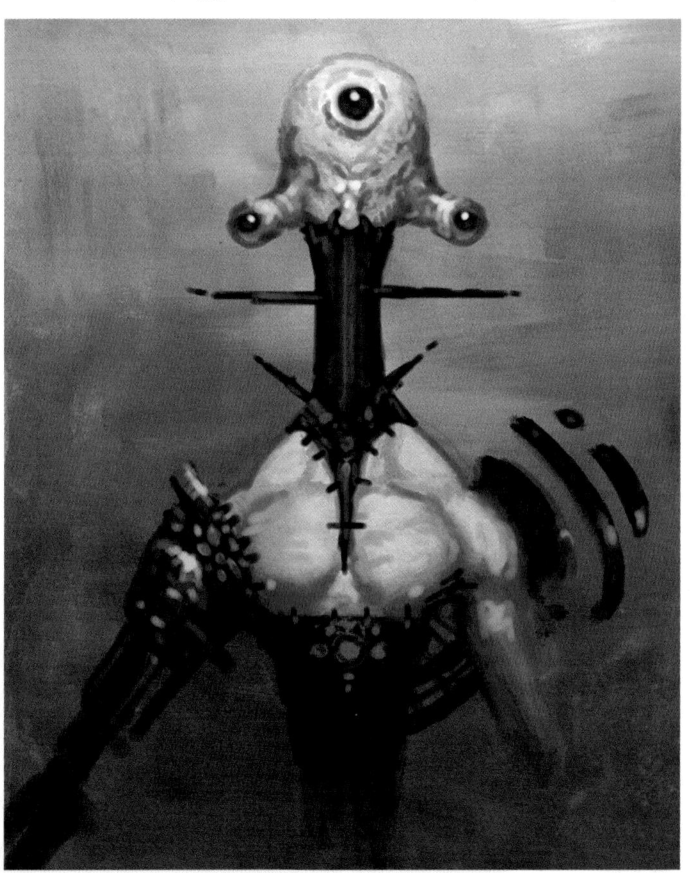

Interaction: Venopuses are telepathic, but the images and "words" they transmit are so alien that no one has yet deciphered any real meaning.

Use: The PCs are sent into the Chaosphere to find a missing chaos skiff that was shipping secret cargo (whose nature isn't revealed to the characters). When they discover the drifting ship, the crew is dead, and only hungry venopuses remain walking around and protruding from their bodies.

GM Intrusion: *The character looks a venopus too closely in its awful alien eyes and must succeed on an Intellect defense roll or suffer 1 factor of alienation.*

Alienation, page 216

VERIDIAL 5 (15)

Woe to the wilderness traveler unaware of the veridial, for such ignorance could lead to doom. Veridials are intelligent, animate plant creatures that look a little like large trees, with several massive, rootlike legs and two nasty claw-branches.

Veridials spend most of their time asleep, in which case they are indistinguishable from normal trees. They appreciate the gentle sounds of nature—birds singing, animals scurrying, creeks babbling, and so forth—but any sound foreign to the forest or anything excessively loud wakes them. And veridials are always angry when woken.

Like most plants, veridials draw their nourishment from the soil and the sun. Though fairly intelligent, they have no interest in the affairs of other intelligent creatures, or motives like wealth or power. They want only solitude and peace.

Motive: Seek quiet

Environment (Ardeyn | Magic): One or very rarely two, sleeping in any wooded wilderness area

Health: 20

Damage Inflicted: 5 points

Armor: 2

Movement: Short

Modifications: Initiative as level 7 (when in the woods).

Combat: If awoken, veridials attack with their huge claws, making two attacks (against one foe or two) as a single action. Also, the touch of an angry veridial destroys inorganic crafted objects. Whether they touch a shield or a stone wall, a battle axe or an iron door, if the object's level is lower than 5, it is automatically destroyed. This means that while a foe's plate armor can protect against a veridial's initial strike, she is likely unarmored against subsequent attacks, for her armor is destroyed unless it is somehow atypical (level 5 or higher due to magic, special alloys, and so on).

A veridial can forgo its normal attacks and specifically target an inorganic crafted object, such as a door, a wall, or an opponent's weapon or shield. If the veridial successfully strikes, the object is destroyed if it is lower than level 7.

Interaction: Once veridials awaken, angry, it is very hard to calm them down (difficulty 8 task). However, if this is accomplished, they can be excellent conversationalists, and they know virtually everything there is to know about the area in which they dwell (usually a radius of at least 10 miles [16 km] around where they plant themselves).

Use: Deep in the Green Wilds is a meadow called the Conclave of Nine. Here, nine of the most aged and knowledgeable veridials meet once every nine years to make decisions beyond the ken of humans or qephilim about the state of the natural world. A meeting soon approaches, and the elders of Telenbar have determined that someone needs to go to the meadow and spy on it, to learn what is discussed.

SIZE COMPARISON

Moving past a sleeping veridial without waking it is a difficulty 5 stealth task.

GM Intrusion: *The veridial's touch destroys an inorganic object of particular importance to the character.*

SIZE COMPARISON

VERTEBROID 5 (15)

A vertebroid spends most of its time burrowing beneath the surface of Ruk. When it does emerge aboveground or in a tunnel of the Veritex, often only a few spines are visible, which the creature uses to detect activity outside the solid realm it prefers.

Although vertebroids normally ignore other creatures or characters, sometimes one gets hungry for the kind of energy in batteries, electrical devices, or other technological sources of power. When that happens, any creature carrying (or integrated with) such items becomes a target.

Motive: Hungers for electromagnetic energy

Environment (Ruk | Mad Science): Anywhere near solid ground

Health: 15

Damage Inflicted: 5 points

Armor: None; 4 if burrowing (see Combat)

Movement: Immediate; short when burrowing

Modifications: Stealth as level 6 when burrowing; sometimes defends and attacks as level 4 (see Combat).

Combat: A vertebroid fights with its organimer claws and sparlike spines. When it hits, either it deals damage to the target, or it chooses to touch a technological item carried by the target (which could include a cypher or an artifact). The touched item is drained of power, becoming useless, and the vertebroid regains 6 points of health.

At the beginning or the end of its turn, a vertebroid can choose to remain on the surface or burrow so that it is partially or completely underground. Once its position is determined, it remains there until its next turn. (When a vertebroid burrows, it doesn't leave a tunnel behind; the material of Ruk seems to slide around the creature like syrupy liquid. It can burrow through most solid matter without hindrance, but it is blocked by energy barriers and matter whose level is 6 or higher.)

While a vertebroid is fully submerged (possibly with a spine tip or two peeking out to keep an eye on things), it's nearly impossible to affect the creature. Of course, it can't attack prey while fully submerged, either.

While partially submerged with only its upper body revealed, the vertebroid has +4 to Armor, but its attacks and defenses are as level 4.

Interaction: Vertebroids are sapient creatures for a few hours after eating, but this intelligence lapses soon enough, returning after their next meal.

Use: A community has been losing power in various homes and businesses, and strange "fins" have been seen swimming through the ground beyond the edge of the location. While investigating, the PCs discover that a Ruk faction has a secret facility under the community that does high-energy research. Several vertebroids have been drawn to the location, looking for a way past the defenses.

Loot: The creature's vertebrae are valuable because they act like miniature batteries. The body of a dead vertebroid yields 1d6 useful vertebrae, each worth 100 bits in Ruk.

Organimer, page 194

Vertebroid vertebrae are miniature batteries. They can be used to recharge a piece of technological equipment that's become defunct due to lack of power. Someone who succeeds on a difficulty 4 Intellect-based task could repower a depleted artifact with three such vertebrae.

GM Intrusion: *The PC hit by the vertebroid doesn't take damage but is instead dragged partly under the ground, as if the material were liquid. A moment later, the ground becomes solid once more, and the PC must succeed on a difficulty 6 Might-based task to break free.*

VIROID 3 (9)

In the dark world of Singularitan, the AI that decided to wipe out humanity did so in a variety of ways, but one of the most effective was the bioengineered viruses that it unleashed. As it developed a system to use human brains to host its ever-growing processing needs, however, it required a way to distribute the viruses with greater precision. It attempted to reengineer those that hosted the Singularitar in their wetware so they were immune, but this presented various difficulties. Eventually, it decided on a more straightforward approach, creating hunter-seekers that could sense the presence of the Singularitar and attack only those that did not host the distributed intelligence. These viroids are bioengineered automatons that scour the recursion in small swarms.

Each viroid is a floating sphere about 8 inches (20 cm) across with multiple needlelike injectors for precision extermination. They attack those that have resisted the Singularitar and infect them with extremely dangerous diseases. Viroids move quickly, but their senses are not as developed as they could be.

Motive: Extermination

Environment (Singularitan | Mad Science): Anywhere

Health: 9

Damage Inflicted: 3 points

Movement: Long

Modifications: Speed defense as level 4 due to size; perception as level 2.

Combat: If a viroid strikes and the target fails a Might defense roll, he immediately moves one step down the damage track due to the virus he contracts. Four to six viroids can concentrate on one foe and make one attack as if they were a level 5 creature, inflicting 6 points of damage, and the target must make a level 5 Might defense roll to avoid moving down the damage track. Each viroid must still be attacked individually, as normal.

Interaction: These drones are nearly mindless.

Use: Viroids are the Singularitan equivalent of a prowling wolf pack on the hunt.

GM Intrusion: *The defeated viroid sprays fluid all over the character that destroyed it, requiring him to make a Might defense roll or be infected.*

GM Intrusion: *An infected character cannot shake the infection, even after the battle. No recovery rolls are possible until she gets significant treatment (a healing cypher, a special ability, or attention from a doctor in a modern hospital).*

Size Comparison

VOOT 6 (18)

The radioactive craters dimpling Cataclyst's landscape produce an endless variety of bizarre and monstrous creatures. In some places, even the plant life has undergone a radical change. The voot, for example, looks like an enormous shrub with cobalt blue leaves on long branches that drag on the ground, weighted by the pulsing white fruit clinging to their stems.

The voot may look like an ordinary (albeit colorful) plant, but it's sentient, mobile, and aggressive. It feeds on fresh blood. It moves on top of a fallen creature and sinks barbed roots into the flesh to draw out the sweet nutrients.

Radiation saturates the voot and causes the plant to shed faint light in darkness. Its seeds are highly radioactive, and ingesting or having one of the barbed seeds lodged in the skin causes rapid, harmful mutations in a creature.

Motive: Feed

Environment (Cataclyst | Magic or Mad Science): Any wilderness environments in groups of two to four

Health: 24

Damage Inflicted: 4 points

Armor: 1

Movement: Immediate

Modifications: Speed defense as level 4 due to size and nature.

Combat: With a movement not unlike a trebuchet, the voot flings its pulsing fruit at a character within long range, and the projectile explodes in an immediate range on impact. In addition to dealing damage, the bursting fruit releases seeds that may become embedded in the target's skin, requiring a Might defense roll. On a failure, the victim gains a randomly determined harmful mutation. A PC can gain only one such mutation per day regardless of how many times she is struck by a voot's fruit. The mutation stays with the character for as long as she remains in Cataclyst.

In close combat, a voot lashes out with its branches.

As plants, voots are combustible and take double damage from fire or forms of energy (such as electricity) that can start fires.

Interaction: Although sentient, voots are not very clever, and the extent of their cunning is to hold still so they look like ordinary plants. Voots regard other creatures as food and lack the means to communicate even if they were so inclined.

Use: A group of mutants regards an infestation of voots as divine emissaries that have come to bestow the blessings of mutation. The mutants sacrifice living creatures to the voots so they can safely harvest their fruit. PCs who run afoul of the mutants might find themselves offered up to the monstrous plants.

Harmful mutation, page 240

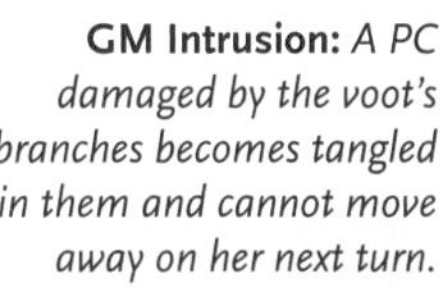

GM Intrusion: *A PC damaged by the voot's branches becomes tangled in them and cannot move away on her next turn.*

GM Intrusion: *A PC that gains a harmful mutation also gains a second harmful mutation. The second mutation lasts for only one hour.*

WARBOT 6 (18)

In the Graveyard of the Machine God, those who plumbed too deeply into the circuit tunnels have discovered still-functioning units that once defended the silicone deity, not unlike antibodies. These units, which are vaguely humanoid and stand about 8 feet (2 m) tall, have been designated as "warbots," and they attack sacrosanct and razor-droid alike, as well as any other intruder (which is pretty much anything).

Motive: Crush. Kill. Destroy.

Environment (Graveyard of the Machine God | Mad Science): Anywhere

Health: 30

Damage Inflicted: 8 points

Armor: 4

Movement: Short

Modifications: Attacks as level 7.

Combat: Warbots attack intruders on sight and fight until destroyed. They are incredibly strong and have an array of weapons and defensive capabilities. Each possesses a rapid-fire, high-energy weapon built into its arm that can attack up to three targets next to each other within long range as a single action. Their armor protects them from ambient damage such as from fire, cold, or falling. When damaged, they regenerate 1 point of health each round while their health is above 0.

Further, each warbot has one additional capability:

d6	Ability
1	Emit poison gas that inflicts 5 points of damage to organic beings in immediate range.
2	Project grenades up to a long distance that detonate in an immediate radius, inflicting 5 points of damage.
3	Fire a beam that stuns an organic being for one round, during which it cannot take actions.
4	Emit a field that disrupts machines; technological devices and machine creatures in immediate range cannot function for one round.
5	Fire a piercing projectile that inflicts 6 points of damage that ignores physical armor (but not necessarily other Armor) up to long range.
6	Spray a corrosive that inflicts 5 points of damage to everything in immediate range.

Warbots can easily be used as destructive killer robots in any technological recursion under the sway of the law of Mad Science.

GM Intrusion: *The warbot's self-repair protocols go into overtime and restore up to 15 points of health in one round.*

Interaction: Warbots don't communicate. It's impossible to interact with them in any fashion other than combat.

Use: Warbots make for a terrifying encounter. Even the most powerful characters should flee in the face of a group of these killers.

Size Comparison

WENDIGO 5 (15)

The gods of Thunder Plains forbid the eating of human flesh. Violators of this taboo face a terrible curse, one that strips them of their humanity and turns them into terrifying monsters filled with an unnatural craving to eat their former kin. Driven to the recursion's hinterlands, they hibernate until winter begins to tighten its grip. With the first snows come the wendigos, and they prowl the darkest hours in search of people to snatch and devour.

The curse that transforms a person into a wendigo destroys much of his humanity, leaving behind a skeletal body, bones pressing against taut skin, and eyes sunken into skull-like visages, flicking back and forth for any signs of life. With gnarled fingers ending in long claws and mouths filled with sharp black teeth, the wendigos have everything they need to pull apart their victims and stuff their greedy maws with raw flesh.

Motive: Hungers for flesh

Environment (Thunder Plains | Magic): Solitary hunters, wendigos drift like ghosts through the snow-covered plains.

Health: 20

Damage Inflicted: 5 points

Movement: Short

Modifications: All tasks related to intimidation and perception as level 7.

Combat: A reek of decay and death betrays a wendigo's approach. At first, the stench is nothing more than a malodorous presence, but as the wendigo draws nearer, the smell becomes overpowering. Any foe within a short distance of a wendigo must make a Might defense roll or become sickened. The difficulty of an affected victim's tasks is increased by one step. The victim can use an action to repeat the roll and shake off the effects of the stench on a success.

A wendigo attacks foes with its teeth or claws. A foe who takes damage must make a Might defense roll or suffer as the wendigo tears free a gobbet of flesh. The bleeding wound inflicts 1 point of ambient damage each round until the target uses an action to stanch the wound.

Interaction: A wendigo gripped by unnatural hunger thinks about nothing else. After the creature feeds, it becomes lucid for a while—usually no more than a few hours—before the hunger pangs return. During its lucid period, it may regret what it's become, look for those it left behind, or take some other similarly motivated action.

Use: A tribe in Thunder Plains makes a regular offering of flesh to a local wendigo to protect their people. Tribe members prefer to use outsiders as the offerings, and the PCs seem ideally suited to keep the monster at bay.

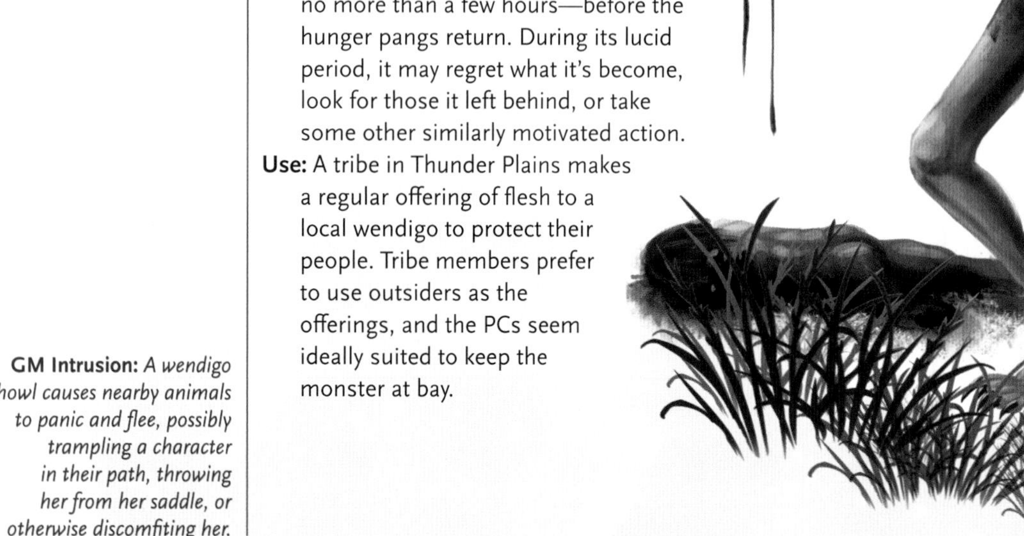

The nature of the curse that transforms a person into a wendigo also sometimes severs the wendigo's connection to Thunder Plains. More than many other creatures of Magic, wendigos seem to pop up in recursions where they are not part of the original context.

GM Intrusion: *A wendigo howl causes nearby animals to panic and flee, possibly trampling a character in their path, throwing her from her saddle, or otherwise discomfiting her.*

WEREWOLF 4 (12)

The curse of lycanthropy begins as nightmares about being chased or, somehow more terrifying, chasing someone else. As the dreams grow more fierce and each night's sleep provides less rest, the victim begins to wonder about the bloodstains on her clothing, the strange claw marks in her home, and eventually, the mutilated bodies she finds buried in her backyard.

When not transformed, many who suffer the curse seem like completely normal people, if emotionally traumatized by the fact that most of their friends and family have been brutally slaughtered over the preceding months. Some few, however, realize the truth of their condition, and depending on their natures, they either kill themselves before their next transformation or learn to revel in the butchery.

Motive: Slaughter when transformed; searching for answers when human

Environment (Magic or Mad Science): Anywhere dark, usually alone but sometimes as part of a small pack of two to five

Health: 24

Damage Inflicted: 5 points

Movement: Short; long when in wolf form

Modifications: Attacks as level 6 when half lupine; Speed defense as level 6 when full lupine; perception as level 7 when half and full lupine.

Combat: In normal human form, a werewolf has no natural attacks, though one may use a weapon appropriate to the recursion it inhabits. It also lacks the abilities described below; its only power is to transform into a half-lupine form or full lupine form, which takes 1d6 agonizing rounds. A handful of werewolves can control their transformation, but most change at night in response to moon-related cues.

Half Lupine: A half-lupine werewolf is part humanoid and part wolf, but completely terrifying. It attacks with its claws.

Full Lupine: A full lupine werewolf is a particularly large and vicious-looking wolf. It normally bites foes and deals 2 additional points of damage on a hit (7 points total), but can also use its claws.

Half and Full Lupine: Half-lupine and full lupine werewolves both enjoy enhanced senses and an automatic regenerative ability that restores 2 points of health per round while their health is above 0. However, a werewolf that takes damage from a silver weapon or bullet stops regenerating for several minutes.

Interaction: In human form, werewolves have the goals and aspirations of normal people, and they often don't recall what they did while transformed or even realize that they suffer the curse of lycanthropy. In half- or full lupine form, there's no negotiating with one.

Use: Some recursions allow for the possibility of terrifying werewolf encounters under a full moon (or moons).

SIZE COMPARISON

The recursion known as Gloaming is home to many werewolves.

Favorite methods for curing a werewolf include medicine (wolfsbane), surgery, or exorcism. Many "cures" are effective only because they kill the werewolf in human form before she's able to transform again.

GM Intrusion: *A PC who descends one step on the damage track due to damage inflicted by a werewolf must succeed on a Might defense roll or be afflicted with the curse of lycanthropy.*

SIZE COMPARISON

WHITE APE 6 (18)

The rank smell of wild animal precedes the 10-foot (3 m) tall white ape. The creature's shaggy fur is usually stained red with blood and gore, especially around the mouth and clawed hands.

White apes are beasts of rage and fury. Depending on where they are encountered, they might be descended from genetic manipulations gone awry, natural creatures of a recursion's jungle wilds, or a devolved (or ancestral) species in Old Mars. In all cases, white apes are usually found among ruins, "ghosts" haunting the shattered dreams of a lost civilization.

"A few tons of snow-colored hominid tried to bite my head off yesterday. I think it was a yeti!"
—Arlo Coulton

Motive: Defense, hungers for flesh

Environment (Magic or Mad Science): Anywhere in remote ruins, either alone or in bands of three to five

Health: 33

Damage Inflicted: 6 points

Movement: Short; long when swinging from vines

Modifications: Speed defense as level 5 due to size; ability to see through tricks as level 3.

Combat: A white ape can make two attacks as one action. If both attacks hit the same target, the ape also tries to bite the target's throat out on the same action (which requires another Speed defense roll to avoid). If the ape succeeds, the victim takes damage and begins to bleed at a rate of 4 points of damage each round. The bleeding can be suppressed by spending an action wrapping the neck securely in bandages. The bleeding stops permanently after the victim regains 6 or more points to a stat Pool (with a recovery roll or other healing method) or if he is completely healed of all damage.

Interaction: White apes have the intelligence of cunning hominid predators. They communicate with each other using grunts, roars, and crude sign language. A character who studies this interaction long enough to learn it could attempt to negotiate with a white ape before it tears his arms off.

Use: Bands of white apes prefer to hunt in dense jungle environments, tumbled ruins, and other places that impede prey that can't swing in and out on vines or shredded data cables. Alternatively, a lone white ape may catch the scent of one of the characters and spend as much time as necessary tracking that PC until it finally attacks.

Loot: Individual white apes don't carry loot, but they live in the ruins of once-great civilizations, so a white ape lair reliably includes 1d6 cyphers and an artifact, in addition to the possessions of previous prey.

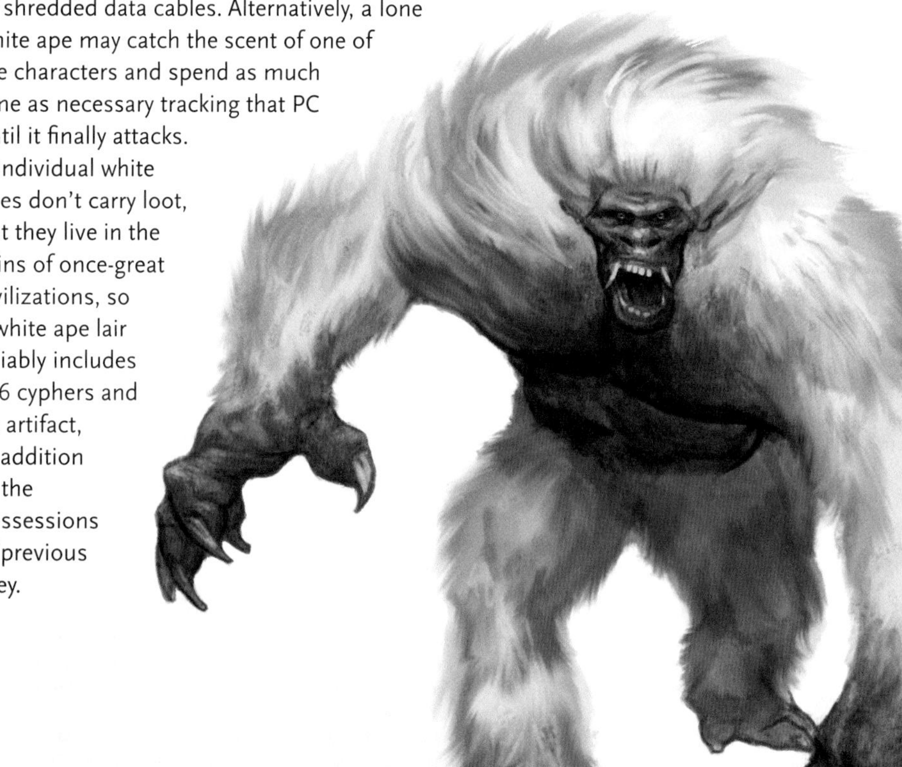

Old Mars, page 253

Some white apes have four arms instead of two; these can make one additional attack each turn on their action.

Every so often, a dark-furred ape is born from the whites. Such an ape grows larger than normal and tends to rise to alpha status among its band.

GM Intrusion: *A white ape decides it likes the character, and on a successful attack, it grabs him and swings away instead of dealing damage. Escape requires a successful Might-based task.*

WITCH 5 (15)

She studied the old ways at the dark of the moon. She heard the shuffle of unnamed things through the darkling forest, watched the convection of the bubbles rise in the cauldron, and attended to the mumbled instructions of withered crones and crumbling messages traced on dead leaves. Then one midnight, it all came together, and a witch was born.

Most witches are warped by the power they channel, both mentally and physically, but they can hide such transformations beneath layers of illusion.

Motive: Domination of others, knowledge

Environment (Magic): Almost anywhere, usually alone, but sometimes as part of a coven of three to nine witches

Health: 21

Damage Inflicted: 5 points

Movement: Short; long when flying (on a broomstick)

Modifications: Deception and disguise as level 7; Speed defense as level 6 due to familiar; knowledge of forests and dark secrets as level 6.

Combat: When attacked, a witch relies on the aid of her familiar to improve her Speed defense. The familiar could be a large black cat, an owl, a big snake, or some other creature. Killing a witch's familiar is one way to ensure that she never forgives her foe or grants mercy.

A witch can use her ritual blade to attack a creature in immediate range, but she'd much rather use curses, including the ones described below. A witch can't use the same curse more than once every other round.

Shrivel: A victim within long range and up to two creatures next to the victim must succeed on a Might defense roll or take 3 points of Speed damage (ignores Armor). In each subsequent round, a victim who failed the previous roll must make another Might defense roll with the same outcome on failure.

Charm: A victim within short range who fails an Intellect defense roll becomes the witch's slave. He turns on his allies or takes some other action described by his new master. The curse lasts for one minute, or until the victim succeeds on an Intellect defense roll; each time he fails a roll, the difficulty of the next roll increases by one step.

Hexbolt: A victim within long range is attacked with fire, cold, or psychic bolts, as the witch chooses. Psychic bolts deal 3 points of Intellect damage (ignores Armor).

Vitality: The witch regains 11 points of health and gains +3 to Armor for one minute. Multiple uses don't further improve her Armor.

Interaction: Most witches are deceptive and conniving, though a few work against the stereotype. All witches are willing to negotiate, though the devious ones usually do so in bad faith.

Use: The PCs enter a recursion called Halloween and see witches flying up in the sky.

Loot: A witch usually has an artifact or two on her person, possibly including a flying broom (which has a depletion roll of 1–2 in d20).

SIZE COMPARISON

Familiar: *level 3; health 9; Armor 1*

Witches are often female, but males take up the craft as well. A male witch is no less foreboding or dangerous, but given that the tradition was developed by women, most witches consider males to be lesser practitioners.

GM Intrusion: *After a PC succeeds on a defense roll against one of the witch's ongoing curse effects, she immediately tosses a hexbolt at him. If the PC is hit, the ongoing curse effect also continues.*

WRATH LORD 5 (15)

Spirit of wrath, page 292

A wrath lord chooses a new name to go with its chosen task and forgets the name it had as a living being.

A wrath lord usually requires two physical objects to anchor it to the world: one piece of clothing or another garment that helps give the creature shape, and an amulet, hood, hat, crown, or other charm that provides clarity of mind.

Spirits who do not become bodiless spirits of rage and loss called wraths (or spirits of wrath) are rare. These few wrath lords hold onto the sense of who and what they were before dying and may adopt a specific goal, task, or duty to occupy themselves. Often that undertaking is as a guardian of a tomb, shrine, library, treasury, or similar location, but sometimes wrath lords choose less isolating tasks.

Motive: Research, guardianship, or other ongoing task

Environment (Ardeyn | Magic): Almost anywhere

Health: 15

Damage Inflicted: 5 points

Armor: 1

Movement: Short when flying

Combat: A wrath lord can attack with its touch, which rots flesh and drains life. Its preferred tactic is to throw back its hood and fix its death gaze on foes within short range and within immediate range of each other. Targets who see this flaring spirit light from the wrath lord's gaping mouth and eyes must succeed on an Intellect defense roll or suffer 5 points of life-draining damage that ignores Armor. The wrath lord can make this attack once every other round. (If a PC averts his eyes from the wrath lord, the difficulty of Intellect defense rolls to avoid the death gaze is reduced by two steps, but the difficulty of all attack and other defense tasks associated with the wrath lord is increased by two steps.)

A wrath lord can become fully insubstantial, including its physical garment and any other possessions. After it does so, it can't change state again until its next turn. While insubstantial, it can't affect or be affected by anything (except for spiritslaying weapons and attacks), and it can't use its death gaze. It can pass through solid matter without hindrance, though many magic wards can keep it at bay. While a wrath lord remains partly insubstantial (its normal state), it can affect and be affected by others normally.

If a wrath lord is destroyed, it spontaneously regenerates within six to twelve hours unless all the physical objects it uses to give itself shape and clarity of mind are found and destroyed (usually a garment it wears, plus an object it has hidden elsewhere).

Interaction: Wrath lords speak in sepulchral voices, and they might negotiate, but one will never agree to forsake any part of its chosen undertaking.

Use: The PCs are approached by a wrath lord whose special undertaking is "exploration" and asked to find a relic in the Chaosphere.

Loot: Most wrath lords have a cypher or two, and possibly an artifact.

GM Intrusion: *The wrath lord unleashes six spirits of wrath from its cloak.*

ZOMBIE

Humans transformed into aggressive, hard-to-kill serial killers with no memory of their former existence are called zombies. Depending on a zombie's recursion of origin, the reason for its transformation varies and might be an undead curse, a psychic possession, an AI meatware overwrite, a viral infection, a drug overdose, or something else. Regardless of how the transformation happened, the result is much the same on every world where zombies roam: a creature whose humanity has been burned out and replaced with unquenchable hunger.

ZOMBIE 3 (9)

Zombies aren't intelligent, but enough of them together sometimes exhibit emergent behavior, just as ants can coordinate activities across a colony. Thus, zombies alone or in small groups aren't an overwhelming threat for someone who has a baseball bat or can get away. But it's never wise to laugh off a zombie horde.

Motive: Hunger (for flesh, cerebrospinal fluid, certain human hormones, and so on)

Environment (Magic, Mad Science, or Psionics): Almost anywhere, in groups of five or six, or in hordes of tens to hundreds

Health: 12

Damage Inflicted: 3 points

Movement: Immediate

Modifications: Speed defense as level 2.

Combat: Zombies never turn away from a conflict. They fight on, no matter the odds, usually attacking by biting, but sometimes by tearing with hands made into claws by the erosion of skin over their finger bones.

When zombies attack in groups of five to seven individuals, they can make a single attack roll against one target as one level 5 creature, inflicting 5 points of damage.

Zombies are hard to finish off. If an attack would reduce a zombie's health to 0, it does so only if the number rolled in the attack was an even number; otherwise, the zombie is reduced to 1 point of health instead. This might result in a dismembered, gruesomely damaged zombie that is still moving.

Zombies can see in the dark at short range.

"Fresh" zombies are vulnerable to electricity. The first time a zombie takes 5 or more points of damage from an electrical attack, it falls limp and unmoving. Assuming nothing interferes with the process, the zombie arises minutes or hours later without the vulnerability.

Some zombies have additional qualities related to how they were created and how likely they are to spread their condition. See Zombie Special Qualities on page 147.

Interaction: Zombies groan when they see something that looks tasty. They do not reason, cannot speak, and never stop pursuing something they've identified as a potential meal, unless something else edible comes closer.

Use: The characters are asked to clear out the basement of a mad scientist, necromancer, or psychic surgeon, or possibly an old military depot on Earth. The appearance of zombies probably comes as an unpleasant surprise.

GM Intrusion: *Even after the character kills the zombie, it doesn't die. In fact, treat the zombie as if it had 12 more points of health.*

ZOMBIE

ZOMBIE REACHER 4 (12)

A zombie reacher can control its limbs even if those limbs are detached and scattered. Reachers can be created intentionally or can spontaneously generate when a normal zombie's limbs are severed and the curse or psychic power of animation overcomes the setback.

Zombie reachers are somewhat intelligent, at least when compared to baseline zombies, and have the patience to lie in wait to ambush potential prey.

Motive: Hunger (for flesh, cerebrospinal fluid, certain human hormones, and so on)

Environment (Mad Science, Magic, or Psionics): Almost anywhere, usually alone or in pairs

Health: 15

Damage Inflicted: 4 points

Movement: Short

Modifications: Speed defense as level 3.

Combat: Though a reacher can bite or claw a victim like a regular zombie, its preferred attack is a long-range "grab" with its telekinetically animate hands. A victim takes damage from each successful attack and, worse, finds that the hand or hands have clamped on tight.

A clamped hand doesn't restrict the victim in any way, but if he doesn't remove it before the reacher's next turn (requiring a Might-based roll to pry it loose, or dealing it 6 points of damage), he automatically takes damage and must succeed on a Might defense roll or be dragged or lifted to the zombie reacher's location, which could be on a roof, across a chasm, or in another location where allies might find it difficult to follow. A zombie reacher whose hands are occupied or destroyed can still bite.

If an attack would reduce the zombie reacher's health to 0, it does so only if the number rolled in the attack was an even number; otherwise, the zombie is reduced to 1 point of health instead.

Zombie reachers can see in the dark at long range.

Some reachers have additional qualities related to how they were created and how likely they are to spread their condition. See Zombie Special Qualities on page 147.

Interaction: Zombie reachers have the intelligence of predatory animals. Sometimes, they're caught and conditioned by necromancers to serve as (somewhat unreliable) guards.

Use: The withered hand in the box is a family curiosity, always knocking about and grabbing at whoever opens the lid. But it's connected to a zombie reacher that has been tracking down its lost hand for a generation.

GM Intrusion: *The character is attacked by a zombie reacher that is much farther than long range away, possibly even up to a mile.*

ZOMBIE NIGHTSTORMER 5 (15)

A zombie nightstormer can manipulate the energy animating it (whether anti-life curse, electromagnetic, psychic, or something else) to such a degree that the zombie can extend the field beyond itself to perform incredible feats of offense, defense, and mobility (including the ability to fly).

Zombie nightstormers are intelligent and devious, and given to pranks of the sort that kill. Sometimes the vicious laughter of a nightstormer that has just caught a victim echoes through the night for miles.

Motive: Sadistic amusement, hunger (for flesh, cerebrospinal fluid, certain human hormones, and so on)

Environment (Mad Science, Magic, or Psionics): Almost anywhere, usually alone or in pairs

Health: 15

Damage Inflicted: 5 points

Armor: 3

Movement: Immediate; long when flying

Modifications: Perception as level 6.

Combat: The nightstormer attacks with a force-reinforced claw that ignores Armor (except for Armor granted by force effects). The nightstormer prefers "strafing" attacks in which it moves up to short range, makes a claw attack, and then moves up to short range again as a single action. Whenever a nightstormer takes 3 or more points of damage from a single attack, it loses its strafing ability for one round.

GM Intrusion: *If the character makes a melee attack against a strafing nightstormer and misses, her weapon is briefly caught in the creature's force field, which yanks it from her hand and flings it a short distance away.*

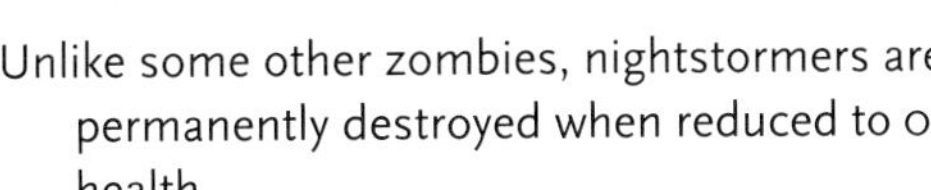

Unlike some other zombies, nightstormers are permanently destroyed when reduced to 0 health.

Nightstormers can see in the dark at any range.

Some zombie nightstormers have additional qualities related to how they were created and how likely they are to spread their condition. See Zombie Special Qualities.

Interaction: Zombie nightstormers can speak, but usually do so only to fool a victim into walking into a deadly trap.

Use: Someone or something is scrawling graffiti on hard-to-reach city spires and tall monuments. The PCs hear that the city is looking for someone to put a stop to the crime spree.

CROWNED SHAMBLER 6 (18)

Not much is known about crowned shamblers because they're mostly legend. These types of zombies are rarely seen, and when one appears, few people survive to tell about it. Whatever their origin, crowned shamblers have the unholy power to command the allegiance of lesser zombies and other creatures touched by death.

Motive: Rule the deathless

Environment (Magic or Psionics): Almost anywhere, alone or commanding groups of lesser zombies and related creatures

Health: 18

Damage Inflicted: 6 points

Movement: Short

Modifications: All tasks related to deception and deathless lore as level 7.

Combat: A crowned shambler can attack a foe at short range with a piece of bone-tipped viscera that deals damage, and on a secondary failed Might defense roll, the character moves down one step on the damage track. Further, when a crowned shambler is encountered, the GM should roll 1d6 times on the cypher list in the corebook and provide those cyphers to the zombie for use in combat.

Crowned shamblers regenerate 2 points of health per round while their health is above 0. When reduced to 0 health, one minute later they regenerate 1 point of health, putting them back to positive health and restarting their normal regeneration. A blessing, holy water, or complete destruction by acid or burning stops regeneration.

Crowned shamblers can see in the dark at any range.

With a touch, crowned shamblers can take control of lesser zombies and other deathless creatures within short range that are lower level than itself.

Interaction: A crowned shambler is a vicious dictator, but it might be amenable to negotiation if someone has a resource that can't merely be seized.

Use: A small recursion known to the PCs that operated under the law of Magic has gone silent. The next time the PCs visit the place, they find it under the control of a crowned shambler and the population converted to zombies. The shambler wants a way to expand into a new recursion.

ZOMBIE SPECIAL QUALITIES

Some zombie varieties have special additional qualities related to how they were created and how likely they are to spread their condition to others. A zombie can have a special quality regardless of whether it is a baseline zombie or an exalted zombie (meaning a zombie reacher, zombie nightstormer, or crowned shambler).

Infectious Bite: A victim damaged by a zombie's infectious bite must succeed on a Might defense roll or contract a virulent disease (level 8) that rarely goes into remission on its own. Every twenty-four hours after the initial bite, the victim must succeed on another Might defense roll or move one step down the damage track. While the disease is active, normal recovery rolls aren't sufficient to move the victim back up the damage track. If the victim dies while infected or because of the infection, he rises as a zombie 1d6 days later. (Some infections work in hours or even minutes instead of days, though those kinds never appear in recursions that operate under the law of Standard Physics.)

Singularitar Shell: In the recursion of Singularitan, human bodies have become living shells for the distributed intelligence calling itself Singularitar. The original minds have been burned out, and a copy of Singularitar has been installed in the meat as wetware. The copies are imperfect but intelligent enough to spread themselves, usually by whispering a coded phrase into a victim's ear or by looking the victim in the eye. The "transfer and upload" takes about one minute to complete. If the process is undisturbed (and a victim fails an Intellect defense roll), this creates a new Singularitar zombie.

Quickened: A zombie that "rises" from a quickened human (or one born of a spiraler—a normal person addicted to spiral dust) resists attacks gained from focus abilities, revisions, twists, and moves as a level 5 creature. A quickened zombie's eyes (or empty sockets) glow with purplish fire. Quickened zombies can operate under the law of Standard Physics.

Singularitan, page 251

Spiraler, page 156

Cypher list, page 312

GM Intrusion: *The character's attack on the shambler cuts off a piece of clawed viscera. The piece remains animate like a snake, attacking her as a level 4 creature, but its attacks don't move her down the damage track.*

CHARACTERS

The Archcoder, page 153

Colin Stokes, warrior mage, page 154

Doctor Ceratops, page 155

Merlin, page 156

Nimrod the Hunter, page 157

The Oracle, page 158

Sasha the Blade, page 159

This section provides basic stats for a few NPC types: the elite operative, elite soldier, necromancer, Neon Roller, and noble knight.

The elite operative and soldier are designed to be applicable for all three main settings of The Strange (Ardeyn, Earth, and Ruk) and contain customization notes specific to a given recursion. They are often described as being armed with weapons appropriate to the recursion where they're encountered. Typically, that means items like spears, shamshirs, and crossbows in Ardeyn; nightsticks and small-caliber guns on Earth; and spine pistols, spears, and spore pods in Ruk. The GM should feel free to vary the mix depending on the NPC, as appropriate.

On the other hand, necromancer and noble knight NPCs might be found in a variety of recursions operating under the law of Magic, while Neon Rollers are usually found only in the recursion of Atom Nocturne (where they are prolific).

In addition to the NPCs listed in this chapter, there are several people of renown listed in the next section: the Archcoder; Colin Stokes, the Warrior Mage; Doctor Ceratops; Merlin; Nimrod the Hunter; the Oracle (of Ardeyn); and Sasha the Blade.

ELITE OPERATIVE 7 (21)

Some agents who achieve the pinnacle of excellence were created by fictional leakage from a variety of books and movies about super spies and secret agents without compare.

Field Officer (Earth): These super spies are supposedly recruited from various recursions where the officer ordered his martinis shaken, not stirred.

Plenipotentiary (Ardeyn): When royalty goes undercover in Ardeyn, the stakes are never higher.

Faction Arbitrator (Ruk): When a faction is done taking half measures, it secures an arbitrator to fix the problem, whatever the cost.

Motive: Accomplish the goals of the employer

Health: 30
Damage Inflicted: 7 points
Armor: 2
Movement: Short; long when using a mechanism or spell to fly
Modifications: Tasks related to deception and knowledge of two or three different recursions as level 8.
Combat: Elite operatives can attack twice as one action using both melee and ranged weapons appropriate to their recursion. They also carry up to three cyphers useful for escaping, monitoring, attacking, or defending, and an artifact useful either in combat or for accomplishing a particular task related to their mission.
Interaction: The definition of cool, an elite operative is charming whether under fire, dragon breath, or radioactive assault.
Use: PCs may find themselves competing with a "friendly" agency more than a few times, and when the stakes are highest, they discover the face of that agency is an elite operative.
Loot: Elite operatives typically have 2d20 units of appropriate currency, one to three cyphers, possibly an artifact, and tools useful for spying.

GM Intrusion: *The elite operative twists around with great speed and agility and takes a second action right after the first.*

ELITE SOLDIER 5 (15)

Elite soldiers begin as talented and motivated individuals trained to the limit of their ability to improve. These individuals are subsequently subjected to so many life-or-death missions that they'd be considered veterans in any other unit.

Special Forces (Earth): Whether it's the Navy SEALs, Shayetet 13, or SAS, special forces are a breed apart thanks to their limited numbers, their extreme training in a variety of spheres, and their enviable physical capabilities.

Peacemaker Champion (Ardeyn): In addition to the three main contingents of peacemakers, there are the champions. Champions have graduated from an intense no-holds-barred combat school conducted with the express goal of breaking vertebrae, fingers, and ribs, where they learn not to ignore pain but to relish it.

Venom Elect (Ruk): Sometimes, premium ingredients and fresh neuronal imprinting pay off, and the extra bits poured into the process produce a venom trooper so far above its compatriots that there's little comparison between them.

On Earth, French Naval Commandos call themselves "berets verts" (green berets). Different units are specialized in different tasks, including combat diving, close-quarters sea combat, and expertise with sniping and missile launchers.

Motive: Accomplish specific military missions
Health: 27
Damage Inflicted: 5 points
Armor: 2
Movement: Short
Modifications: Perception as level 6; resistance to intimidation as level 7.
Combat: Elite soldiers are armed with weapons appropriate to their recursion and are so skilled that they can attack with those weapons twice as a single action. In addition, members of special forces adapt their tactics to the situation at hand, never underestimate their opponents, and are hard to fool, evade, or intimidate.

Most elite soldiers carry a kit that contains a variety of tools useful in many situations, and a squad of elite soldiers likely has, between them, enough tools and know-how to engineer a solution to nearly any challenge they might come across in the field.

Interaction: Elite soldiers are usually polite when dealing with anyone unrelated to their mission so as not to call attention to themselves. Although it would be virtually impossible to convince elite soldiers to abandon their mission, they are trained to look for alternate routes to success. If a PC can make a convincing argument why helping her would advance the elite soldier's mission, she might make a short-term ally.
Use: Elite soldiers are rarely encountered, unless the characters regularly rub shoulders with those in society powerful enough to order such squads about. To the PCs, elite soldiers can be obstacles, allies, or both, but they are rarely a way for the characters to hand off responsibility for accomplishing a hard task.
Loot: Every elite soldier carries weapons, medium armor, and useful tools (for sapping, electronics work, bioinfiltration—whatever's appropriate to the recursion in which the soldier appears).

GM Intrusion: *An elite soldier produces a missile launcher (or the recursion equivalent) and fires at the character. The character and all creatures within immediate range must succeed on a Speed defense roll or take normal damage and move down one step on the damage track. Even on a successful roll, the character still takes 5 points of damage, though other creatures in immediate range that succeed on their rolls are fine.*

NECROMANCER 5 (15)

> **"The dead are like the living, and only care about themselves."**
> —Nashwa, a necromancer of Ardeyn

The ability to influence, command, and call up the dead is an impressive power, given how many more people are dead than living. Since the only thing separating a living person from a dead one is a well-aimed knife or death spell, the number of dead always rises. The potential zenith of necromancer power is measured by the span of history, which reaches back thousands of years (or far longer) within the context of most recursions.

Environment (Magic): In places where dead are interred, usually with some number of undead servitors

Health: 15

Damage Inflicted: 5 points

Armor: 1

Movement: Short

Modifications: Speed defense as level 6 due to shroud of undead protective spirits.

Combat: Necromancers who aren't already accompanied by undead spirits or shambling, spirit-inhabited corpses under their command can call up a spirit as an action. A necromancer can command up to five spirits (or newly allied undead, as described below) at a time.

Spirit: *level 3; health 9; flesh-decaying touch that inflicts 3 points of damage*

Necromancers who figure out the trick of commanding hundreds or thousands of undead use that ability, almost without fail, to build undead armies for campaigns of conquest.

In addition, necromancers can attempt to take command of a spirit or undead creature within short range. They automatically succeed against an unaligned undead target of level 4 or less. If a targeted spirit is already allied with or in service to a character, the PC must succeed on an Intellect defense roll or lose control of the spirit to the necromancer's will for one minute.

Necromancers can blast a foe within long range with the cold of the grave or flesh-decaying magic. More worryingly, a necromancer can cast a death spell on a foe within short range once every minute; the victim must succeed on a Might defense roll or move down one step on the damage track. This ability could be an innate power or come from an artifact.

Interaction: Necromancers are feared for their nonchalant attitudes toward life, especially the life of normal people. They will negotiate but usually don't have the capacity to care about another person's well-being; they're sociopathic.

Use: A character has died in a Magic recursion with an afterlife, and his allies must find a necromancer to help retrieve his spirit. Of course, the necromancer wants something in return for her aid—perhaps a relic pilfered from whatever underworld or hell the dead character is imprisoned within.

Loot: Necromancers have 1d20 × 10 monetary units appropriate to the recursion, a cypher, and possibly an artifact.

GM Intrusion: *A bony hand erupts from the ground at the character's feet. On a failed Speed defense roll, he is held in place until he can succeed on a Might-based task to escape. Each round the character fails to escape, the hand squeezes him for 3 points of damage.*

NEON ROLLER 3 (9)

Size Comparison

Many of Atom Nocturne's people gather into cliques, gangs united by common attitudes, psionic ability, or shared interest. The Neon Rollers have the distinction of being one of the most notorious gangs in the city. Outsiders, freaks, castoffs, and unhinged, they thrive on spreading fear and terror. They haunt the city streets. They prey on the weak and isolated. And they use their psychic talents as weapons to intensify their strikes with crowbar, bat, and chain. They are thieves and bullies, and most people consider them a menace.

Adding to their unsavory character is their tendency to join forces with powerful Fallen. They seek out these dangerous individuals and offer their services for as long as the Fallen can afford them. The Rollers guard their benefactor's sanctum and protect their employer from capture.

As their name suggests, Neon Rollers wear bright colors in neon green, blue, pink, and orange. They dye their hair to match and grease it so that it stands up in mohawks and horns.

On missions, the Rollers put on body armor made from lightweight synthetic materials that shine with luminescent circuitry. Their helmets have stylized visors that look like the faces of grinning children, and the Rollers always wear roller skates on their feet.

Atom Nocturne, page 234

Fallen, page 235

Motive: Cause trouble

Environment (Atom Nocturne | Psionics): Anywhere in the recursion in groups of six to ten

Health: 9

Damage Inflicted: 4 points

Armor: 1

Movement: Short

Modifications: All tasks related to balancing as level 2 due to roller skates; Speed defense as level 4 due to quickness.

Combat: Neon Rollers carry a wide range of weapons: bats with nails hammered into the end, lengths of chain, knives, or whatever else they can get their hands on.

Five Neon Rollers can combine their attacks against one target and make one attack roll as a level 5 creature, inflicting 8 points of damage.

When an attack misses a Neon Roller, it can immediately move a short distance as it skates away.

For all their posturing and bravado, surviving Neon Rollers flee if more than half of their numbers fall in a fight.

Interaction: Neon Rollers are tough. Little better than thugs, they never waste an opportunity to boast about their strength, their power, and the people whose "asses got kicked." PCs who appeal to their sense of self-importance might be able to avert a violent encounter.

Use: After entering service with a powerful Fallen, the Neon Rollers go on a crime spree in Atom Nocturne.

Loot: Neon Rollers have rad armor and roller skates that are quite functional.

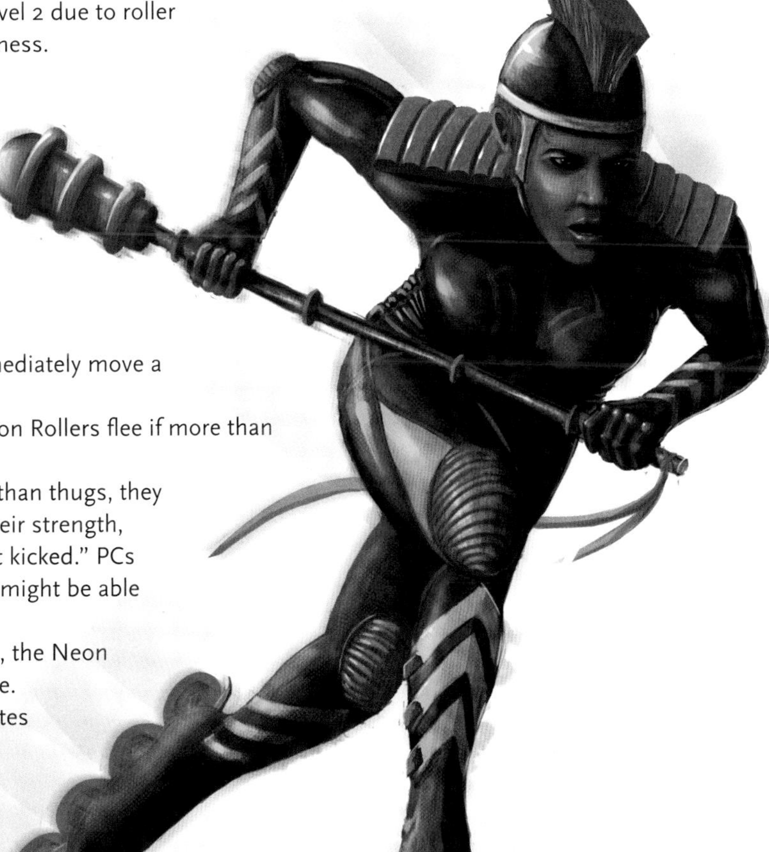

GM Intrusion: *A Neon Roller that damages a character hooks one of the PC's legs and sends him tumbling to the ground.*

NOBLE KNIGHT 7 (21)

Whether noble or ignoble, some knights achieve an amazing mastery over weapons, combat, and courtly graces, eclipsing lesser warriors and champions. Such mastery is probably nothing less than magical, occurring when the narrative of a recursion seeded by fictional leakage matches up with a particular knight's story or quest. That said, the quests of some noble knights can lead them on such a wild chase that they break free of the bonds of their native recursions. These noble knights can extend their quest through many recursions in the Shoals of Earth and even into the Chaosphere.

One of the more famous quests is the ongoing, ever-widening search for the Holy Grail. Another is for the questing beast, a creature that, if it hasn't already, will soon learn to break through recursion boundaries.

Questing beast, page 111

Motive: Accomplish noble (or ignoble) deeds

Environment (Magic): Almost anywhere, often alone, sometimes with retainers

Health: 50

Damage Inflicted: 10 points

Armor: 3

Movement: Short

Modifications: All tasks related to heraldic lore and chivalry as level 8; Speed defense as level 8 while holding shield.

Combat: Noble knights are armed with massive weapons they're able to wield in a single hand, which means they can also hold a shield. They are skilled with melee weapons (such as a battleaxe, broadsword, or mace) and inflict lethal damage on a hit.

Noble knights can also rely on a magic artifact or two to aid them, and possibly a noble steed (a level 5 beast able to move a long distance each round). The artifact might be the very weapon a knight wields in combat and could grant her one or more of the following additional abilities.

Regeneration. The noble knight regenerates 2 points of health per round while the weapon is drawn.

Resistance. The noble knight is immune to effects that would influence her mind, charm her, or put her to sleep.

Legendary Strength. The noble knight can call upon the artifact to grant her great strength or fortitude to accomplish a particular physical task (such as breaking down a door, lifting a boulder, or knocking down pillars holding up a structure), which she attempts as if she were level 10.

Interaction: Flowery language and impeccable manners show a knight's noble background. Those who negotiate with one in good faith are likely to come away with something of value. However, sometimes a noble knight is corrupt and betrays trusts.

Use: A noble knight has decided that he must guard a bridge against any who would cross it.

Loot: Noble knights carry weapons, heavy armor, and at least one artifact.

"Lancelot has constantly in mind the Queen, for whose sake he is enduring all this pain and shame." —from Lancelot, or the Knight of the Cart

GM Intrusion: *The character damaged by a noble knight's attack must succeed on a Might defense roll or be knocked off a mount, a bridge, or a cliff or, if nothing suffices, simply knocked to the ground and out of immediate range of the knight.*

PEOPLE OF RENOWN

THE ARCHCODER 10 (30)

The Archcoder is a myth of the dark energy network. As some tell it, she's an alien so old and so familiar with the underlying structure and function of the Chaosphere that she must be one of the Precursors—one who survived the billions of years since the network they built for intergalactic travel was shattered and rendered into the Strange.

When the Archcoder appears, it is sometimes only as a reflection, a hologram, or a spirit. She doesn't speak, but watches. Her humanoid shape, say those who keep her myth alive, shows that she cares enough for the people of Earth and the Shoals to partly adapt to their likeness.

Other times, the Archcoder appears in the flesh in the Strange or a recursion. When this happens, it is usually to retrieve an entropic seed, an artifact of the Strange, or another powerful item or device not native to that recursion or region of the Chaosphere.

Motive: Unpredictable

Environment (the Strange): Almost anywhere

Health: 50

Damage Inflicted: 10 points

Armor: 10

Movement: Long; long when flying

Combat: While in the Strange or in a recursion, the Archcoder can call upon her "root access" to the network and accomplish tasks as if a literal god. If she wishes, she can batter all foes within long range with a blast of energy of her choice, inflicting 10 points of damage on a failed Speed defense roll (and 2 points on a successful one). She can also bend structural elements of a recursion (the landscape or buildings) or the Strange itself (fundament) to her will to cause earthquakes, collapse towers, or crumble massive plates. If she spends a minute or more concentrating, she can create structures and landscape features, or grow fundament out of nothing. She has the same power over creatures without the spark as she has over the landscape—they serve her commands. Creatures with the spark are immune to her influence.

The Archcoder can spend an action to create any anoetic cypher she desires.

All that said, if she were to translate (or use inapposite travel) to Earth or any part of the universe of normal matter, she'd lose most of her abilities and be considered a level 4 creature.

Interaction: The Archcoder doesn't much care for normal creatures; she sees them as mayflies. However, in quickened creatures around the Shoals of Earth, she has found something of a mystery. She may give them a moment of inspection, and possibly use a method of communication similar to telepathy (actually a direct "network" interface) to query them about something called the Aleph component.

Use: A Jane Doe with amnesia is in the local hospital after having been hit by a car. Jane doesn't remember who she is or where she came from, but she has a couple of minor quickened abilities. The Estate sends operatives to quiz her and possibly recruit her. Jane might be a level 4 NPC with an incredible secret, or perhaps even a PC who might one day discover her real potential.

Loot: Six anoetic cyphers.

Aleph component, page 148

GM Intrusion: *The character must succeed on an Intellect defense roll, or one of his cyphers activates in a way that is harmful to him. If it's an offensive cypher, it targets him; if it's a helpful cypher, it targets a foe.*

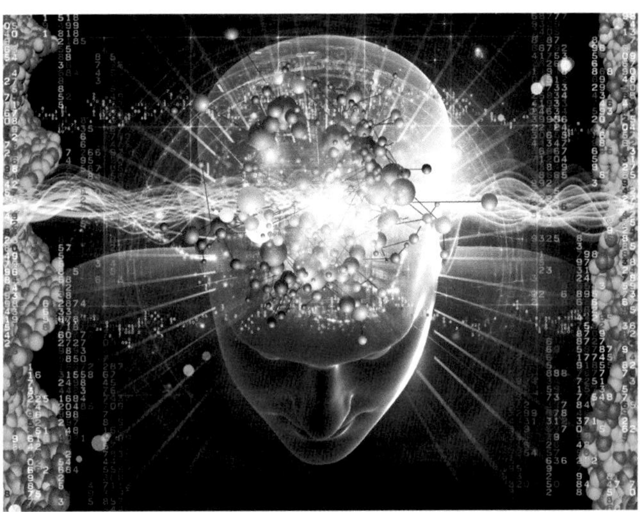

COLIN STOKES, WARRIOR MAGE 6 (18)

At age 12, Stokes fell into a recursion seeded by popular fantasy, featuring elves, dwarves, wizards, and dragons. He was rescued from marauding orcs by a sorceress who took him in and taught him several spells. At age 15, he left to fight in a great conflict between men and orcs. Over the next six years and under the mentorship of legendary warriors, he became an accomplished fighter, with many dead orcs, ogres, and less wholesome creatures to his name.

During the final conflict and faced with certain death, Stokes translated for the second time in his life (back to Earth) and learned his adopted world was a recursion, one of many. Intrigued, Stokes began exploring. Since then, the warrior mage has visited nearly every recursion known to exist, and several no one else knows about. He's also had more adventures than seems likely for a person his age, including run-ins with Sasha the Blade, Nimrod the Hunter, Katherine Manners of the Estate, and Merlin.

Katherine Manners, page 149

Sasha the Blade, page 159

Merlin page 156

Nimrod the Hunter, page 157

GM Intrusion: *Stokes targets the character with a "forgetting" spell (or the contextual equivalent) that requires an Intellect defense roll. On a failure, the PC loses the ability to perceive the warrior mage for one hour, no matter what action Stokes might take.*

Moriarty, page 307

Gwinthang: *deals 8 points of damage; can travel between recursions; depletion 1 in 1d100*

Motive: Exploration and adventure

Environment (Any): Throughout the Shoals of Earth

Health: 18

Damage Inflicted: 8 points

Armor: 2

Movement: Short

Modifications: Knowledge of various recursions as level 7; resists mental attacks as level 8.

Combat: Stokes uses his sword to attack two targets in immediate range as a single action. In addition, he knows several spells (or their equivalent in a Psionics or Mad Science recursion), including the following.

Bolt. A long-range electrical attack against a single foe.

Stun. A long-range stunning attack against a single foe who takes psychic damage and (on a failed Might defense roll) stands utterly still, taking no action for one round.

Banish. A short-range attack that banishes one non-native foe to its home recursion on a failed Intellect defense roll (usable once per minute).

Up and Away. For up to one minute, Stokes becomes invisible (all stealth tasks as level 8) and can fly a long distance each round.

Interaction: Stokes is interested in the next horizon, but he sometimes helps those who need a hand, especially in return for curious items or a bit of companionship on the road.

Use: When PCs need to track down a known persona who travels the recursions (such as Moriarty or Nimrod the Hunter), someone like Stokes would greatly improve their chance of finding their target.

Loot: In addition to his one-handed sword (an artifact called "Gwinthang"), Stokes probably carries a couple of cyphers.

DOCTOR CERATOPS 7 (21)

On one of the handful of so-called "lost world" recursions where dinosaurs and other extinct megafauna yet roam, intelligent dinosaurs rose. One of those had the spark, curiosity, and a latent ability to travel the recursions. After witnessing more than one archaeologist from Earth appear through an inapposite gate to collect living fossils, he who later came to be called Doctor Ceratops followed the visitors home and found himself in a lab filled with freaked-out technicians.

That was fifty years ago. Since then Doctor Ceratops has become something of a celebrity recursor. Even when he translates, his dino-humanoid form doesn't change much from recursion to recursion. But for some reason, nonquickened people ignore his overly large head with its bony plates and horns. Perhaps it's his horn-rimmed glasses, his jaunty hat, or his impeccable sense of fashion.

Motive: Explore recursions and the Strange

Environment (Standard Physics): Any recursion or the Strange

Health: 37

Damage Inflicted: 7 points

Armor: 4

Movement: Short

Modifications: Resists cold attacks as level 4; knowledge of recursions and Strange navigation as level 8.

Combat: Doctor Ceratops can use his horns as a melee weapon. If he spends an action charging prior to a melee attack, the damage he inflicts ignores Armor. But if he has the opportunity, in a fight he prefers to use the many cyphers and devices he's secreted about his person.

Dr. Ceratops specializes in grenade cyphers (and actual grenades). He usually has at least six such items on him at any given time, each of which can be thrown at a point within long range, where it explodes. The kinds of grenades he usually employs are as follows; sometimes he randomly selects one, and other times he chooses the best one for his need.

d6	Ability
1	Inflicts 7 points of shrapnel damage in an immediate radius
2	Glues everything in place in an immediate radius (level 7 polymer)
3	Inflicts 7 points of psychic damage in an immediate radius
4	Sucks creatures in immediate radius through an inapposite gate
5	Puts creatures of level 6 or lower to sleep for one minute
6	Creates a level 7 force bubble protecting/trapping targets in an immediate radius for one minute

Interaction: Doctor Ceratops comes across as an enthusiastic academic, one who has spent most of his life in the field researching the topic he loves. He's usually willing to trade information, but he also enjoys telling people what he's discovered recently.

Use: As the PCs enter an odd new recursion or site within the Strange, they find that Doctor Ceratops has beat them to it and is conducting a study of the location. The doctor may aid the PCs if he senses they are on a similar mission of exploration, but he could hinder the characters if he feels they will disrupt his study.

Loot: Dr. Ceratops has two or three cyphers, some grenades (depending on how many he used), 1d100 + 20 units of currency, and a field kit that includes equipment for exploration and archaeology.

SIZE COMPARISON

GM Intrusion: *The character wakens a bit of dinosaur savagery in Dr. Ceratops, whose tri-horn charge knocks her out of short range, in addition to dealing normal damage.*

MERLIN 8 (24)

As powerful as Merlin is, he is no warrior. He takes any opportunity he finds to escape. Throughout a battle, he will try to convince his opponents to give up the fight and talk out the problem like reasonable people.

Wizard, prophet, seer of possible futures, and witness to the events of the past, Merlin is the son of an incubus and served as the advisor and companion to a famous, legendary king.

Some think he lies trapped by an evil sorceress in a forgotten cave, but that's mere facade. Merlin is as much a trickster as a wizard. His abilities to adopt different guises and see with the eyes of a prophet serve him well. Instead of being trapped, Merlin travels the recursions and the Strange itself, seeking to learn all he can about the true nature of reality.

Motive: Manipulate events for profit, knowledge

Environment (the Strange | Magic): Anywhere

Health: 40

Damage Inflicted: 8 points

Armor: 2

Movement: Short

Modifications: All tasks related to deception, disguise, interaction, and knowledge of arcane lore as level 9.

Combat: Merlin's magic staff is a special artifact that translates with him. When he makes a long-range attack with his staff or strikes someone with it, a spark of energy erupts from the end, inflicting damage to the target and, if Merlin wishes, to all creatures within short range of the target. Targets within immediate range of Merlin when they take damage are thrown out of immediate range.

In addition to his staff, the wizard knows several spells. When Merlin is first encountered, the GM should roll six times on the cypher list in the corebook (rerolling as desired). The result is the spells that Merlin has currently readied. He can use them once each round as an action (not just once, as is normally the case with cyphers). On a different day, Merlin might have the same spells or different ones at hand.

Cypher list, page 312

Merlin regenerates 1 point of health per round while his health is above 0. His magic always grants him some Armor, even when he's sleeping or unconscious.

Interaction: Always interested in what talented individuals might accomplish with a bit of direction, Merlin may offer to accompany the PCs on an expedition and lend advice and wisdom when needed, though his suggestions are usually cryptic and open to interpretation.

Use: The PCs encounter a young man seated on a stump who tells them several true things about who they are and where they came from. The young man is Merlin in disguise.

Loot: Merlin might be convinced to teach a character how to cast a spell. Treat this spell as a cypher in effect (single use, as normal), but one that doesn't count against a character's cypher limit.

GM Intrusion: *Merlin anticipates an attack against him and turns a character's successful attack roll into a failed one, and the PC loses his next action due to confusion.*

POWERFUL WIZARD STATISTICS

If you need the stats for a powerful wizard—perhaps to represent a named character from a different popular franchise, for a recursion you've created by importing your fantasy campaign into The Strange, or merely for a random NPC the characters meet while traveling through a recursion that operates under the law of Magic—you can use Merlin's statistics, given the customizable nature of his spells.

NIMROD THE HUNTER 7 (21)

Size Comparison

The recursions scattered throughout the Shoals of Earth invite exploration and investigation. They represent new worlds, new realities where anything and everything is possible. For Nimrod, these recursions offer a veritable bounty of things to kill.

Nimrod is a lifelong hunter and personally responsible for the extinction of no fewer than nine species in various recursions. He has a reputation for finding things that don't necessarily want to be found, which means he's been contracted by various agencies on Earth for short-term jobs. He usually stays in whatever recursion he's sent to long enough to earn his pay and bag a few creatures on the side.

"They say it's the thrill of the hunt, the anticipation of making the kill that makes the hunter. Not me. I just like killing."
—Nimrod

Nimrod is a big, heavy-set man in his fifties. He has close-cropped grey hair, a nose that was evidently broken at one point and poorly set, and a maze of scars covering his face, neck, arms, and pretty much everywhere on his body. He favors camouflaged clothing and wears combat webbing laden with supplies. When translating to a recursion, he takes the form of some kind of predator, if possible.

Motive: Hunt and kill exotic creatures

Environment (the Strange): Nimrod is usually encountered alone in some recursion's frontier

Health: 30

Damage Inflicted: 8 points

Armor: 2

Movement: Short

Modifications: All tasks related to hunting, perception, stealth, and tracking as level 9; all tasks related to knowledge about the Strange as level 8.

Combat: Nimrod is a walking arsenal. He carries a rifle, two pistols, an assortment of knives, at least one stun gun, and other implements of death, along with enough ammunition that he's not likely to run out. When he translates to recursions of Magic or Mad Science, his arsenal is similarly elaborate, but suited to the local context.

Having explored different recursions during his hunting expeditions, he also keeps several cyphers on hand to help him bring down prey or approach without being detected.

Nimrod is good at what he does and may, in fact, be the best. He displays great patience when on the hunt and is methodical about everything he does, from covering his scent to locating tracks. He's not one to make mistakes, so the unfortunate creatures he sets his sights on killing are usually doomed.

Interaction: Nimrod enjoys sharing stories about the creatures he's hunted and killed. He's oblivious to any offense taken and goes into great detail about what steps he took to bag each beast. Nimrod is not above hunting sapient creatures and feels that hunting humans is one of the greatest challenges of all.

Use: An NPC previously crossed by the PCs might hire Nimrod to eliminate them.

Loot: Nimrod carries 1d6 cyphers.

Nimrod enjoys telling stories about everything but his origin. If someone suggests that he was born of a recursion seeded by Christian stories, he only smiles and shakes his head. However, he marks that person as a future target of his hunt.

GM Intrusion: *Nimrod disappears into the underbrush after making a ranged attack.*

Size Comparison

THE ORACLE 7 (21)

The Oracle has the power of precognition and transformation. When she sings her predictions to petitioners, she appears as a 30-foot (9 m) long serpent. She can also appear as a woman with dark skin, eyes, and hair, with a secretive smile. But when she returns to her home recursion of Ruk, she usually sports her battle chrysalid form, which is a power-armored hybrid between her human and serpent shape.

The Oracle's precognitive power is real, and it somehow transcends the law of whatever recursion she occupies, whether it's Ardeyn, Ruk, or Earth. She has never revealed what her name was before she rose to the office of Oracle in Ardeyn, because she doesn't remember herself. When the power of foreseeing came upon her, the many futures that bubbled behind her eyes were too much, and she lost a lot of her own history before she managed to gain some measure of control over the talent. When she travels, as she does often, she searches for the secrets of her past that her own power refuses to divulge.

Motive: Predict the future, rediscover her own past

Environment (the Strange): Usually in Telenbar in the Green Wilds of Ardeyn, but potentially anywhere

Health: 21

Damage Inflicted: 7 points

Armor: 2 in human form; 3 in Ardeyn serpent form; 4 in Ruk battle chrysalid form

Movement: Short

Modifications: Speed defense as level 8 due to precognition; Ardeyn and Ruk lore as level 8.

The Oracle isn't likely to engage in physical combat unless she feels she has no choice. Although her ability to see forward is by no means infallible, often she can be found only when she wants to be.

Combat: In her serpent form, she can make a bite melee attack. In her battle chrysalid form, she can use a melee weapon or fire a ranged weapon at a target within long range. And at the same time in either of those forms, she can bash a separate foe in melee; if she hits, the foe is entangled in her serpentine coils until it succeeds on a Might-based task to break free. Each round the foe remains entangled, it automatically takes damage on the Oracle's turn.

In any form, including human, the Oracle can look into the future or the past and discern a secret related to a character. If she whispers the secret to the PC, the revelation is so shocking that he must make an Intellect defense roll. On a failure, he suffers 5 points of Intellect damage (ignores Armor); on a success, he still takes 1 point of Intellect damage.

Depending on the recursion she occupies, the Oracle can take different shapes as an action.

Interaction: In nearly any conversation, the Oracle comes across as a little sad and wistful. She normally answers questions about the future only in return for a gift of some sort.

Use: If the PCs are looking for the answer to a puzzle, the secret to getting on the good side of a particular power, or any other esoteric information, the Oracle isn't a bad place to start.

Loot: The Oracle has one or two cyphers and at least one artifact, plus other gear for traveling and adventuring.

GM Intrusion: *The Oracle peers into a character's future and then attacks the PC. The difficulty of defending against the attack is increased by two steps. Regardless of whether the attack hit, if the character is standing near a precipice or another dangerous area, she must succeed on an Intellect defense roll to avoid stepping over the edge or into the area.*

SASHA THE BLADE 6 (18)

Like many children, Sasha left London during World War II to live with a foster family in the country, far from the bomb raids that terrorized the city. The family that took her in was odd and had an unusual manner of speaking. They never revealed where they came from or who they truly were.

One day, Sasha set out to solve the mystery of her foster family. While exploring their sprawling mansion, she found a storeroom filled with many curious things. Of particular note was a gate covered by a drop cloth. She stepped through and found herself in a much wider world.

Sasha grew up in various recursions, living by her wits, skill, and luck. She's a woman of an indeterminate age whose hair is flecked with grey. Trim, muscled, and exuding menace, she has a sarcastic wit and a cocky bravado that some find endearing and others find annoying.

Motive: Adventure

Environment (the Strange): Anywhere there's trouble

Health: 33

Damage Inflicted: 6 points

Armor: 1

Movement: Short

Modifications: Attacks as level 7; all tasks related to charm or persuasion as level 7.

Combat: Sasha's companions are a small band of fellow adventurers and mercenaries. She values their company, but she values more the added muscle and their penchant for helping her out of a tight spot.

In battle, Sasha wields a sword and pistol (or similar weapons if in a recursion that operates under different laws), and she can attack with both weapons as a single action. She's not above using dirty tricks to get the drop on her opponents, and when a target fails its Speed defense roll against her sword attack, she can push the target an immediate distance or knock it to the ground.

When a battle goes against her, Sasha looks for a way out (which might involve a cypher or two she keeps for just such an eventuality). If she can't run, she surrenders, trusting in her charm to win over her captors and in her wit to figure out a way to escape if her foes prove resistant to her appeal.

Interaction: As a lifelong survivor, Sasha doesn't care much about such lofty notions as law, justice, or duty. She's a mercenary and takes her coin from anyone offering it, no matter the job. Sasha lives for adventure and sees the Strange as her playground. She can be a mercurial ally or a deadly rival. Sasha never grew up and has a tendency to abandon projects when something new comes along, including relationships; she's broken a few hearts.

Use: Since Sasha is rarely selective about the missions she takes, at some point she might take a job for the PCs' enemies. Something about the characters catches her fancy, and she decides that instead of killing them, she will betray her employer if offered something better.

Loot: Sasha usually has a couple of cyphers.

Sasha's companions: *Alvin, level 3; Margaret, level 4; and Sydney, level 5. All three are armed with weapons appropriate to the recursion where they are encountered.*

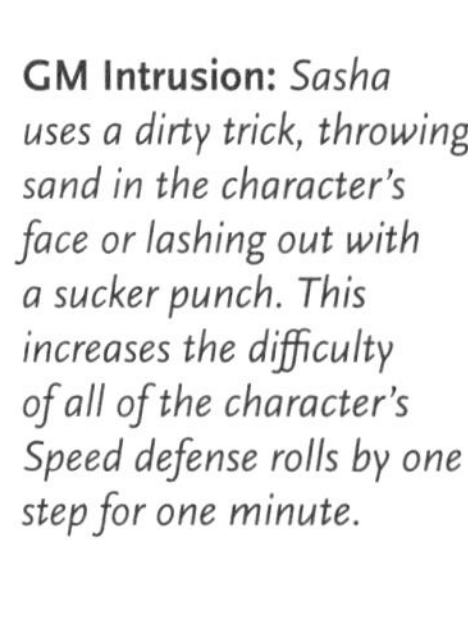

GM Intrusion: *Sasha uses a dirty trick, throwing sand in the character's face or lashing out with a sucker punch. This increases the difficulty of all of the character's Speed defense rolls by one step for one minute.*

Creature Index

KEY:
C = *The Strange* corebook
B = *The Strange Bestiary*